Praise for *The Last Atoll*

"It's wonderful to have another book fr(
beloved Hawai'i—this time about its fa.
fragile, contaminated, and plundered worlds unchronicled and previously ignored in our letters. She lives among its monk seals, short-tailed albatrosses, rails, petrels, and Laysan ducks, hopping island to atoll, lagoon to fringing reef over the course of ten years of patient exploration and research. From this, an inspiring personal odyssey, she brings us a book in the ecological tradition of Rachel Carson's *Silent Spring* that is also like a piece of extended war reportáge—for these islands were once indeed a combat zone and its dear creatures victims of our cold and riotous pillage. Homage to Ms. Frierson and homage to this living, precious world she brings to us."

—GARRETT HONGO, author of *Coral Road*

"*The Last Atoll* draws a vivid portrait of what might just be my favorite place on earth (and that's saying something), the secret islands northwest of Hawai'i. It's a place that still feels like the original world, like earth before us. There the nations are of seabirds, the world is almost entirely ocean, and the air roars with the calls of them in their millions. It feels like Life at full burn. But as Pamela Frierson's work shows, there is much more, even, than first greets the eye."

—CARL SAFINA, author of *The View from Lazy Point*

"As with her previous book, *The Burning Island*, Pamela Frierson takes readers to one of the most remote and ecologically fragile places on the planet. Gracefully written in the tradition of Rachel Carson, *The Last Atoll* is a personal trek to a chain of tiny, northwest Hawaiian islands, where Frierson brings us nose-to-nose with endangered Hawaiian monk seals, coral polyps, green sea turtles, and golden gooneys—alongside the fossils of long-extinct species, the bones of animals on the edge of vanishing, and the ravages of guano mining, coral dredging, and military bases. *The Last Atoll* skillfully travels through myth, culture, and history and arrives at present-day attempts to preserve islands that are as biologically significant as the Galápagos."

—FRANK STEWART, editor of *Mānoa*

THE LAST ATOLL

THE LAST ATOLL

Exploring Hawai'i's Endangered Ecosystems

PAMELA FRIERSON

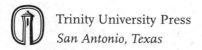

Trinity University Press
San Antonio, Texas

The publisher gratefully acknowledges the support of the Atherton Family Foundation in the publication of this book.

Published by Trinity University Press
San Antonio, Texas 78212
Copyright © 2012 by Pamela Frierson

Cover design by Nicole Hayward
Book design by BookMatters, Berkeley
Jacket illustration: ©iStockphoto.com/Alexandr Tkachuk

Trinity University Press strives to produce its books using methods and materials in an environmentally sensitive manner. We favor working with manufacturers that practice sustainable management of all natural resources, produce paper using recycled stock, and manage forests with the best possible practices for people, biodiversity, and sustainability. The press is a member of the Green Press Initiative, a nonprofit program dedicated to supporting publishers in their efforts to reduce their impacts on endangered forests, climate change, and forest-dependent communities.

The paper used in this publication meets the minimum requirements of the American National Standard for Information Sciences—Permanence of Paper for Printed Library Materials, ANSI 39.48–1992.

Library of Congress Cataloging-in-Publication Data

Frierson, Pamela.
The last atoll : exploring Hawai'i's endangered ecosystems / Pamela Frierson.
       p.   cm.
    Includes bibliographical references and index.
    ISBN 978-1-59534-130-3 (pbk.)
    1. Endangered ecosystems—Hawaii—Leeward Islands. 2. Endangered species—Hawaii—Leeward Islands. 3. Biotic communities—Hawaii—Leeward Islands. 4. Natural history—Hawaii—Leeward Islands. 5. Leeward Islands (Hawaii) I. Title.
QH76.5.H3F45 2012
578.6809969—dc23   2012006349

16 15 14 13 12 | 5 4 3 2 1

To Peter

Contents

Prologue

Over a decade ago, I found myself on a Hawaiian island that only a short time earlier I (like most of my contemporaries raised in Hawai'i) had no idea even existed.

When I first learned of this place, it seemed strange indeed that a Hawaiian island—and, as it turned out, a string of islands and atolls that extend the Hawaiian archipelago far into the North Pacific—could be nearly absent from history. Hawai'i is one of the most geographically isolated places on earth, but it has a long and complicated history of human habitation. Its capital city, Honolulu, is popularly known as "the hub of the Pacific." It is one of the world's major tourist destinations and possibly the world's biggest purveyor of images of tropical "paradise." A virtually unknown Hawaiian destination? I knew I had to find a way to get there.

A year later I stepped down from a five-seater plane onto a surreal version of the classic desert island: a tiny landfall with a maximum altitude of six feet, corseted by rusting sheet piling. Situated on this few dozen acres of sand and shrubs were a coral runway and a few aging concrete buildings, but these signs of human presence were nearly eclipsed by a wildlife population so dense that I wondered for a moment if all the seabirds, seals, and turtles that had disappeared from the Main Hawaiian Islands had simply moved here.

This particular place—Tern Island, within the circling reef of the atoll French Frigate Shoals, 550 miles northwest of Honolulu—would seem an unlikely candidate for a critical wildlife refuge. Tern Island's strange mix of the wild and the trammeled was a startling but, as it would turn out, fitting introduction to this hidden half of the Hawaiian archipelago, a paradoxical world both plundered and pristine.

When I was growing up on Oʻahu, we were taught that the volcanic islands that make up the Hawaiian chain numbered eight, and starting with the most southerly and youngest, we learned to recite their names: Hawaiʻi (the "Big Island"), Maui, Kahoʻolawe, Lānaʻi, Molokaʻi, Oʻahu, Kauaʻi, and Niʻihau. Even now, looking at a world atlas, I find only these islands depicted, with not even a dot to suggest the 1,200-mile stretch of islands, atolls, and coral reefs to the northwest.

Over the course of the next decade I traveled, mostly by research vessel, to some of the remotest islands in the world and to the farthest end of the Hawaiian chain. The journeys brought me to a shadow world of the Hawaiʻi I was taught to perceive. In these distant waters were sharp-spined remnants of ancient volcanoes, nearly inaccessible, yet crowned with Polynesian shrines, where stone human figures unlike any produced by the ancient Hawaiians had been found. There were shoals and atolls, too, where coral had fashioned enormous mazes and circles on the tabletops of drowned basalt islands. Giant fish patrolled the reefs, seabirds claimed every inch of dry land, monk seals lounged like fat odalisques on the beaches. Nīhoa, Mokumanamana, French Frigate Shoals, Laysan, Lisianski, Pearl and Hermes, Midway, Kure.

In some ways this hidden end of the archipelago was the antipode of those southern high islands known as Hawai'i: a vast reef wilderness with island life distilled into tiny landfalls. In such a world the parallel human stories of discovery and destruction play out in microcosm. To go there is to live that history.

I lived in tents on islands like Laysan, whose 1.6 square miles still support two species of landbird found nowhere else in the world. Laysan is one of a handful of places outside the Galápagos (Lord Howe Island in the Tasman Sea and Palmyra Atoll in the equatorial Pacific are two others) where ecosystems formed by the riotous evolution that occurs on isolated tropical and subtropical islands remained undisturbed long enough to be recorded. To be in such places—even just to read about them—is to peer into a deep well of time.

Such moments of islophiliac ecstasy are too often fleeting in an ocean world threatened not only by a legacy of damaging human activities but also by changes in climate, sea level rise, and ocean chemistry. At Midway Atoll I observed the closure of a sixty-year-old naval fortress and Cold War spy station, an event also witnessed, from every remaining bare patch of ground, by a million nesting albatrosses. I met researchers measuring global pollutants in seabirds that inhabit one of the most isolated places on earth. I came to realize that the US military had not been totally blind to the complex web of life that unites far distant islands. A military-funded research project in the 1960s contributed the first comprehensive survey of that web in the region, but its purpose seems to have been to determine whether seabirds could be used as vectors in biowarfare. On islands that could provide a baseline for measuring climate change, a clandestine past still casts a long shadow.

In June 2006, the northwestern end of the Hawaiian chain entered the world stage as the nation's newest and largest (nearly half the size of Texas) national monument, to the astonishment of many people, in Hawai'i and elsewhere. It was as if history had failed to record the existence of a major portion of the Galápagos.

How did these biological treasures remain nearly unknown into the twenty-first century? Ancient Hawaiian chants suggest that voyaging canoes sailed to some of the Northwestern Islands in the distant past. At the time of Captain Cook's arrival in 1778, Hawaiians still spoke of journeys to places beyond what was then the most northerly inhabited island, Ni'ihau, to gather feathers and hunt turtle. But in the turbulent years that followed Western discovery of the archipelago, these ancestral landfalls were nearly forgotten.

In the last two hundred years the Northwestern Islands have been visited by small numbers of Westerners, but still the region never registered in the Western imagination as more than isolated bits of land strewn randomly in a watery waste, an oceanic desert.

It is hard to see through the veil of our own perceptions of Pacific islands as inexhaustible cornucopia to an idea of what they may have been like in their untouched state. The land colludes in that veiling, for it is indeed fertile, and it has accommodated introduced flora and fauna from the tropics and subtropics of the world. The ease of colonizing such a land feeds our vision of Pacific islands as welcoming paradise.

"Paradise" is an imported vision, but islanders embrace it

because it fits with an unspoken assumption: that our insulation protects us from the most egregious damage afflicted on the landlocked regions of the earth. But in the "paradise" I hail from, a mounting tally of environmental ills is eroding that sense of unspoiled Eden: among conservation biologists, at least, the Hawaiian Islands now carry the dubious title "Extinction Capital of the World." We will, it seems certain, have to adjust to a new and uncomfortable view: that islands are the earth's proverbial canaries in the mine, microcosms where the forces that will shape our global future are already beginning to reveal themselves.

As miniature worlds, islands provide living laboratories for exploring how ecosystems evolve, how they fail, and how they may be restored. But perhaps even more important, as participants in an oceanic web, these water-girt worlds offer us a chance to revise our own isolated perceptions of the world and our role in it—to see that no island stands alone.

PART I

French Frigate Shoals

ONE

Island in a Steel Corset

I stood on a patch of sand and coral rubble in the middle of Tern Island and stared at the odd arrangement of objects at my feet. Dark wing feathers outlined the body of a large bird, spread-eagled. The hollow, polished bones of the legs curved down to long toes where paper-thin webbing still clung. The ribs attached to the breastbone were as fragile as the tines of a long, delicate ivory comb. A beak twice the length of the streamlined skull ended in a sharp hook. The upper bill was ridged on either side with short, tubelike nostrils, a conduit for the excess salt of a seawater-drinking bird. To judge from the bits of down that still clung to the skull, the seabird must have been young.

Bones and feathers all fanned outward from the body cavity, and like a feather-lined bowl, the bird's remains cradled the contents where its stomach had been. The black wedges of squid beaks were no surprise, but mixed in was a breadloaf's weight of plastic objects: several bottlecaps; numerous brightly colored, unidentifiable shards; and a pink Bic lighter. My hand reached for the lighter, then drew back as my mind registered what I was seeing. This four-inch capsule of fuel, presumably swooped up from the sea by its parent, may have been the fledgling's last meal.

I and this bird, or what remained of it, were about as far away as you can get from most of the rest of the world: 2,000 miles from the nearest continent, 450 miles from the nearest island larger than downtown Boise. We were on a speck of land no higher than a doorway, so small that no Western ship appears to have found its way here until one nearly wrecked on a surrounding reef in 1789. Yet here at my feet was a bolus of the world's garbage, nested in what had once been the gut of an albatross.

That was how I met the mariner's bird of fortune, famously described by Samuel Taylor Coleridge as the one "that made the wind to blow," the wild familiar that had lived inside my head since childhood. It was not a first encounter I could have imagined. But then very little on this steel-corseted island was turning out to be what I expected.

When I started making inquiries in the early 1990s about visiting the Northwestern Hawaiian Islands, I found no way to get to them. With the exception of Midway, at that time still a Naval Air Facility, and the soon-to-be-abandoned coast guard LORAN (long-range navigation) station at Kure Atoll, these far islands were protected wildlife refuges, off-limits to the general public. Outside Midway there were only two other working runways: coral strips at French Frigate Shoals and Kure. Research vessels anchored outside reefs and lowered inflatable boats to provide access to other islands for research and periodic field camps for the two conservators: the US Fish & Wildlife Service and the National Marine Fisheries Service (or NMFS, pronounced "nymphs").

But in the summer of 1993, Ken McDermond, refuge manager for the Northwestern Islands in Fish & Wildlife's Honolulu headquarters, said he could put me on as a volunteer at their remote field station at French Frigate Shoals if I were willing to fly in and out of Tern Island on the Piper Apache that delivered mail and food every six weeks, when weather permitted. It was not the time of year I wanted to go—the albatrosses, said to be there in great numbers, would be done with nesting, the chicks fledged and all gone to sea—but it might be the only chance.

In August I was on that tiny plane. I sat behind the pilot, next to the only other passenger: biologist George Balazs, the world's expert on Hawaiian green sea turtles. It was too noisy for conversation, though. The sky was overcast, and the sea from ten thousand feet up looked thick-skinned, with a metallic gloss like a dull mirror. There was nothing to do but wonder what had got me here, flying off the map in a plane that seemed much too small for the journey.

My parents, who had met in Honolulu during World War II but left the Islands shortly thereafter, returned in 1950 to settle on Oahu's windward coast, on a dusty patch of what was formerly a watermelon farm. They happily filled the yard with imported tropical plants without a thought to what native plants might once have grown there. They took ocean dips daily but never, that I can recall, donned a mask to look under the surface. Nonetheless, as a very young transplant, I became viscerally attached to a natural world that barely figured in either my parents' lives or my formal education.

In those days, school, for natives and immigrants alike, meant indoctrination into a world foreign to the Islands. *Dick and Jane* readers suggested to us that the ideal landscape looked like the

American Midwest. Yet even on crowded Oʻahu, shadows lingered of a former world. Hawaiians my grandfather's age talked about times when the sea turtles nested and basked on the beaches. They had known an era when the big fish were plentiful, as were sharks, which had special meaning for many Hawaiians. The esteemed Hawaiian cultural expert Mary Pūkuʻi, who died in 1986, spoke of watching, as a child, while her great uncle fed a shark who was a family guardian, an ʻaumakua. I, who had never seen a shark or the great schools of fish old fishermen described, and had only once or twice seen a sea turtle, longed for a glimpse of this wild abundance.

If there was a moment that made me wonder whether these shadows of the past might yet still exist in some remote corner of the Hawaiian archipelago, it was my encounter, some time in young adulthood, with the mystery of the feathers. On that day I entered a room filled with trophies from a lost world.

The room, in the main hall of the Bishop Museum, a Victorian stone pile now surrounded incongruously by Honolulu suburb, is richly paneled with burnished koa wood. The air is hushed and musty with the smell of age, and the light is muted, the objects in the room seeming to soak it up. Slender poles, some of them rising nearly twenty feet to the ceiling, line the room. Shaped from turtle shell, native wood, whalebone, or human bone, they are crowned by great cylinders made entirely of feathers, hundreds of thousands of them.

These cylinders are *kāhili*, the ultimate symbol of Hawaiian royalty. In 1825, the Reverend Charles Stewart, attending the funeral of Liholiho, the son of Kamehameha, and his queen, Kamāmalu, saw "poles near thirty feet high with hulumanu [literally, "bird-feather cluster"] . . . twelve to fourteen feet long."

Photographs of state occasions taken during the late 1800s, in the last years of the Hawaiian monarchy, show seated royalty dwarfed by a dozen *kāhili* standing like exotic topiary. Here, crowded into a room at the museum, they were no less impressive, and much more disturbing.

There is nothing that conjures up more vividly the tragic loss of native species on the Islands than traditional Hawaiian featherwork. I was raised on stories and images of ancient Hawai'i that depicted magnificent capes made from the feathers of now-extinct native forest birds like the beautiful yellow and black *o'o*, or the still-surviving red-feathered *'i'iwi*. The *kāhili* at the Bishop Museum are made up of these feathers as well, but what predominate are seabird feathers.

In my childhood on the shore, I had looked out every day on the conjoining of ocean and empty sky. Inland, the streets and gardens were noisy with birds, all non-native: raucous Indian mynahs, cooing Chinese doves, melodious Java thrushes. But there was silence along the shores, and seabirds were a rare sight. Once in a while the night call of a shearwater startled us out of sleep. Occasionally, riding high in the thermal gyres, would appear the pterodactyl shapes of *'iwa*, the frigatebirds, soaring on their long, slender wings, like visitors from another world.

Now, at the museum, I stood before a *kāhili* glinting with the green-black metallic sheen of frigatebird feathers, attached as thickly as blades of grass, the tufted mass of feathers thirty-six inches high. Some cylinders included the long, elegant tail feathers—only two to each bird—of *koa'e 'ula*, the red-tailed tropicbird, and the flight feathers of brown noddies and sooty terns. Others were made up of the soft chest feathers of two species of albatross, Laysan and black-footed. I took in, at last, their mute testimony: somewhere in the Hawaiian Islands, at least at one time, lived great legions of these birds.

Journeys northwest along the Hawaiian chain are a form of geological time travel, moving deeper and deeper into the past until one encounters, at the very end of the Hawaiian archipelago, 29-million-year-old Kure Atoll. Like all Hawaiian islands, Kure was once a high volcanic island birthed over the "hot spot," an upwelling of magma located now under still-growing Hawaiʻi Island. This stationary volcanic plume pierces the earth's largest crustal plate, the Pacific Plate, which underlies most of that ocean. Like all crustal plates, this one is in slow motion, pushed by magma also upwelling along long rifts. As Hawaiian volcanoes build up atop the crustal floor, they are slowly rafted northwest, away from the island-creating forces of their birthplace.

Although a full picture of this longest of volcanic archipelagoes had to wait for instruments developed in the last few decades that could pierce the opaque surface of the sea, the age progression of Hawaiian islands is dramatically visible in their varied topography. The Hawaiians noted it carefully and codified their knowledge in chants to the fiery deity Pele, who arrives on some unspecified low, flat island and journeys down the chain, settling at active Kīlauea volcano on Hawaiʻi Island. My home for many years has been on that youthful island, where the towering humps of shield volcanoes fill the sky. If life feels too tame I can contemplate the fact that I live virtually over the "hot spot," that fissure beginning deep in the earth's molten innards that has been birthing volcanoes, and sometimes islands, for tens of millions of years.

On the flight to French Frigate Shoals, we skirted the west side of Kauaʻi, looking down on the deep cleft of Waimea Canyon and the razor-sharp ridges of the valleys erosion had carved into this old, high volcanic island. Then we were over the low back, deeply cut by streams, of privately owned Ni'ihau, the island I had thought of most of my life as the last Hawaiian landfall. I felt a twinge of vertigo as we headed off the map of the Hawai'i of my memory.

Two hours and 150 miles later, the first northwestern Hawaiian island—a craggy volcanic remnant called Nīhoa—appeared: a jagged tooth piercing the shining foil of the sea. With sheer cliffs surrounded by deep water and no sign of reefs or shallows, it looked like the loneliest place in the world. Another hundred miles brought us over Mokumanamana (Necker), an even more forbidding sea-dragon spine of an island. Those heights, I had read, were covered with ancient shrines where those strange stone figures had been found.

An hour later, the horizon took on a green iridescence that widened as we approached. A curve of wave-pounded atoll reef passed under our wings and we were over the waters of a huge lagoon: brilliant aqua in its sandy shallows, shading to lime green over patches of coral. We passed islets—a few partly covered with green shrub, others brilliant ovals of white sand, strewn with dark shapes, like scones laced with raisins. "Seals," mouthed George, "and turtles."

Then there, unmistakable, was our destination: a flat stretch of sand and coral dredged out and molded by sheet piling into the shape of an aircraft carrier. Spilling from gaps in the sheet piling, as though the ship leaked sand, tiny beaches could be seen. Tern Island was mostly runway, but buildings clustered at one end like a ship's bridge added to the carrier effect. On each side of the runway ran green bands of shrubbery.

The air above the island was dark with seabirds. "Hang on,"

announced the pilot. "When I see an opening I'm going in fast."
He dove toward the island as though we were on a bombing raid.
There was a thump as we hit a bird. We bounced on the ground,
past a sign that read "Welcome to Tern Island. Elevation 6 feet.
Population 6," and rolled up to a long cinder-block building.

The crew of the good ship Tern Island had been busy chasing
birds off the runway, which looked to be a futile task. Now they
approached the plane, mouths open, shouting greetings, but all
I could hear was an avian din. I clambered out on the wing and
dropped to the ground, into heat and glare and noise, and followed George into the building. We entered a large room where
banks of windows covered with tattered military-drab shades let
in a dim, green-tinged light. Two dilapidated couches, a large TV,
and an Exercycle filled one corner; desks and an aquarium with
murky water occupied another. A pool table laden with diving
gear, binoculars, life vests, and other items stood in the center.
An alcove was stocked with radio equipment, files, and shelves
of three-ring binders, and an adjoining closet-sized room held an
array of photovoltaic equipment and batteries.

We sat down at an expanse of four cafeteria tables pushed
together, piled in the center with bird bands, notebooks, tattered
paperbacks, and a cribbage board. I watched as six sunburned
people, two females and four males, scurried around, stowing
the plane's cargo—the first delivery of fresh food in six weeks.
Not until everything was carefully rewrapped, labeled, and stored
did they join us at the table, unceremoniously tossing down various sandwich makings. The sliced turkey bore a new label pasted
over the old: "Roast breast of domesticated wildfowl."

After lunch the plane took off, bearing away the volunteer I was
replacing. Cris, the refuge manager, who had come across at first

as affable and laid-back, was immediately all business. In his early thirties, he had the bleached-hair boyish look of a surfer but the confidence of someone used to running his own small fiefdom—honed, I would learn, from years of working in the field in Alaska.

One of my duties, Cris explained, would be to monitor daily various marked-out bird nesting areas. He gave me the cold appraisal of one weary of working with nonprofessionals. "This isn't some bogus eco-tourist busywork," he said. "It needs to be done right. The daily log is our basis for seeing how bird populations are doing. This is the only place in the Northwestern Islands where daily logs are kept. Seabirds are indicator species for the whole ocean ecosystem.

"The health of the North Pacific is in your hands," he added, and then laughed at his own pomposity, handing me a Rite in the Rain all-weather notepad, the bird-banding log, and a fanny pack containing tools for banding. He pointed out a wall chart with photos of seabirds, brief descriptions, and acronyms for the names of each species. I counted them—nineteen species in all: albatrosses, tropicbirds, terns, noddies, boobies, petrels, shearwaters, frigatebirds.

"They're not all here at one time," Cris said. "That's part of how they manage to share such a small area of land. Kind of a time-share, you could say. One of our biggest populations of birds, the albatrosses, is all gone. The last fledglings took off a month ago, and a new cycle won't start until November."

"Where do they go?" I asked.

"They feed as far away as the Aleutians or the West Coast," Cris said. "The young birds stay away, living on the wing or occasionally resting on the water, for the first years of their lives."

Nearly the entire world population of Laysan and black-footed albatrosses, he explained, nest in the Northwestern Hawaiian Islands. "In the case of the Laysans, that means over two and a half million birds, but the largest colonies are north of here, at Laysan Island and Midway Atoll. Huge colonies of them were exterminated from other Pacific islands, such as Wake Island or Johnston Atoll, by either bird-feather hunters at the turn of the twentieth century or military activities during World War II."

Vulnerability, I was beginning to see, was the flip side of island isolation. Birds who lived a near-mythological life of open ocean and air were herded by their hormones, once they reached breeding age, into small spaces that could be refuges—or fatal traps. The feather poachers had been on Tern Island too, and later the military had remodeled this ark to suit its own convenience. Bird colonies had survived here only, it appeared, because those activities had not gone on long enough.

I followed Cris out onto the runway, into blinding light and a bedlam of birds. "I'll take you for a tour of the bird plots you'll be working in," he said, handing me a broom handle. "You might want this to keep them from diving at your head."

The three-thousand-foot crushed coral runway ran roughly east to west, cutting a huge swath from bow to stern of the narrow island. Outside the cluster of one-story cinder-block buildings, water tanks, and three huge, derelict fuel tanks, dense vegetation crowded the runway's margins. An enormous congregation of seabirds, of a dozen shapes and sizes, nested on the ground among sedge puncture vine and long tendrils of morning glory. Capon-sized, dun-colored seabirds blanketed this, the western end of the runway, and several wobbled on pink, webbed, oversized feet toward my sneakers. "Sex-starved juvenile wedge-tailed shearwaters," Cris shouted. "They'll go for anything."

To the north I could see the outer reef of the atoll a few hundred feet beyond the island, pummeled by huge combers that curled rhythmically out of the deep blue of open ocean. Inside the reef, the lagoon waters rippled gently, glowing beyond the bleached expanse of runway as though all of the rich color that land usually holds had drained into the sea.

The waves breaking on the reef must have been making a great thunder, but we could hear nothing over the clamor of birds. As we walked along, dozens of white and black terns flew up from the runway and hovered just above our heads, emitting raucous, three-syllable shrieks that sounded like "paddy-whack, paddy-whack." I raised my broom handle up like a majorette's baton. It didn't faze the birds. "Sooty terns," shouted Cris. "Most of them are gone. There's several hundred thousand when they're all here. They probably won't dive at you. It's the brown noddies you have to watch for. They're still nesting."

He gestured off to the side of the runway. Pigeon-sized noddies, chocolate colored, with a cap of gray like a daub of paint on their heads, brooded eggs on every available space between patches of ground cover. The patchy ground gave way to bushes festooned with much larger birds: red-footed boobies and frigatebirds. The latter had a baleful look about them, perching with their long, black wings drooping batlike. The air was laced with the acidic pungency of dried guano, a fecund but not unpleasant odor, like the back room of a garden supply. The wind had picked up and the sky deepened toward cerulean in the afternoon light. Perhaps a hundred more frigatebirds rode thermal gyres high overhead.

A clamorous throng of noddies and terns now wheeled above our heads, and Cris shouted instructions I couldn't hear. It was like being schooled while someone held a pot over your head and beat triple-time with a spoon. I trailed clumsily after him as he picked his way through the nesting birds.

The sandy earth beneath me gave way suddenly, and my right foot dropped two feet into a hole. I pulled myself out and my left foot sank abruptly. Cris waved me back and then inexplicably dropped to his knees, digging the sand out from the hole with both hands, like a mammoth squirrel. I hoped this wasn't part of my job. He stood up. "Bird burrows," he said. "Shearwaters, mainly, on this island. Other islands have lots of petrels, too. If you cave in a burrow entrance you've got to dig it out. If there's a bird in there, it might need help getting out."

I stepped backward and immediately sank down into another burrow. Under Cris's watchful eye I dug out the sand. Something sharp and pincerlike grabbed at my fingers. I yanked back my hand.

Cris grinned. "Somebody home?" He started off again. "Try to step where the birds have piled up the sand when they dig," he shouted over his shoulder. "That's often opposite the way the burrow goes."

By treading in Cris's footsteps I managed to navigate over the burrowed sand to the stand of large shrubs. They were *Tournefortia*, or tree heliotrope—a hardy plant with fleshy, drought-resistant leaves found throughout the Pacific. Their gnarly branches were heavily laden with guano, the droppings sealing together large, messy piles of sticks that made up the birds' nests. We were now eye level with nesting frigatebirds and red-footed boobies, who clattered their beaks at us like castanets and reached out, hoping to get in a jab or two.

Among boobies, heavy-bodied birds the size of a small goose, red-foots are the only members that perch, wrapping the long, webbed toes of their bright red feet around branches. Most of the booby nests held chicks—balls of white down with bodies as large as their parents' and stubby, half-formed wings. There were half-grown frigate chicks nesting in the shrubs as well. With ruffs of white down around their necks above emerging black scapular feathers, and heads scantily covered with orange down, they reminded me of some famous portrait of Elizabeth the First.

"You'll be banding red-tailed tropicbirds," Cris said. He pulled a banding kit out of his fanny pack and, using a piece of stick, demonstrated how to fit the band and squeeze the aluminum together with the pliers. "It'll be up to you to check the area every day for tropicbird chicks that are ready for banding," he said. "You need to catch them just as they're nearly fledged, when their legs are full-grown. Otherwise the band will end up being too tight."

"These birds are ground nesters," Cris went on, now down on his knees, peering under the branches. "And here's a likely candidate."

Red-tailed tropicbirds are the size of small chickens, a brilliant white as adults, with startlingly red bills and two long tail feathers like thin red streamers. They are beautiful birds with fierce temperaments and thoroughly unlovely, raucous voices. Cris grabbed this young one, still in its fledgling attire of white with black bars, slipping one hand over the head to hold the murderous-looking bill shut and clamping the bird against his chest to pin its wings. Somehow, in the same motion, he managed to back out from under the bush and stand up.

The bird was squalling loudly and drooling a fishy liquid. A large lump of something bulged in its throat. Cris instructed me to stroke its throat downward. "It's nice for you and for him if he doesn't lose his dinner—it might be a while before he gets another one."

I retrieved a size 5 from a necklace of aluminum bands strung on a wire loop and gingerly extracted one bird leg from the folds of Cris's shirt. The webbed toes wrapped around my finger with a reptilian grip. I pried up the toes, fitted the open-ended band over the leg just above the foot, and began, clumsily, to clamp down with the pliers. Clamp too hard and the band will flatten and pinch, and you'll have to pull it apart with needle-nosed pliers while holding the leg of a very angry bird. I was taking too long, clamping cautiously, and the chick struggled and disgorged over my hand three partly digested squid, each the size of a jumbo fishing lure. Finally the band was squeezed into a circle around the bony leg, and we hastily released the bird under the bush.

The frigatebirds perched on top of the bush were watching nervously. The males had folds of bright red skin at the throat, like miniature turkey wattles. (These were pouches that inflated like heart-shaped balloons during courtship—as blatant a come-on as a baboon's bottom.) Their bills were three times as long as their heads, wickedly hooked at the end. I stepped back, narrowly missing another burrow, and dodged around the bush, away from those sharp bills.

The seal I nearly tumbled into was lying like a soft log half under the low branches. Its eyes were shut tightly above fat jowls and a catlike muzzle with large whisker pores. I could see the characteristic rolls of fat at the neck whose vague resemblance to a monk's cowl may have led to the "monk seal" name. The seal's yellowed fur was tinged with patches of green, like a doormat left out too long in the rain; it was molting, shedding its pelt in chunks, showing dark new fur beneath. Near its neck was an enormous healed wound surrounded by folds of scar tissue in the shape of a large shark's bite.

This, one of the world's rarest animals, was the reigning species of French Frigate Shoals. The seal opened its eyes, then
raised its head and looked at me with what seemed disgruntle-
ment rather than alarm. I backed up slowly. The seal lowered
its head and belched. To my relief, Cris signaled a return to the
runway, and we retraced our steps to the packed coral, creating a
wave of bird pandemonium as we went.

We stood at the edge of the runway while Cris pointed out the
"facilities." Just to the east of the low, concrete barracks that furnished living and office space was the cement rectangle of an old
tennis court, now used, Cris said, for water catchment. Beside
the old court were three huge redwood water tanks. "Rainwater
is our only supply of freshwater," he said. "Don't expect too many
showers."

We walked east toward a second concrete building where
rusted iron doors bore a HAZARDOUS: DO NOT ENTER sign. Cris
swung one door open. "In 1979 the coast guard could walk away
from a building with asbestos contamination," he said. "They
wouldn't be able to do that now. Or at least not so blatantly." The
room we peered into held the hulks of four huge rusting generators that once powered the radio transmitters of the LORAN
station, providing tracking and navigation aid for both navy and
civilian ships until rendered obsolete with the advent of satel-
lites. Instrument panels sprouted tangled wires, encrusted with
bird droppings. I had headed out to the middle of nowhere,
toward what I thought was one of the world's last wild places; I
had landed in a post–Cold War ghost town.

As Cris and I headed back to the barracks I thought of the
little history I had dug up about this place. The first Western

ships to encounter French Frigate Shoals did so in a moment of near-calamity. On November 6, 1786, the French explorer Jean-François de Galaup, comte de Lapérouse, was on his way from Alaska to Macau with a cargo of furs to trade. His two frigates were sailing abreast on a tranquil sea in the middle of the night. No watch saw the breakers until the ships were nearly on top of them. Brought about in minutes by highly trained crews, the ships passed within five hundred feet of the atoll's encircling reef and the pounding waves. As a consequence Lapérouse named his new discovery Basse de Frégates Françaises, or Shoal of the French Frigates.

Little record was made of the atoll in the next half century until, in October 1858, the US schooner *Fenimore Cooper*, under the command of Lieutenant John Brooke, was sent to the North Pacific to make soundings for an underwater telegraph cable route. Brooke took formal possession of French Frigate Shoals for the United States under the land-grabbing Guano Act of 1856. According to this legislation, any unoccupied, unclaimed island with commercially exploitable quantities of bird guano could be claimed in the name of the US government. Bird guano was prized as fertilizer and used in the making of saltpeter, but the impetus was already imperial, an unspoken recognition that remote Pacific islands might have value to an empire-building nation. (The United States would ultimately claim over fifty islands under the Guano Act, eight of which remain possessions today.)

The Shoals' accumulation of guano proved too small to mine profitably, but the atoll's position and name were now inked in on the navigational charts of the day. Fishermen and traders took note, and it was not long before vessels like the *Ada* arrived and took their fill of the abundant wildlife Lieutenant Brooke had described. The *Ada*, Japanese-owned but American-chartered, departed French Frigate Shoals in 1882 with a cargo of not only bird feathers to supply the millinery trade, but also shark meat, fins, and oil; turtle meat and shells; and dried and salted bêches-de-mer, or sea cucumbers. Such plundering undoubtedly took place throughout the Northwestern Hawaiian Islands in this period but left little trace in the record books.

In 1895, two years after a cabal led by American business-men overthrew Hawaiian queen Lili'uokalani, a cutter was sent to French Frigate Shoals to plant the flag of the new provisional government. In 1898, despite vigorous protest from Native Hawaiians, President Grover Cleveland's administration, lobbied by sugar planters and other business interests, formally annexed Hawai'i, and in the process all lands that had belonged to the monarchy passed officially into the hands of the new territorial government, and eventually to the state of Hawai'i. After the Northwestern Islands (excluding Midway, already in the sights of the US Navy) became a Federal Bird Reservation in 1909, on the heels of reports of wholesale slaughter of seabirds in order to harvest their feathers, wildlife enjoyed a brief respite as US vessels patrolled occasionally to keep poachers out. But the shoals would not be left to the wildlife for long: human events in very distant places would soon bring great changes even to a place as remote as a then-uninhabited Hawaiian atoll.

The famous Battle of Midway (June 1942), the World War II battle that broke the back of Japanese sea power, was just the culmination of two decades of maneuvering for control in the Pacific. In a treaty signed in 1921, the United States and Japan had promised each other not to arm their oceanic possessions, but in fact the race was on. Under the guise of developing commercial interests, both nations had begun to build up remote outposts and prepare for possible combat. By 1932, the US military was conducting exercises in the French Frigate Shoals' lagoon, and had flown seaplanes the 586 miles from Honolulu to the atoll in what was hailed as the first long-distance flight in the Central Pacific.

After the Battle of Midway, the US Navy decided that both French Frigate Shoals and Midway needed better military protection and more development. Fighter planes could not carry enough fuel to make the 1,300-mile trip to Midway from Honolulu. An air base at the Shoals offered a solution, but no islands there were large enough for a runway. Thus began the demolition and reconstruction of Tern Island, eleven acres of sand, shrub, and wildlife turned into the semblance of a fifty-three-acre aircraft carrier by mid-1943.

The island served as a naval facility for the remainder of the war. No birds were allowed to nest, Cris told me. "The commanding officer wouldn't even allow a blade of grass to grow," he went on. "Imagine this place with hardly a shred of vegetation and no wildlife. It would be like living on a permanently marooned ship." The navy, it appeared, had forgotten—or had chosen to ignore—that the atoll was part of a federal wildlife reservation.

After the war ended, the navy handed administration of the Shoals over to the US Coast Guard. The Tern Island LORAN building was constructed a decade later, and continued in use until 1979. An officer and crew and a few dogs lived at Tern, serviced, like the island's tenants when I visited, with biweekly plane deliveries of fresh food and mail. One crew member, it was said, hanged himself, and a few biologists who came later claimed to have felt his ghostly presence in the dark corridors of the barracks.

It was nearly sundown when we returned to the barracks. Cris handed me some folded linens and a solar-powered lamp. "If you put it outside first thing in the morning," he said, "It'll give you a half-hour of light if you're lucky." He pointed me down a long hallway to my room: a monastic cell, with a metal-frame bed, a chair, and a wooden desk that had once been painted blue. The exoskeleton of the largest lobster I had ever seen was fastened like an icon on the wall over the head of the bed. Bizarre, but somehow appropriate: living for long in this isolation would require a religious devotion to wild nature.

Bird down drifted in the corners of the room, and droppings had made long runnels down the outside of the louvered windows. I opened up a sheet. A small oval of sun-baked bird shit decorated one side. I considered it for a moment, then spread that side facedown and made up the bed. I sat on the desk and gazed out the windows.

The rooms in this wing of the building faced the lagoon, a hundred feet away. Several shrubs laden with birds partly blocked my view. There was a small concrete bunker near the narrow strip of beach, with what looked like old carpet rolled up against it. Suddenly the carpet came alive, flicking up a flipper. A white tern flared its angelic wings in the last light before settling onto the window ledge.

The color of the lagoon deepened with the dusk, blending so smoothly into the crepuscular sky that there seemed to be no horizon. Only the lone vestige of volcanic rock in the Shoals, La Pérouse Pinnacle, several miles out toward the center of the lagoon, broke that seamless joining. From this angle, the 120-foot sea stack seemed to rise from a narrow base, flaring slightly near the top, like a hand thrust up from the drowned island.

All night long the air was filled with the caterwauling of the shearwaters, the sudden racket of the birds in bushes outside my window. In the distance I heard rollers breaking against the outer reef, the only protection from open ocean. The shape of the island was branded on my retinas from the day's light and heat, as bright as the afterimage that comes from staring out a window into the glare. The bird sounds were utterly demented. Somewhere a window was banging in a rising wind. I could imagine too easily the rollers breaching over the reef, the island slipping from its moorings and beginning to drift like a rudderless ship. Was I catching one last glimpse of the world before the Flood from the patched-together deck of the ark? Or was it that the waters had already risen and retreated, and here, at the wrecked edges of the world, the animals were returning home?

TWO

The Drowned Island

Days on Tern Island passed in a fog from little sleep and too much heat. I returned from my bird plot surveys each afternoon, ears deafened, to a communal life poised somewhere between college dorm and lifeboat. At dusk the shearwaters began the crazed caterwauls they kept up all night—a thousand cats in heat, a miniature city of lost souls wailing. Or a ship of the damned adrift. Coleridge would have loved this place.

Our days were a delicate dance of trying to carry out myriad tasks of conservation with the least disturbance to the wildlife. The daily monitoring work in the bird plots was simple enough: tracking the survival rates for this year's crop of white terns and tropicbirds, and making sure those that made it to full fledge were tagged before they took their maiden flight.

But various weekly and biweekly tasks sometimes required all of us for hours on end and left me finishing my daily tallies only as darkness settled in. On one day, we banded the few dozen juvenile red boobies; on another we fanned out and marched in a line down the island, tickers in hand, to do the monthly count of migrant shorebirds: tattlers, sanderlings, plovers, ruddy turnstones, and a couple of bristle-thighed curlews.

There were cleaning and maintenance days, and cooking rotation. Chef duty was taken very seriously: the cardinal sin in our tiny universe was failure to produce a tasty meal, and it required sweat and ingenuity to create a winning dish from our limited food supply. Cris did not exempt himself, but claimed the executive privilege of producing pizzas—a sure winner even with Bisquick crust. Evening meals were eaten out on the deck to watch the spectacular marine sunsets speckled with the winged forms of birds returning to the island. Boobies and tropicbirds lumbered in laden with squid, and frigatebirds dropped like missiles from the sky to intercept them, harassing them until they dropped their catch. It wasn't often that the frigates missed the falling booty, but there were times when we lunged to cover our plates as a squid hurtled toward someone's dried-shrimp creole.

Several weeks went by before I had time free to explore the island, but at last I headed out in the tempered sun of late afternoon. As I walked down the runway, I accumulated a hovering escort of sooty terns, soon joined by some white terns and a juvenile red-footed booby who maneuvered his heavy body with surprising skill just over my head. Once I determined none of them were trying to get in a jab, I felt an odd sort of beatitude surrounded by this aerial crowd.

Through gaps in the vegetation lining the runway I could see the rusting sheet piling that ran the entire length of the island along the side facing the outer reef. On the lagoon side, Tern was only partly rimmed with steel, allowing for the beach that my room looked out upon—a narrow strand we left to the seals, except for one end where we splashed on no-shower days.

At the far end of the island, the runway stopped several feet short of another seawall. Sand had accumulated beyond into a long, beautifully sculpted spit, with gentle waves meeting at the end. On the side of the island that faced the reef, where the bottom had been dredged for runway fill, the water was deep blue; on the other side the sand sloped out gently, washed by bright water shading into the aquamarine of the lagoon.

I sat at the top of the spit with my back against the seawall and turned gratefully away from the airstrip. The sand near me was hummocked with nesting pits turtles had dug. Their flippers left regular tracks, like those of small recreational vehicles, leading to and from the water. A more deeply plowed, irregular track showed where a seal had hunched up the beach and into one of the half-dug nesting pits to rest. Above me seabirds flew in low from the ocean, their shadows swooping up the spit and imprinting me for an instant with the shape of wings. Around the curve of the spit swam a flotilla of spotted eagle rays, several males courting a larger female, eerily birdlike in their slow-motion aqueous flight.

Something splashed just beyond the sheet piling behind me, and I climbed back up on the seawall to investigate. Through a hole in the corroded metal I could see two young seals not six feet away. They floated in the shallow water, heads together, languorously rotating, so that the light fur on one belly and then the other flashed in the sun. They seemed to be blowing bubbles into each other's whiskers.

Watching them made me ache with a deep mixture of pleasure and pain, like a recollection of lost love. What else to call so deep a longing? I was feeling profoundly disoriented, never having expected to find here a world of such extremes. Here was an island so altered by human hand that it was difficult to imagine what once it might have been like. Yet the sea around me teemed with wildlife, and on the island itself animals were everywhere we did not forcibly exclude them, and few of the creatures seemed to bear the instinctive fear of humans I had anticipated.

From this perspective, even my home island of Hawai'i Island, celebrated because its forests and lava lands still harbored endemic species vanished from other islands—the nēnē goose, the Hawaiian hawk, wonderful honeycreepers like the scimitar-billed 'akiapola'au, the native bat—by comparison seemed eerily stripped of its wildlife. Seabirds were seldom seen on the Big Island, and turtles nested very rarely on its beaches. I had never seen a monk seal, and only once had I seen a shark.

Yet Tern itself was less like an ark than a shipwreck. The biologists spent less time doing research than they did mitigating introduced problems. We had already rescued a frigatebird and a turtle trapped in the crumbling metal of the seawall. This bulwark held together the added acres of sand and coral, making it possible to have a runway. And a runway meant a biological field station, and research. But did the work we did here justify the impact of being here? Did that work add up to conservation?

With the heat and confinement of Tern Island, the crumbling buildings and other signs of human damage, the sense of taking up space at the expense of the wildlife, I was finding it easy to feel superfluous. I was unused to daily traffic with death, to such unremitting exposure to the great wheels of biology, where individual lives count for little. In the bird plots, I cataloged survival, but what I remembered was the opposite: a brown noddy chick the size of a feathered thumb, shivering under bunchgrass, weakening after a few days when no parent returned; a white tern with two small fish held crosswise in its long bill, sitting patiently on a ledge, waiting to feed its chick, but the chick gone, perhaps carried off by a frigatebird. And everywhere the dried carcasses of fledgling albatrosses, the ones whose parents couldn't fatten them enough to survive the month when they were no longer fed and who were beaten down by the summer heat before their adult feathers grew long enough to release them from the land.

One of the first things Cris told newcomers to Tern was "We can't play Dr. Dolittle here. If we did, we'd soon be overwhelmed. If I find a bird with, say, a broken wing, I put it out of its misery. What you decide to do is up to you, but don't bring it back to nurse."

I was still thinking of the brown noddy chick I found the day before, lying at the water line. It was very thin, and wet, as though it had washed into the water and back onshore, but still feebly alive. Sand crabs had already begun to tear a hole in its belly. I couldn't bring myself to wring its neck, so I held it underwater for a minute. It came up still alive. Finally, too tentatively, I hit it with a rock. It took more than one blow.

I had watched Cris carrying injured birds off toward the refuse pit, where he would dispatch them, and I sensed that though he had done it many times, he didn't find the killing any easier. It seemed one of the ironies of field biology that what drew many to the work—an empathy with animals—was a trait one often had to suppress. Cris spoke with exasperation that masked a certain admiration of one former Tern Island field biologist named Cynthia. She had, he said, an almost uncanny ability to read animal behavior, "and a way overdeveloped Dolittle complex. She even brooded an abandoned red-footed booby egg in her armpit—carried it around, slept with it at night. Found parents for it. End of story. Don't even think about pulling any stunts like that."

I suspected Cynthia hadn't made it too far up the corporate field biologist ladder, but I sure wanted to meet her, to borrow some of the courage of her convictions. I found myself thinking back nearly twenty years to a visit I had made to another Hawaiian island, much larger than this one, and damaged, it seemed, beyond repair. It was Kaho'olawe, smallest of the eight Main Hawaiian Islands, six miles off the resort-encrusted shoreline of west Maui and used by the military for bombing practice.

In 1976, as a journalist working in Honolulu, I interviewed two young Hawaiian men who had been charged with making an illegal landing on the uninhabited island, which was under the jurisdiction of the US Navy. Like many Hawaiians, the two men felt that the military appropriation of Kaho'olawe (by executive order the day after Japan attacked Pearl Harbor) and the island's continued use and abuse were symbolic of a larger destruction of indigenous nature and culture. Hawaiians at the time were beginning to speak out about what they saw as the theft of their land.

The prevailing perception among the residents of Hawai'i in the 1970s was that Kaho'olawe, stripped of most of its vegetation by introduced goats, had never been much more than a wasteland. But Hawaiian elders knew that the 29,000-acre island, crown lands taken over by the new territorial government after Queen Lili'uokalani was forced off her throne in 1893, had supported cattle ranching for many years before the military took over. Some could recall traditions that spoke of the island's important role as the point of arrival and departure for ancestral sea voyages between Hawai'i and Southern Polynesia. The stories suggested a very different place than the one I knew growing up, with dryland forest of sandalwood and the beautiful wiliwili tree, abundant pili grass for thatching houses, and soil rich enough to grow sweet potato.

I learned these things while writing a piece on the island and the formation of a Hawaiian activist group called the Protect

Kahoʻolawe ʻOhana (*ʻohana* means "family"), or PKO for short. Its founders included Walter Ritte and Richard Sawyer, the two Hawaiians who had been arrested and removed from the island by the coast guard; a young doctor, Emmett Aluli; and a talented Hawaiian musician, George Helm. The article I wrote, sensationally titled "Paradise Bombed," sprang from my surprise at the strength of feeling these men expressed for the desolate island.

Sawyer and Ritte had not meant to stay on the island: they were off exploring, and when they looked down to the beach and saw the coast guard intercept their companions in their hasty scramble to boats, they decided not to reveal themselves. Days later, when the coast guard crew eventually pulled Ritte and Sawyer off Kahoʻolawe, they were flummoxed to see from the two young men, not smiles of gratitude for being rescued from one of the most godforsaken places on earth, but tears of grief. The Hawaiians spoke of the island's rugged grandeur, of coming across ancestral shrines and native plants in the shelter of steep gulches. They struggled for words to express how the silent land had moved them, how it pained them to find the red topsoil—exposed by overgrazing, then blasted by bombs—blown into the gullies, and thence washed by the rain into the sea when it rained, staining the mouths of coves red, like blood.

As Kahoʻolawe became a rallying point for Hawaiians, George Helm, raised on a Molokaʻi farm, emerged as a leader, his eloquence in music able to move the older, more conservative generation when his words failed to reach them. He found a way to link for his listeners the music—Hawaiian songs that celebrated place—and *aloha ʻāina*, the traditional concept of a spiritual connection to the land. I began to drop in at the Honolulu nightclub where he played, sometimes sitting with him afterward and talking about the meaning of the songs, and about Kahoʻolawe.

I was particularly fascinated by the lyrics of one song of pro-test, "Mele 'Ai Pōhaku," or "The Stone-Eating Song." It had been written, George explained, in 1893, the year the Hawaiian mon-archy was overthrown. The song claimed that "the children of Hawai'i, ever loyal to the land," would never be tempted into sell-ing their native civil rights. It ended with these intriguing words:

Ua lawa mākou i ka pōhaku
I ka 'ai kamaha'o o ka 'āina

We are satisfied with the stones,
The astonishing food of the land.

I puzzled over those words. I understood how stone, in a vol-canic landscape where one could actually witness the birth of rock from its molten source, could exude a life force as powerful as that of plants and animals. In Hawaiian tradition, natural for-mations of stone were often embodiments of the gods. But there was a level of attachment to the land, expressed here in exquisite defiance, irony, and tenderness, that I could not comprehend.

In early January 1977 a state archaeological team reported that a sample survey of Kaho'olawe had turned up a surpris-ingly large number of prehistoric shrines and agricultural sites, suggesting that the island might once have supported at least a small population. Later that month, Walter Ritte, George Helm, Richard Sawyer, and two other PKO members returned to Kaho'olawe. They explored the island for two days, walking at night by moonlight to avoid detection by military patrols. Three of the men, including Helm, were picked up on the third day, but Ritte and Sawyer, supplied with water and some dried food, asked Helm to publicize their intention to remain on the island as a deterrent to the bombing.

Military troops searched the island for the two men. After

nine days had passed and "no evidence of intruders" had been found, the navy declared it would resume target practice.

On Valentine's Day, two weeks after Ritte and Sawyer had been left with a fourteen-day supply of food and water on Kahoʻolawe, I flew to the island in a navy helicopter. Congressional delegates and press had been invited to witness a "demonstration bombing."

I went into the cockpit to photograph the island when it came into view. But I was so stunned by the sight that I never lifted the camera to my eyes. I knew the island's size in terms of acreage, but its role as expendable military target had shrunk the island in my imagination. Now it loomed ahead. Steep cliffs rose straight from deep waters, scored here and there by gulches sheltering pockets of green. As we flew over Kahoʻolawe, its broad back unrolled like a vast savannah, rising gently to a thousand feet at the top of a shield-shaped cinder cone. The gray-greens and dusty golds of dryland shrubs and grasses seemed to have been peeled back in the bombed center of the island to reveal the red volcanic soil.

We landed in a cloud of red dust on hardpan next to a large, shallow pit rimmed with sandbags. I stood to the right of Senator Daniel Inouye, who was looking at the sky in the direction the bombers would come. The rocky silence asserted itself, reaching deep inside me.

F-4 jets appeared, falling out of the sky before the sound could reach us. I looked at Inouye's face turned upward, frozen into a look of profound worry. The jets had already dropped their payload—not the usual five-hundred-pounders but dummy bombs with an explosive device the size of a 12-gauge shotgun shell— and streaked upward. Puffs of white smoke mixed with red dust blossomed from the target area, a few hundred yards away.

Two days earlier, on February 12, George Helm had addressed the state House of Representatives, asking them to support a resolution to halt the bombing. "We are motivated to protect whatever is left of our culture," he said. Echoing the state motto, he added, "Our [Hawaiian] culture only exists if the life of the land is perpetuated in righteousness." Many of the legislators were moved to tears, and the resolution passed.

But the bombing continued, and Helm grew very worried about Ritte and Sawyer. In early March, he traveled to Maui, determined to go to Kahoʻolawe to look for the two men. Two Hawaiians known as excellent watermen, Kimo Mitchell and Billy Mitchell (no relation) agreed to accompany him. A boat dropped the three men on March 6. On March 8, Billy Mitchell was picked up on Kahoʻolawe by a military patrol who told him Ritte and Sawyer had flagged a coast guard vessel and been taken off the island two days before. Billy said he had been walking all night, trying to make contact, to get help for George and Kimo. The day before, after a pickup boat failed to show up at the prearranged time, the three men had paddled away from the island on the two surfboards they had brought to float supplies from boat to shore, heading for the tiny islet of Molokini in the eight-mile channel between Maui and Kahoʻolawe. The seas had become rough. When it was clear they weren't going to make it, Billy paddled back on his own to Kahoʻolawe to look for help.

A massive air search launched the next day netted the other surfboard, drifting several miles northwest. George and Kimo were never found.

The loss of both men was deeply felt in the Hawaiian community, but it did not slow the movement to stop the Kahoʻolawe desecration. A successful lawsuit brought by PKO against the navy to halt the bombing and require an inventory of archaeological sites led to a survey stretching over several thousand acres of the island. The results were astounding. Kahoʻolawe had at one time been extensively settled. Over five hundred sites had been documented; radiocarbon dates suggested human occupation reaching back several hundred years.

PKO then won a suit for the right to conduct religious ceremonies at the prehistoric shrines on the island, and with state lawmakers now backing them, brought the bombing entirely to a halt in the next few years. There was talk of setting up a Hawaiian commission as official caretakers for the island. At one of the island's few bays, where reefs forced the boats to anchor offshore and goods were passed hand over hand to the beach, Hawaiians painstakingly transported native plants at each visit to begin a restoration that could take centuries if it succeeded at all.

I mourned the death of George Helm, and applauded the end to the bombing; I admired the visionary energy that had galvanized the Hawaiian community. But increasingly I felt like an outsider in the land where I had grown up. It would take a *people*, I thought, to bring back to health an island nearly stripped to its bare bones. I was a second-generation colonist: what could I offer? Or, perhaps more to the point, how much was I willing to give?

What I remembered about Kahoʻolawe was my first sight, from the helicopter, of its huge, scarred back, pitted from the bombs, frightening in its scale of damage and need. On that brief visit I was not granted what had sustained George Helm, and all who continued to dream of healing Kahoʻolawe: glimpses of its remnant wild community—native plants still clinging to the gullies, turtles basking on its sands.

Here on Tern Island nearly thirty years later, an island as damaged as Kahoʻolawe, albeit in different ways, I was being granted a vision of a natural world both generative and regenerative. At the end of the spit a large turtle hauled its armored body out of the water, looking so primeval that I felt I was watching the first amphibian emerge onto dry land. It lumbered up the sand with surprising speed, rolling up and over two pits dug and abandoned, and heading purposefully back toward the water. Was it the last female of the season, looking for a good nesting site?

French Frigate Shoals is nearly the exclusive nesting ground for the Hawaiian green sea turtle, a distinct population of the *Chelonia mydas* found in tropical and temperate seas around the globe. Over 90 percent of the adult female turtles migrate from all the other islands in the archipelago, and from Johnston Atoll, to lay their eggs at this handful of sand and coral islets that altogether add up to less than one square mile.

Green turtles once nested on all the Hawaiian Islands, and old-timers remember them coming ashore to lay their eggs on beaches of Oʻahu, Lānaʻi, and Kauaʻi. But only a handful of turtle nesting sites remain on the Main Islands. Turtles have been taken as food since humans arrived in the Islands, and by the mid-twentieth century their numbers had declined drastically throughout the archipelago. The state of Hawaiʻi passed protective laws against commercial exploitation of sea turtles in 1974, but there was little enforcement. Finally, in 1978, the Hawaiian green sea turtle was listed as a threatened species under the 1973 US Endangered Species Act, which granted full protection. Though their numbers are recovering, they still remain vulnerable, putting nearly all their eggs in the sand-basket of French Frigate Shoals.

A few of the turtles that nest at the Shoals swim down from

the islands and atolls farther northwest. Most of them, however, travel from foraging grounds along the coasts of the Main Islands. If they come from the island of Hawai'i, they have swum through more than seven hundred miles of open ocean. No one knows for certain how they find their way.

George Balazs pioneered studies of Hawaiian sea turtle migration. We had barely seen Balazs, who spent all his time camping on East Island with a couple of National Marine Fisheries Service biologists, sleeping in the ovenlike atmosphere of their tents during the day and staying up all night to tag the females after they've laid their eggs on shore. Females will lay one to six egg clutches. The males, who possess legendary libidos, attempt to copulate with the females between bouts of laying, sometimes pursuing them ashore. Both sexes bask on the beaches, often next to the seals. Such basking behavior in green sea turtles is found nowhere outside the Hawaiian Islands, and only rarely down around the Main Islands.

We did have some brief moments with Balazs before he flew back to Honolulu to ask about the three turtles he had fitted with satellite transmitters the year before at French Frigate Shoals. The turtle that had been identified via a tag on its flipper as having come from Johnston Atoll, he said, had headed back out to sea a couple of weeks after the transmitter was attached. She had kept a nearly straight course to Johnston, making the 515-mile trip in twenty-two days. Satellite transmissions from this turtle continued to come from Johnston for six months before stopping (presumably the transmitter stopped working or fell off). It had been previously thought, Balazs said, that turtles used the islands and shoals of the archipelago as navigational landposts, but like the Johnston turtle the two other turtles (one untagged, the other bearing a tag from Kāne'ohe Bay, O'ahu) swam in deep ocean out of sight of land, one leaving two weeks later than the other but both taking fairly identical routes. Both turtles followed routes that took them south of the island of O'ahu, each then making an abrupt turn northward to reach their Kāne'ohe Bay destination. In each case they swam mainly against the prevailing winds and currents, one taking twenty-three days and the other twenty-six, each swimming an average distance of seven hundred miles.

Was the route taken by the two females similar to ones taken by other turtles who spent part of the year foraging at Kāne'ohe Bay? Satellite transmitters were very expensive, so Balazs had to choose his turtles carefully. This year he had put transmitters on two more females first tagged at Kāne'ohe Bay, and next year he hoped to do the same with two males, to see whether their routes deviated from those the females took. What Balasz was discovering about Hawaiian turtle migrations marked the Shoals as a place whose conservation affected the entire archipelago.

For a few weeks I had been going along with Cris on the early-morning "turtle walk" to look for new nests. Every nest was marked with a numbered stick placed a few feet inland. Figuring out what was a nest was an art: females are picky about finding just the right spot, and sometimes they excavate more than one pit before getting down to business.

On my first walk Cris showed me how to read the signs. We waited until the morning sun had climbed high enough to lure the seals from their nighttime resting places down to water's edge, where several now lay with their muzzles washed by the gentle lap of waves.

We skirted along the berm above them, searching for the symmetrical tractor-tread marks of turtle flippers levering up the beach. Cris followed one set of tracks to a bowl-like depression dug in the sand, partly filled in by mounded sand. "She started digging a pit here, and then abandoned it," he said. "See, the tracks continue." Twenty yards along the berm was another pit and another mound, this one with two humps like a camel's back. "Here's where she laid," Cris said.

What are turtles looking for when they dig a nest? Eager as they are to rid themselves of their pressing burden of eggs, they choose carefully. Nests must be safe from flooding, but able to maintain a steady temperature and a certain level of moisture. The turtle selects a place on the beach, then digs the body pit to the depth she needs to provide the best environment for the eggs. Standing in the body pit, she carves out the nest chamber with her back flippers. In his classic account, *So Excellent a Fishe*, renowned turtle expert Archie Carr describes the green sea turtle nest as "an elegantly flask-shaped, slightly lopsided, spherical chamber that communicates with the surface by a narrow neck."

Cris was down on his knees, patting one hump of sand as though testing the doneness of a cake. "When she's done laying, she mounds and then packs the sand with her back flippers," he said. "You can feel that it's more compact than the sand she threw up to dig the body pit."

The average nest at the Shoals holds a clutch of ninety-two eggs. It takes a lot of eggs to keep a turtle population going: if all hatch, the odds are only one turtle of that number will survive to maturity.

As we left the beach, entering the rough coral and sand of the artificial fill that formed the island's interior, Cris found a single rubbery white egg case—a tiny collapsed balloon. He eyed an uneven mound. "Unless a bird dropped this, there must be a nest here. Not a great place for one, in this coral rubble. There may be some hatchlings trapped. Before this island was made over, turtles probably nested everywhere on it."

Cris kneeled down and scooped the sand from a small depression in the center of the mound. A tiny waving flipper the size of a young child's thumb appeared. He probed gently with his fingers and lifted up a hatchling not much bigger than a silver dollar, pedaling its flippers furiously. A terrible smell emanated from the sand from which it had been pulled. Carrying the hatchling, Cris went back to the barracks for a couple of plastic toy shovels and a bucket. He took the bucket down to the beach and filled the bottom with wet sand.

Scarcely breathing, we scooped back more layers of sand and coral. At the end we had sixteen hatchlings trying to scale the walls of the bucket. We left four dead ones in the hole, with a few rotten eggs and a lot of empty egg cases, and carried the bucket inside. Cris put the bucket in a dark corner of the pantry. "If it's dark they'll stay active," he said. "We want them to develop their muscles for the big night ahead."

That night, a half-moon illuminating the water, Cris picked up the bucketful of hatchlings from the dark pantry and we carried it down to the beach near their nest. This was the lagoon side, washed by gentle wavelets—giant combers to these tiny beings. We lined them up on the sand partway up the beach. As they scrambled toward the water, we could just make out their tiny forms and the frothy edge of waves licking toward them. The first turtle entered the wave and was swept back up the beach and stranded on the sand. The hatchling scrambled immediately toward the water again, paddling furiously as the next wave lifted it. This time it didn't reappear. Other hatchlings were being cast back up on the beach, but in five minutes all were gone. Our presence had probably kept marauding ghost crabs away, but I wondered what lurked just offshore. The enemies of baby turtles were legion. Where the turtles found safety, or simply how they survived, was still a mystery.

These creatures were setting off on a journey that would last several years, perhaps drifting with the great gyres of the North Pacific. Through some of the deepest water in the world, they find their way back as juveniles, browsing mainly in seaweed pastures around the Main Islands, though a few show up around the Northwestern Islands. The slow-growing animals take nearly two decades to reach a breeding size of two hundred pounds or more. Adult green turtles return to their natal site at the Shoals once every two to five years to mate or lay their eggs.

Were the migrations of the turtles, I wondered, a pattern that evolved over the 12-million-year life span of French Frigate Shoals? In the Shoals' long journey from new volcanic island to a lush, mature island of deep carved valleys, plains, beaches, and fringing reefs, and its inchmeal transformation into an atoll, did the turtles begin to undertake increasingly longer migrations in search of the shallow algae pastures found most abundantly around the younger islands?

The sand was beginning to cool under me now, where I sat in the long shadow of the seawall. The sun had sunk down to shine fitfully through low, dark clouds tinged blue-green by light reflected off atoll waters. Its long rays pierced the rain squalls and fell on tiny, bare Trig Island a half mile away, its sand brilliantly lit, symmetrical as a template from this distance. It was a bright shard, a white bone half buried in the sea, like a fossil from the drowned volcanic island.

The eerie thing, I thought, in flying to the Shoals, was seeing that luminous aqua disk appear in an indigo sea, and suddenly realizing what lies below those bright lagoon waters. The reef forms a ragged crescent partly circling an enormous oval platform; as you approach you can see that the submerged land extends way beyond the reef, giving a brief sense of the titanic presence of the mountain below the fragile coral atoll.

The ability to map that underwater world was a recent product of the urge toward empire. In 1980 President Ronald Reagan had proclaimed an Exclusive Economic Zone extending two hundred miles offshore from all US territory. Bathymetric scanning along the entire Hawaiian archipelago ensued, using a submersible vehicle towed along some one hundred feet below the surface that could provide an acoustic backscatter image for a depth of three miles and a distance of thirty miles.

Maps produced by this method gave the first three-dimensional view of the drowned island reborn as coral atoll that we call French Frigate Shoals. Once a lofty island of somewhere near the size of Oʻahu, it was born where all Hawaiian islands are born, from the "hot spot," the thermal plume of volcanism that is currently feeding active Kīlauea Volcano on Hawaiʻi Island, and undersea Lōʻihi, just south of that island.

The hot spot has been birthing islands for over 70 million years, but the oldest, carried far to the northwest, have long since drowned, pared down by erosion and carried under by their own weight. The oldest dry land in the archipelago is found on the nearly 30-million-year-old Kure Atoll. Kure, having rafted on the Pacific Plate over 1,500 miles northwest, is now the most northerly atoll in the world. Although it marks the end of the archipelago, it is not the end of the Hawaiian chain. The range of volcanic mountains continues northwestward beneath the waves until it takes a sharp swerve north (for reasons geologists are still trying to understand) at a distance of 2,100 miles from the chain's most southerly point, marked by very active Lō'ihi. Beyond the bend to the north the submerged mountain range continues under the name Emperor Seamounts, each seamount (or guyot, the name given to a flat-topped seamount that once was an atoll) increasingly older until, at another 1,400 miles and nearly to the Aleutians, you come to Meiji, a guyot around 70 million years old. In its entirety the Hawaiian-Emperor chain is the longest and oldest volcanic mountain range in the world.

Looking out from Tern Island at the thin line of barrier reef that allows this islet, little more than a sandspit, to exist, I wrestle with the idea that the longest-lived islands in Hawai'i owe their lives to trillions of tiny coral polyps, busily secreting over an enormous span of time enough calcium carbonate to encircle and harbor these rich lagoon worlds. French Frigate Shoals is the apex of coral reef architecture in the archipelago, with 230,000 acres of reef habitat that supports a great diversity of corals— more than forty-one different species. The enormous volcanic mountain has now been claimed almost entirely by the sea as it sinks under its own weight, and a million years from now, the waters will close over the eroding basalt of La Pérouse Pinnacle. But as long as its reefs grow apace with its slow subsidence, this drowning island may persist for millions of years as platform for an atoll, with the lives of millions of creatures cupped within its coral crown.

From the shadow of the seawall I stood up and turned to go, catching a glimpse of the Pinnacle. Black in the dying light, leaning its guano-laden rigging away from Tern Island, the rocky stack was a ghostly frigate sailing northwest.

But it is the entire Shoals, this island with its atoll crown, that is sailing northwest at the stately pace of seven centimeters a year. In an unchanging world the Shoals would arrive, in another 16 million years or so, at the northerly latitude Kure now occupies and become the last landfall in the Hawaiian chain. It would have traveled nearly 25 degrees in longitude and 9 degrees in latitude from where its life began. It would then be approaching what is called the Darwin Point, that thermal River Styx where the atoll's coral growth, slowed by cooling water temperatures, can no longer keep pace with the settling of the great mountain beneath. As Kure is now, French Frigate Shoals would become the most northerly atoll in the world, gradually relinquishing its sand islets to the waves. For a long time it might live on as wave-washed shoals—a hazard for ships, if there *are* such things as ships then.

But the earth was entering a time of unprecedented, human-caused change. I had dreamed of finding among these far islands a pristine world where the wheels of animal migrations, the cycle of seasons, were knit whole cloth into the formal procession of geological time. Now this dream seemed like an idyll from another world, another time. It was not, I suspected, the vision of a true islander. Island cultures, in their changeable worlds, were unlikely to give much credence to permanence and linear progress.

But equally foreign to them would be a world in which human-caused climate change could alter the fate of islands. In the Hawaiian creation chant "Kumulipo," the coral polyp is the first creature to emerge from primordial night. Islanders aptly saw coral as an essential foundation of their world. That atmospheric pollution from distant industrial nations could fundamentally alter ocean temperatures and chemistry, threatening the future of coral reefs, was inconceivable. Coral polyps are exquisitely sensitive to changing conditions. These very simple invertebrates are, like their close cousins the anemones, little more than tentacles and a basic digestive system. Coral capture tiny fish and plankton, but most of their nutrients come to them as by-products of photosynthesis from microscopic plants that take shelter with them.

When coral is stressed, it boots out these algae, called zoo-xanthellae. Since the plants are the source of a reef's color, coral bereft of its tiny partners appears "bleached." Small-scale coral bleaching in response to local stressors, such as sedimentation or pollution, has long been observed, but in the 1980s bleaching on a large scale was recorded in tropical seas around the globe, and it appeared to be linked to rising ocean temperatures. Scientists were predicting that massive bleaching and die-off of coral reefs could occur as seas warmed under the greenhouse effect of increased carbon dioxide in the atmosphere. (Those predictions would turn into harsh reality a few years after my time on Tern Island. The first major bleaching events in the Northwestern islands hit Midway and Kure in 1996. In 1998, catastrophic bleaching would occur on tropical reefs around the world, devastating up to 79 percent of the coral in areas like the Caribbean.)

Warmer sea surface temperatures were not entirely to blame. Much of the carbon dioxide added to the atmosphere through burning fossil fuels was being taken up by the ocean, shifting the delicate pH balance toward acidic, adding further stress to reefs already coping with warming and rising seas.

The Northwestern Islands were no strangers to change. Over their life span the oceans had cooled and warmed, sea levels fallen and risen, great gyres of wind shifted latitude, currents changed their course. It's possible that the communities of life on some of the low-lying islands had been entirely extinguished in rising seas deep in the past, only to be reseeded from other islands in the chain. But now as greenhouse effects from CO_2 emissions warm the seas and melt the ice sheets, ocean conditions are changing at an unprecedented rate.

Like these islands, all of us are being pulled into unknown waters, into a different climate, with the dynamics of earth systems increasingly driven by human-caused alterations. Islands, not singly so much as bound together in the ocean's watery web, had something to teach us, I felt, about cycles of life in a changing world.

THREE

Monk Seals at Home

Preparing for my trip to French Frigate Shoals, I had sought out Sheila Conant, a zoologist at the University of Hawaiʻi who had spent months doing research in the Northwestern Islands. Her descriptions were mesmerizing: seabirds wheeling in great clouds over huge lagoons and tiny islands, sea turtles swarming ashore to dig nests. Waters that teemed with marine life, not just multitudinous fish but the big predators: giant trevally (ulua), groupers, and many sharks.

But it was her stories about seeing lines of monk seals basking on atoll beaches that conjured up an unimagined wildness. At the end of the twentieth century the Hawaiian monk seal, one of the most endangered marine mammals in the world, was so rare among the Main Islands that I had not met anyone who had seen one outside the Honolulu Aquarium.

Now I was nearly bedding down with them. The same seal made a nightly visit to the crawl space under my Tern Island floor. His belches wafted rank, fishy odors up through my window, and his booming sneezes (I learned that seals are plagued by nasal mites) were amplified by the cinder-block walls, compounded by the sound of his head involuntarily knocking the drainpipe against the wall. The noise would wake a row of white terns perched on my windowsill, and they would start to quarrel among themselves. The noddies in nearby bushes joined in, and I heard the clamor spread through the island's bird colonies like incendiary words passed through a mob. Through the night and into the early morning too my downstairs tenant usually remained, his head under the building but his body protruding: a torpedo shape ending in rubbery flippers.

Their onshore manners seemed less than regal, but as the only endemic mammal in the Northwestern Hawaiian Islands (there are in fact only two endemic mammals in the entire archipelago—the monk seal and 'ōpe'ape'a, the Hawaiian hoary bat), and critically endangered, the seal was king in conservation efforts. "If it weren't for the seals," Cris said, "some of the schemes our state senators have come up with for exploiting the Northwestern Islands might have been pushed through. Try fish factory. Or prison. No kidding. And, of course, nuclear waste dump."

Cris went on to give me a crash course in the heritage of my basement tenant. Monk seals are phocids, or "earless" seals, so named because the ears have no external features and are hidden beneath the hair. Of three species—Caribbean, Mediterranean, and Hawaiian—the first is extinct, and the latter two highly endangered.

Hawaiian monk seals most likely evolved into a separate species around 3 million years ago, branching off from a large population of monk seals that once occupied the Caribbean, in the food-rich waters of the equatorial current that swept through the gap at that time separating the two Americas. A population may have become isolated in the Pacific as the gap slowly closed, and found their way to the Hawaiian Islands. The new home must

have proved easy to adapt to, for the Hawaiian monk seal is nota-
ble for having retained certain "primitive" features. Other monk
seals from the Caribbean stock migrated east across the Atlantic
and founded the Mediterranean population; these seals adapted
to some changing conditions in ways the Hawaiian monk seal
did not, developing a better hearing apparatus and more efficient
flippers, for example. Adapting to the growing presence of *Homo
sapiens* was another story.

The Caribbean population of monk seals, whom Columbus
encountered and called "sea wolves," dwindled in the face of
hunting and expanding human settlement; the last Caribbean
monk seal was seen in 1952. The Mediterranean population,
common enough in Homer's time to have been given the epi-
thet "brine children" in the *Odyssey*, held on, with the rugged
shorelines of the region offering some protection. But now the
fishing boats go everywhere, the coasts are developed, and the
seal population is down to less than six hundred, mostly around
Greek islands in the Aegean and on the western Sahara coast,
and unlikely to survive much longer.

The Hawaiian monk seal population gives biologists a
glimpse into the deep past of the genus. Being branded a "living
relict" has been more of a curse than a blessing, however. Some
in the scientific community argue that the Hawaiian monk seal
faces a natural extinction, having made a home along the coasts
of islands that are drifting slowly deeper into the nutrient-poor
North Pacific. Until a short time ago, this viewpoint was sometimes put forth as reason not to do anything about their plight.
Even Hawaiian tradition seemed to concur that these animals
were rarely seen around the Main Islands, inhabiting only tiny
islets far from most human traffic. Surely, the argument went,
humans could have no blame in their diminishing numbers.

In the first years after World War II, along with coast guard operations, commercial fishing disturbed monk seal and turtle populations at the Shoals. Though the atoll was nominally managed as a refuge by agencies of the Territory of Hawai'i, fishing went on uncontrolled in the lagoon and around the atoll. Turtles were harvested and flown out, along with fish, to Honolulu; one fisherman, for example, took two hundred turtles from the Shoals between 1946 and 1948.

By the 1950s, seal and turtle populations had sunk dramatically. At French Frigate Shoals human intrusion on their pupping beaches kept the seal population from recovering from earlier depredation by sealers, feather poachers, and shipwrecked crews. A seal count conducted from the air in 1957 documented only thirty-five seals on the beaches of all the islets in the entire Shoals. (The standard estimate is that for every seal that has hauled itself out at water's edge, there are 2.5 more in the water.)

The US Fish & Wildlife Service opened an office in Honolulu in 1964 and inaugurated some survey work among the Northwestern Islands. When the Tern Island LORAN station closed in 1979, Fish & Wildlife lobbied for a permanent field station at the Shoals. They were opposed by commercial fishing interests, who dreamed of a fish-packing facility out in the rich northwestern waters, and by the Hawai'i State Department of Land and Natural Resources, who were fighting to secure state interests and continuing a long battle over who controlled the Northwestern Islands—the federal government or Hawai'i.

In the following decade, however, various federal conservation laws gave some power to Fish & Wildlife. Pacific green sea turtles were declared a threatened species in 1978 under the Endangered Species Act. Under the same act, the National

Marine Fisheries Service (NMFS) became charged with conservation of the Hawaiian monk seal.

In 1980, NMFS rather reluctantly accepted the mandate to pull the monk seal back from the brink of extinction by forming a Monk Seal Recovery Task Force. With their entry into active conservation of marine mammals (a "problematic" mantle for an agency primarily charged with supporting the commerce of fisheries, Cris pointed out), they entered into an agreement with Fish & Wildlife worthy of King Solomon. Fish & Wildlife remained primary managers in the Northwestern Islands and in charge of the new field station at Tern Island. The welfare of monk seals while on land was in their hands, but seals in the water became wards of NMFS. (The same odd split responsibility applies to turtles, who are also both land and sea animals.) As the monk seal population at the Shoals began a slow recovery after the coast guard left and the area was closed to fishing boats, it became clear that the atoll was the prime pupping ground for the animals. At French Frigate Shoals—and throughout the Northwestern Islands—the monk seal was now king. Fish & Wildlife managers were reluctant courtiers, responsible but with little authority when conservation decisions were made, but they saw the writing on the wall: without NMFS and its overseer, the National Oceanic and Atmospheric Administration (NOAA), they had little money and no ships.

The NMFS monk seal team on Tern Island, headed by Steve, a soft-spoken tri-athlete and marine biologist, and his two volunteer assistants, Kyler and Berta, were often out all day in one of the two Boston Whalers, patrolling the atoll's islets and sandbars: East, Whale-Skate, Round, Trig, Shark, Gin, Little Gin, and Disappearing Island. If they had a chance to sneak up on an unmarked seal snoozing on the beach, they bleached a number into the fur with a squirt of Lady Clairol Blonde from a squeeze bottle. The numbers made identification easier but only lasted until the next molting, so every day the NMFS team updated a computer database with other identifications—sometimes tags they could read, but often going by scars or other markings. They also looked for recently weaned pups to tag on the rear flippers with bright plastic tags, color-coded yellow for French Frigate Shoals.

The team kept an eye out for pups in trouble—abandoned, or weaned too early, with not enough fat on them to get through the first lean months on their own. If an underweight pup was female, it was brought in for captive care, held in a shallow plastic pool at the far end of the barracks and force-fed on a diet of imported (frozen) herring. When the next plane flight came, the pup would be sent to the NMFS compound in Honolulu, where it would be coaxed to catch live fish. Most such pups were released back into the wild, to build up troubled populations at other sites in the Northwestern Islands.

There were two pups in the pool now; their bawling could be heard even above the bird clatter. They caterpillared over to the edge of the pool whenever a human came near, peering out with huge, liquid eyes. Despite the rough treatment of having herring shoved down their throats, they seemed eager for contact. But it would not serve them well, if they were to return to the wild, to regard humans as friends.

We were under strict orders from Steve to have no contact with the seals outside their basic care, but I found I could stand unseen at the back window of the building and watch them tussle and mouth each other like young dogs. They were very appealing animals, I thought, in the pup stage. I had often heard conservationists lament that Hawai'i had no large endemic mammal—an island equivalent of the Chinese panda—that could serve as poster child for preserving Hawaiian wilderness. It would be hard to make a poster child of an animal virtually unknown even to the last several generations of Native Hawaiians. In the rare instances when a seal had pupped on a beach in the Main Islands, NMFS had made an effort to close off an area around them. But there were few Hawaiian beaches unused by people, and both tourists and locals had been upset by loss of access to their favorite stretch of sand. And certainly no beach in the Main Islands had ever been taken away from human use and returned to the wild.

One night I dreamed of home—that a pack of large and aggressive seals had moved in and I was wondering where I was going to find enough squid to feed them. The next day the Piper Apache flew in, bearing fresh food and Tim Ragen.

A tall, fair-skinned man in his early forties, Tim was second in command on the monk seal task force. He was a little manic but had a soft voice and a keen wit. Tim had come out to Tern to put satellite transmitters on three seals. We were all enlisted to help with the seal capture and were briefed the next morning. The transmitters would provide data on where seals foraged and how deep they dove, broadcasting position and recording time and depth. Little data had been collected on these crucial aspects of monk seal behavior. As Tim pointed out, with an ironic smile, the traditional NMFS approach to protecting species was to wait until there was an obvious problem—a clear drop in annual fish harvest, for example—and only then begin the scientific studies. The recovery team operated in the constant awareness that both time and money were running out for monk seals. The transmitter work was essential, but tricky, and the equipment expensive. (Each transmitter cost around three thousand dollars.) To attach a satellite transmitter on a wild animal you have to subdue it and dope it, and if the species is critically endangered such handling is a tough call. The previous year three seals had been fitted with transmitters, and one died during the process. "It happened with the first one we grabbed," Tim said. "They can go into a stress response, and suddenly they'll be gone."

The transmitter—about the size of a paperback, with a short antenna—is epoxied to the back of the seal. "It's more than a one-step process," Tim explained. "You have to apply one element, wait a precise number of minutes, then apply the other to bond it. The stuff is tricky. You have to work fast and accurately. The seal needs to be sedated so we can hold it still, but not so sedated that it can't recover quickly once it goes into the water. Otherwise, it'll be an easy target for sharks."

Several mornings later Steve radioed in from East Island that he and his team had found a candidate seal sleeping on the beach. Tim, Cris, and I loaded ourselves into a Boston Whaler and motored over to the island in thirty minutes. We crawled up the berm, dragging our equipment, and positioned ourselves. The seal by this time had moved down halfway to the water, snoozing on his belly facing the waves.

Steve and Kyler were able to get directly behind the animal with their hoop net and cast it over the seal's head. He woke with a start, flinging his head and throwing the net off. They got it over him again and both men were on the seal's back, pinning the animal until Berta and Cris could move in to secure its rear flippers. I started recording: time of capture, 10:42. The seal heaved up when Tim injected the Valium. He was down fast, though not out entirely, making a sputtering growl, his eyes still half open. Tim tried to get the needle into a vein for a blood sample but gave up after two tries. With a brush and detergent he scrubbed and dried an area on the back to epoxy the satellite transmitter. I timed minutes from mixing epoxy to time to attach. Everyone talked quietly, all of us staying behind the seal's line of sight.

When the transmitter was affixed, we rounded up gear, released the seal, and backed off. He moved groggily toward the water, the transmitter with its antenna incongruously perched on his back like a remote-operated road toy. "Hope he doesn't meet a tiger shark," someone said.

Tim was meticulous in his fieldwork but clearly more at home with the analytical side of his work. Hoping to finish the current status report on the Hawaiian monk seal while he was on Tern, he had brought out a hefty statistics textbook and his laptop. I helped him piece together extension cords and snake them down the hall and into his room so he could work as far as he could get from the rock music that blared almost constantly in the common room. We commiserated about being the only middle-aged crew on the Good Ship Tern. "We're the first ones they'll jettison," he said. "Or, rather, you first, since you're older than I am."

Tim could have caught the NOAA research vessel *Townsend Cromwell* back to Honolulu instead of staying on an extra week to wait for the Piper Apache's next flight out. But he was prone to seasickness of the "kill me now and get it over with" variety.

I was glad he was staying on Tern for a couple of weeks. In a life suddenly crowded with Hawaiian monk seals I began, by talking to Tim and reading, to put together a picture of their tenuous position on the earth.

We don't know the size of the monk seal population encoun-tered by the original Polynesian immigrants, who scholars be-lieve arrived in the Hawaiian archipelago about twelve hundred years ago. Though Hawaiians have a name for the monk seal—*ʻīlioholokauaua*, literally, "dog running in the rough seas"—there are no traditional stories regarding the animal. Those first Poly-nesians, who are now thought to have come from the Marquesas Islands, may never have seen a seal before. And Hawaiian his-torian David Malo, who lists the native animals and traditional lore about them in his book *Hawaiian Antiquities* (1898), does not even mention the seal.

A turn-of-the-century zoologist noted that "in 1900 a sick or helpless seal was caught by natives in Hilo Bay [on Hawaiʻi Island], towed ashore, killed, and eaten." "Unfortunately," he wrote, "I was unable to secure any part of the animal for identifi-cation, but the natives assured me that solitary seals occurred on the coast about once in ten years or so. They were very curious as to the habitat of the animal, its nature, food and habits, about which they knew nothing."

Because evidence is lacking that any significant number of seals has ever inhabited the Main Hawaiian Islands, some biolo-gists and have proposed that monk seal population has always been small and restricted to the northwestern end of the archi-pelago. A more plausible argument is that monk seals have been hunted to near-extinction and that concurrent loss of habitat has kept the population from springing back once they were no longer human prey. Early Polynesian settlers would have been attracted to the same protected coastal areas that seals favored. They must have been astounded at the easy bounty of protein seals offered. The seals that escaped two-legged predators would still have faced a steady loss of beaches where they could pup and bask undisturbed.

The earliest Western account of the Hawaiian monk seal is by the Russian explorer Urey Lisianski, who observed seals in 1805 on the sand and coral island given his name, three hundred miles northwest of French Frigate Shoals. Trading ships had followed fast on the heels of Captain Cook's "discovery" of the Hawaiian Islands in 1778, and whalers began putting in to Honolulu harbor as early as 1819. Within a couple of decades there would be more than four hundred ships a year plying the North Pacific. Their crews undoubtedly made landfall on several of the Northwestern Islands.

Shipwrecks and stranded crews were not unusual, and seals were the readiest source of food. In 1837, for example, the English whaleship *Gladstanes* wrecked at Kure. "The master and several seamen patched together a schooner and managed to sail down to the Main Hawaiian Islands," wrote marine historian Lyle Shelmidine. "The rest of the crew stayed behind, no doubt dining on seals and turtles, until eventually rescued by a vessel dispatched from Honolulu."

Less is known about the ships that hunted seals. Fur traders may have brought the monk seal very close to extinction in the early to mid-1800s. Captain N. C. Brooks of the Hawaiian bark *Gambia*, the discoverer of Midway, returned to the Honolulu port in 1859 with a reported "1590 skins." "If this account is true," said Tim, "that number might have been close to the entire seal population of the Northwestern Islands." In any event, by the late 1800s monk seal sightings were a very rare occurrence.

The few accounts mentioning Hawaiian monk seals at the end

of the nineteenth century suggest that the species must indeed have been nearly wiped out. Castaways who were stranded on Midway for fourteen months in 1888–1889 saw no seals, while a scientific expedition to Laysan in the winter of 1912 encountered only one seal. The Tanager Expedition, stopping at French Frigate Shoals in 1923, found none.

When Tim's boss, Bill Gilmartin, inaugurated the Hawaiian monk seal recovery team in 1980, he found that little was known about the seals. The few reports suggested that most of the Northwestern Island population had made a partial recovery from predation by seal hunters, guano miners, and bird-plumage hunters in the early part of the twentieth century, and continued to grow during the war period everywhere but Midway and French Frigate Shoals, but the recovery was short-lived. The first reliable range-wide surveys were conducted in the 1950s, and by the time Gilmartin became head of the task force, it appeared that seal numbers had declined over the preceding three decades by nearly 50 percent.

At the time of my visit to French Frigate Shoals in the fall of 1993, Midway's Naval Air Facility still hosted a skeleton crew but had just been declared operationally closed in preparation for full shutdown as a military base. The atoll's seal population, which may have been extirpated some time after the war, was estimated now to be only nine seals, probably replenished with seals from Kure, sixty miles northwest. Kure had supported a coast guard LORAN station since 1961. By the early 1980s, the number of pups born at the atoll had dropped to zero, and Bill Gilmartin had begun a "head-start" Hawaiian monk seal rehabilitation program there. Undersized, weaned female pups were transported from French Frigate Shoals to Oʻahu, where they were fostered for several months. Transferred then to a shoreline enclosure at Kure, they were provided with live fish to learn feeding skills before being released into the wild, apparently successfully.

The year I visited French Frigate Shoals the coast guard closed the LORAN station at Kure, air flights there had ceased, and the crushed-coral runway was left untended. The logistics of continuing Kure's seal rehabilitation program became too difficult, and efforts were shifted to Midway.

"We're still reeling from our Midway failure," said Tim one evening, as we sat out on the deck and watched the winged shapes of returning birds appear out of the dusk. "We sent twenty juvenile female seals to Midway. Two died before release. Four were found dead after release. The rest we never saw again. We were really counting on building up a healthy population at Midway—one more egg in our basket of seal populations. Some people are pushing for us to try again. But every female seal is incredibly important, when you get down to this few animals left. We don't want to try again until we figure out what went wrong."

"We're in midst of another very controversial program too," Tim said. "Three islands—Laysan, Lisianski, and Mokumana-mana [Necker]—have a skewed ratio of males to females in the breeding population. We don't know what throws the ratio out of balance but the result is instances of 'mobbing': mass mating attempts by several males with one female, or sometimes with juveniles of either sex. In any case, females are injured or killed every year, perpetuating a vicious circle."

"Our first attempt to address this problem was to remove ten adult male seals from Laysan, and move them to Johnston Atoll [an atoll 750 miles southwest of Honolulu that is not part of the Hawaiian chain]," Tim said, uncoiling from his chair and pacing to the window where three white terns were jockeying for space on the ledge. "That may have been a death sentence," he added, over his shoulder. "We never saw them again." He turned back to me and said, "This is a controversial program, to say the least. These are critically endangered animals—you can't just shoot the extra males, unless you want to be sued by various environmental groups. And zoos don't want males; they want females."

In 1992, in a second effort to deal with the mobbing issue at Laysan, ten adult males were injected with a testosterone suppressant that had been tested on captive seals at Sea Life Park on O'ahu the year before. The results of using this drug in the field, Tim said, were ambiguous. Though the drug indeed reduced aggression in the treated seals, its effects only lasted a few weeks, not for the entire breeding season.

"My personal feeling is that a lot of what's done up here, in terms of general wildlife management, is unnecessary," Tim said. "If biologists stopped and asked themselves whether what they are doing is ultimately benefiting the wildlife, they might sometimes decide no.

"But I think we all are at risk of trying to justify our job," he added. "We should be constantly questioning everything we do out here. We should even consider having areas we don't 'manage' at all."

"Have they ever considered setting aside such an area?" I asked.

"You mean all of us agencies—fed, state—agree on something? Vote ourselves out of a job? Dream on." He paused, then added, "Can we walk away from anywhere on this planet, anymore? I'd sure like to think so . . .

"Bill Gilmartin wants to continue this program of putting some Laysan male seals out of action next spring," he went on. "You should persuade him to let you go out to Laysan with him. . . . You can see what you think, experience the full irony of what we do—major interference with the seal population in what feels like the wildest place in the world. And then you should go to Midway. Oooh boy, you want to understand what effect humans have had on these islands. They're about to start an environmental cleanup before they shut down. See if you can get out there before they sweep everything under the rug."

I wanted badly to go to Laysan. Even with its history of guano mining and feather poaching, from what I had heard it promised a wildness I was experiencing only piecemeal, at best, at French Frigate Shoals. I did not yearn to go to Midway for that reason, but I knew there was a link between the fate of islands like Tern and Midway and the fate of other small remote islands in the Pacific: waves of human activity had swept through them, but none more long lasting, perhaps none more damaging, than the military. Their continuing occupation, exempt from most environmental regulation, seemed an extension of the plunder-and-abandon policies of an earlier, more piratical age. The military wave might be withdrawing from Midway, but the occupation continued throughout the Pacific: Johnston Atoll, Wake Island, Guam, the Marshall Islands. Including at home: fifty years after the end of World War II, the military still controlled 5 percent of the land in the Main Hawaiian Islands.

In Hawaiian tradition there is a protocol for making things *pono*—that is, for restoring the natural balance. The first and necessary step is a kind of group confessional: shining light on all that is hidden. The cloak of World War II and Cold War secrecy still spread over the actions of the US military among the Hawaiian Islands, as it did elsewhere in the Pacific. How, I wondered, could you clean up a place like Midway if you didn't know what went on there? I had thought that the most outrageous sins against the natural environment surely happened elsewhere in the Pacific—in places, such as Bikini Atoll (site of twenty nuclear tests by the US military between 1946 and 1958), that few Americans could even find on a map. What then to make of an article I came across at Tern Island, while browsing through a dusty file of scientific articles about the Northwestern Islands?

The article by investigative reporter Ted Gup, which appeared in the *Washington Post* on May 12, 1985, was titled "The Smithsonian secret: Why an investigative bird study project went straight to biological warfare experts at Fort Detrick." Gup's article revisited the 1969 revelation—shocking at the time—that an enormously ambitious Smithsonian-led biological study of the Central Pacific, a project which still forms the baseline for science in a huge region that includes the Northwestern Hawaiian Islands, had been funded by the US military. Under pressure from the US Senate, the Department of Defense admitted it had been gathering information for years on whether testing biological weapons on remote Pacific Islands could be done "safely." Smithsonian officials maintained they had no idea what the DOD needed the research for, which seemed to focus primarily on the migratory patterns of seabirds and of landbirds that overwintered on oceanic islands.

Gup's article probed how much Smithsonian officials knew about why the military wanted the research done but provided no new information about what testing had actually occurred or what the DOD was trying to learn. The Smithsonian's research had resulted in a series of scientific bulletins, though, that cataloged numerous trips to nearly all the Northwestern Islands. *Atoll Research Bulletin Number* 150, published in 1973, was typical: a 180-page catalog of scientific information about the Shoals up to that time. Looking over the log of research visits, I found that the navy vessels Gup claimed had been involved in actual biowarfare tests had visited the atoll numerous times between 1963 and 1968, and personnel from the Smithsonian project had come for lengthy stays.

In the file cabinets there were also *Atoll Research Bulletins* for Laysan, Pearl and Hermes Reef, and Kure. At each island the same naval vessels had brought Smithsonian scientists for lengthy visits. I asked Cris about an Atoll Research Bulletin for Midway. None had ever been released, he said. The navy had tightly controlled access to Midway during the Cold War period, but judging from the number of personnel—"a few thousand people," he estimated—"there must have been a lot going on out there."

Of all the Hawaiian islands, Midway seemed to dwell apart, wrapped in its history, as though human events could physically island—*isolate*, in the root meaning of that word—a link in an archipelago. It seemed to carry into modern times an old mistaken view of the world ocean: that its watery vastness and its islands are only linked together in the human mind, much the way that we pattern the night sky with constellations. Yet the enormous numbers of seabirds alone that the atoll supported, despite sixty years of navy occupation, were testament that Midway was an integral part of a Pan-Pacific ecosystem.

At French Frigate Shoals, tangible evidence of the complex web of Oceania was deposited daily at our feet. Where the sea marked its claim on the land at the high-water line there accumulated among the seaweed and occasional lobster shell a constantly renewed fringe of trash: netting, plastic net floats, lightbulbs, bottles of a popular Japanese soft drink and Suntory whisky, and many other items. From this vantage point Tern Island itself felt less like a wildlife refuge than a collection plate for human debris.

Once a week we collected the larger pieces, hauling wheelbarrow loads down the runway. One huge room in the abandoned generator building was filled to the ceiling with nets and other flotsam. After we collected the trash, we cataloged the items for "the researchers in the problem of pelagic trash," as Cris vaguely put it.

But the small pieces of plastic remained as a bright border high on the beach. With our loads we sidestepped arrangements of feathers and bones that had once been young albatrosses— those who had not survived the long wait for their adult wing feathers that would release them from the land. As often as not, those remains gently cupped a load of plastic. One could shun Tern Island or Midway as a lost cause, hope to land only on Laysan's relatively pristine shores . . . but inevitably, even there, would not a circle of feather, bone, and plastic accost you, like the ancient mariner's glittering eye?

PART II

Laysan

FOUR

Wild Island

For the first few months after I returned from French Frigate Shoals to my Big Island home I couldn't get enough of walking in the mountain forests, among giant koa trees and red-flowered 'ōhi'a. But soon I grew restless and found myself driving to the rocky lava coast in the late afternoons. On this geologically young island the land fell off so steeply into the depths that the sea right up to shore was only a shade lighter than indigo. You rarely saw a seabird. I had always loved the bare-bones emptiness of that stretch of coastline, but now I found the silence unnerving.

On the wall of my office at home I had pinned an aerial photograph of Laysan Island. Seven miles in circumference, the island was roughly ovoid—almost the shape, I thought, of a pregnant seal. There were patches of reef around the southern and western sides of the island, and nearly one hundred thousand acres of deeper reef surrounding the island. Like nearby Lisianski, Laysan is what is known as a *raised* atoll, one that has been lifted up as the tectonic plate on which it rides pulls it across a rise in the seafloor. Such islands do not have a fringing reef encircling a large lagoon, but in Laysan's case there is a small inner lagoon— a shallow, hypersaline body of water in the middle of the island.

Only a handful of biologists were visiting Laysan each year, traveling the nine hundred miles from Honolulu in a research vessel. I had despaired of ever getting there, but eight months after I returned from French Frigate Shoals I was invited to meet with biologist Bill Gilmartin, Tim Ragen's boss, in the Honolulu office of the NMFS.

Gilmartin was rangy, gray-bearded, and weatherbeaten, with a winning smile. He had been championing the cause of Hawaiian monk seals since he was hired to head the recovery program in 1980. He was inviting me to join a Laysan expedition as a volunteer research assistant. For me, it seemed the chance of a lifetime. A National Oceanographic and Atmospheric Administration (NOAA) vessel would drop us off and, six weeks of tent living later, would pick us up again. I had only a vague notion of what I was getting into, but I said yes.

"These will be extremely rugged living conditions," Gilmartin said, looking me over with a dubious expression. "It'll make Tern Island look like the Four Seasons." I had lived in rougher places than Tern, I told him. And I had, though I was much younger then. I took heart from the fact Bill was as solidly middle-aged as I was.

Bill explained what we would be doing. We would be capturing a number of males (to be transported down to the Main Islands and released) in hopes of reducing the injuries, even deaths, caused by mobbing of the females during breeding season, the problem Tim had described to me. A NMFS team was already out at Laysan, tagging newly weaned seal pups, taking the yearly census of the population, and collecting behavioral data on male monk seals—"identifying the perpetrators," said Bill with a wicked grin. "Working up a hit list." We would help them with ongoing seal work, build a pen to hold captive seals, capture the males, and load them on the research vessel, the *Townsend Cromwell*, when it returned to pick us up.

Bill turned me over to Michele, a twenty-six-year-old lieutenant in the NOAA corps. She quickly made it clear that she thought I had no business going on this expedition: "What we need is a second Chad," she commented, referring to the other volunteer, a marine biology graduate student built like a sumo wrestler.

She wasn't happy to be going herself. Michele had been drafted by Gilmartin, even though she was in the midst of preparing for her oral exam for a master's degree in zoology. He had made her scientist-in-charge, giving her the nightmare job of assembling supplies and equipment for what seemed to be a departure date no one had prepared for. But NMFS, Gilmartin said, had to take whatever schedule the research vessel could offer them. Only later would I learn there was another reason: this was not an expedition sanctioned by the NMFS higher-ups, but a Gilmartin expedition, patched together out of what little money was in the monk seal program's budget, pushed through before anyone had a chance to veto it.

On the eve of departure, I met the lieutenant in a cavernous warehouse full of NMFS equipment. Laysan expedition stores ready to be ferried down to the harbor filled one end. "Everything goes in plastic buckets," said Michele, ill concealing her foul mood. "First, double-seal with garbage bags and duct tape. Seal the rim of the bucket with more duct tape. Label if it should go in cabin, hold, or freezer. Anything you don't want fumigated has to go in the freezer. Check everything for seeds or bugs. Just remember, it was somebody like us who accidentally introduced *Cenchrus*, that weed that's taking over the whole bloody island."

As I set to work, I recalled hearing that the two men who had been the Fish & Wildlife *Cenchrus*-weeding team on Laysan the year before had nearly set up enemy camps at separate ends of the island by the end of their six-month stint. (I decided not to mention this story to Josh and Hannah, the young married couple who would be going with us to replace Laysan's current weeding team.) I looked at my completed packing job: eight sealed plastic buckets labeled Hold, Cabin, or Freeze. More books than I need, I thought. Should have substituted booze.

The *Townsend Cromwell* was an old ship, built in 1963 and ready for retirement. It pitched and yawed across the big swells rolling out of the northeast, the direction of the trade winds. It was a classic research vessel, 163 feet long, with a cruising speed of 9 knots. The front deck—what wasn't taken up with the loading crane and saltwater tanks for holding marine specimens, now dry and filled with sealed buckets full of canned and dried food—was crowded with large wooden cages that would hold our captive monk seals on the trip back.

Two days into our voyage, we stopped at French Frigate Shoals to drop off a Spanish biologist, here to learn how to set up a head-start program to foster juvenile Mediterranean monk seals. Then for two more days the sea was empty of islands, but scores of seabirds followed in our wake. I saw albatrosses in flight for the first time—white and black Laysans and the heavier, dusky black-foots—majestic flyers with astoundingly long, thin wings that they held rigid as oars, skimming in and out of the wave troughs, dipping the tip of one wing in the water.

At dawn of the fifth day, we could make out a thin white line of beach topped by a not-much-thicker line of greenery. The day was calm, and we were able to thread our way through the coral banks and across the shallow waters of the shelf surrounding Laysan to anchor a quarter-mile off the west shore.

Disembarking was an all-day affair, with endless loads ferried in on the ship's Zodiac and the Boston Whaler we had brought for our own use. On the *Cromwell*, we were kept busy hoisting supplies up from the hold, bringing them out from cabins, the freezer, the wet lab, and the saltwater tanks. Michele and I were the last Laysan crew off; we had stayed to fill dozens of five-gallon containers with the most precious supply: water.

The Zodiac landed us on a blinding-white expanse of sand. At the vegetation line were four white canvas tents—cook tent, office tent, and sleeping quarters for each of the two NMFS biologists already on the island. A hundred yards inland, at the high point of the island, a sturdier array of tents made up the semipermanent Fish & Wildlife camp. The couple who was departing on the *Cromwell*, both deeply tanned and looking dazed, stood next to their gear and a dozens of buckets marked Glass, Tin, Plastics, Ashes.

I staggered into the cook tent in search of shade. A woman with blonde hair matted in dreadlocks into which shells had been woven was taking voracious bites out of the first apple she had seen in three months. "I'm Cynthia," she said, "*God*, this tastes good."

The cook tent was stifling, messy, and full of flies. Cynthia zipped open the screen door and started manically, ineffectually, shooing the flies. I wondered if she and the others had given up on sanitation, gone a little around the bend. I went out and sat in front of the tent, in shade but covered with flies, and wondered how I was going to endure six weeks of this. It was late afternoon, but the sun's glare on the sand still made my eyes water.

We were short a tent, it turned out. Cynthia offered me hers and moved into the large office tent. Her tent stood high on the berm just in front of a patch of stunted heliotrope trees heavy with nesting white terns, black noddies, and frigatebirds. The advantage, she pointed out, was that it was only a short stroll to the "long drop," a toilet seat and lid perched on top of a box, the island's only latrine. Other than a couple of scraggly ironwoods, adorned like Christmas trees with boobies and frigatebirds, the only other trees visible from camp were some coconut trees way off at one end of the island.

The bird species were nearly all familiar, but here, at last, I met albatrosses face to face. Leaning against the doorway of Cynthia's tent was a huge, brown, fuzzy chick, his webbed feet propped in the air to catch the cooling effects of the slight breeze. He clattered a long hooked bill at me as I zipped open the door. Heading out to the long drop, I saw a few adults among thousands of brown chicks. These were Laysan albatrosses: white around the head and breast, with black backs and wing feathers. Their pink feet seemed gigantic for their body size, which was that of a small goose. The tube-nosed bill shaded from yellow to fleshy pink to a gray-mauve at the hook. The eyes, rimmed with dark feathers, looked sultry and intelligent.

Further along the berm the land was claimed by black-footed albatrosses. They were larger birds, a dark sooty brown with brown bills and black eyes, very handsome and fiercer than the Laysans, a gypsy version of albatross. Inland, the birds clustered as thickly as they did on Tern. An enormous ruckus was announcing my progress toward the long drop. I sat down, in full view of the Fish & Wildlife camp. A goofy-looking albatross chick, all his down gone except patches on his head that looked like muttonchop whiskers, snapped at my leg. I tried to shoo the brown noddies off the box. They moved over a few inches.

I looked out over the water. The sight of the *Cromwell* was comforting. But tomorrow it would be gone.

The flies ceased pestering us at dusk, but the birds continued their bedlam long after. My bed in the tent was a piece of plywood and a ratty piece of foam, balanced on eight cylindrical five-gallon water jugs. I was sleeping on top of my water supply. I took two aspirin to ease aching bones, unrolled my sleeping bag on the foam, spread a sheet over it, and lay down. Little breeze came through the tent's mesh windows. In the bushes behind my tent, frigatebirds landed to feed screeching chicks, with a protesting chorus from noddies, terns, and tropicbirds. Albatrosses all over the island clattered their beaks in small bursts, like sudden applause. Shearwaters had begun their wailing on a scale that made Tern Island's noise pale in comparison. I pried up the lids on several buckets before locating my earplugs.

Bird sounds seemed to taper off around midnight, and I finally drifted off to sleep. At the first hint of dawn the noise rose again to near-deafening pitch, coming from the interior of the island as though being pushed ahead of the sun. I was brought fully awake by a bird landing on my nose.

Laysan has two endemic bird species. One is a duck and the other a finch, both on the endangered list. The finch was not large, but its claws gripped its new perch fiercely. I sat up with a shout. The bird hopped onto the board I had balanced on two buckets for a tabletop and over to the screen door, then exited out the hole he had just pecked in it. The flies had already begun to find their way in.

I got dressed and went over to the cook tent as the sun rose. It was as though someone had opened an oven door. I looked out to sea. It was too late to reconsider: the ship had sailed.

Michele appeared and handed me a piece of white synthetic material. "Put this on the floor of your tent," she said. "It's been treated."

"Treated for what?" I asked.

"For ticks," she said. "Didn't they tell you about tick fever?"

I went out with Cynthia for the morning seal reconnaissance. In front of our camp, three turtles basked in a row at the waterline. We climbed a hundred feet up the beach to the vegetation line to avoid a mother seal at the edge of the water with a newborn pup, glistening black, snuffling beside her, trying to get its mouth around a teat. The placenta lay a few yards away. Further on, there was another female with a fat young one who lay on his back with a look of mindless contentment. Cynthia crawled close with a squeeze bottle filled with Lady Clairol Blonde and squirted a number on the pup's side without waking either the mother or the pup. It should suffice until the pup was weaned a few short weeks from now, when the crew could capture the pup and attach the brown flipper tags that marked it as a Laysan seal.

I watched from the berm, where I could also see back down the crescent of beach to our camp. A few yards inland from where I stood were two battered wooden crosses. "Cheerful spot," I said to Cynthia, when she joined me.

"This is one of my favorites," she said. "Oh, you mean the crosses. Well, at least they aren't wildlife biologists. The story I've heard is that they date from the guano mining. Come down near the water, you can see the sharks."

We climbed onto a wave-washed ledge of exposed coral and looked out across a turquoise stretch of water rimmed by reef. A dorsal fin and a large, pewter-colored tail rose ten feet from me. The tail was deeply notched at the end, like a harpoon, and flicked drops of water toward my knees. Beyond it three dorsal fins emerged at once. I stumbled backward on the slippery surface.

"They've been milling around here nearly every time I've been by in the last few weeks," Cynthia remarked. "They're gray reef sharks. I got in one time so I could look at them. They just kept cruising around. I saw a seal swim right through the middle of them, and they didn't even seem to notice. Don't tell Bill I got in there. He's really paranoid someone will get bit by a shark out here."

Bill and Cynthia were alike in their fierce dedication to this work. But Cynthia was clearly one of those rare individuals with a deeply intuitive understanding of animals. With a veterinarian father, she had been raised in their midst in Southern California. After earning a biology degree she started an aquarium business. On a trip to Hawai'i she had been stunned by the sight of the same fish tank species swimming free.

A job as animal trainer for the navy converted her to the cause of wild animals. She trained captive bottleneck dolphins near Honolulu that the navy wanted to send out on solo runs using the animal's sonar to search for underwater mines.

"I could get this one female to work when no one else could," she had told me, "but I could see it was destroying her. She was scared shitless the whole time. For a social animal like a dolphin, being alone in open ocean must be a horribly vulnerable feeling."

Cynthia left the navy job and met Bill when she volunteered to help NMFS monitor a rare event: a monk seal giving birth on an O'ahu beach. Bill recruited her to help with the monk seal head-start program at Kure. When the program came to a halt she worked at French Frigate Shoals and Midway. NMFS next sent her and coworker Lucy to Kure Atoll to do the annual seal census and then to Laysan. They had now been in the field for six months. "I don't want to go back," she said. "But I've got a bad tooth. And I have an eighteen-year-old daughter I want to see. And, umm, I probably need to file some divorce papers."

We had walked as far as the southern end of the island, where the beach stretched way inland. It was an area favored by the black-footed albatross. The shore was less protected, and the waves broke on coral shelves. Black-foots lay their eggs earlier than Laysan, and the chicks here were nearly free of their golden down. Their new feathers were dark and sleek, and they clattered their bills fiercely at us. When the wind came up, the albatross chicks stretched out their wings and flapped furiously.

There was a bedraggled albatross chick in the water, drifting out from shore. Cynthia stopped and pulled off her shorts and a torn, sleeveless shirt. She was very tanned all over, thin, and quite muscular. She dove into the water and swam out to the chick. It pecked at her, but she got a hand around its neck. Its wings flailed, hitting her in the face. She pinned the wings, but its head got loose. It tried to twist a large chunk of flesh from her shoulder. She wrestled it to shore. "The tiger sharks will be showing up now that some chicks are trying out their wings and ending up in the drink," she remarked, placing the sodden bird high up on the berm.

It was very hot, but I had lost the desire to jump in the water. We had now checked half the island shoreline for new pups. Chad and Lucy would be checking the other half, so we stopped to eat granola bars and quench our thirst. It suddenly occurred to me that this was the Cynthia I had heard about on Tern Island, famous for hatching the booby egg. "Yeah, that was me," she grinned. "Guess I'll never live that down. I should have been a vet like my dad—at least it would be okay to save individual animals."

We headed back overland, through an area of hard-packed sand with sparse vegetation. The land sloped gently upward in the direction of the briny lagoon at the center of the island. There were black-footed albatrosses here too, clustered thickly.

The chicks faced away from the sun, and tipped up their huge veined feet to be cooled by the air. Even so, they were panting in the fierce heat radiating from the sand. I tried to step between two adults. One bird opened its beak and displayed a bright pink gullet, then shrieked and lunged at my legs.

The area was pocked with bird burrows and littered with bird bones—an eerie, desolate expanse. On the hardpan were stumps and branches of what must once have been quite large plants. I picked up a piece. It was dried hard as a fossil.

The fossil branches, I read later, were once part of a small forest of endemic sandalwood. I had brought with me everything I could find on Laysan, which wasn't much. A brief history in a 1973 *Atoll Research Bulletin* was a starting point. And there were bits of information scattered in expedition journals and scientific papers.

In the evenings, lying on my sticky sheet, I tried to piece together the painful tale of the island's entry into human history. In 1828 the navy sent a representative around New England whaling ports to gather information about Pacific islands. He recorded several entries for a Laysan Island but found no one who could explain either the origin of the name or precisely where the island was. The first notes on the natural history of Laysan came from the ship's surgeon on a Russian vessel, *Moller*, which came upon the island in 1828. The surgeon, Karl Isenbeck, was not much of an observer, but his mention of "pygmy palms" and "several species of landbirds" would pique the curiosity of naturalists years later.

In 1859 Captain N. C. Brooks of the Hawaiian bark *Gambia* plundered at Laysan. This was the sealing expedition that had reported fifteen hundred skins (presumably sealskins) when it returned to port in Honolulu and may have driven the monk seal nearly to extinction. The captain was so struck by the unusual vegetation on the island that he made note of it: "a kind of palm tree, and splendid flowering shrubs, very fragrant, resembling plants I have seen in gardens of Honolulu." There were huge colonies of seabirds, and surprisingly, landbirds: "some of the land varieties are small and of beautiful plumage."

Since Cook's third expedition returned to England in 1779, after the captain had been killed in a scuffle with Hawaiians, the Western scientific world had slowly begun to realize that Hawai'i was a biological treasure house. Early explorers obtained a few bird specimens with the help of native bird catchers, but some descriptions would remain tantalizing, hardly believable stories for decades. The bird Hawaiians called "A kee-a roa" (*'akialoa*), for example, was said to be a "honey-eater" six inches long, with a curved bill like a scimitar a third as long as the body (an accurate description, as it turned out). None of these early expeditions, though, sailed up to the Northwestern Hawaiian Islands, or at least left record they had.

News of further Hawaiian natural wonders slowly began to reach America and Europe, soon accompanied by alarms that the endemic birds were disappearing rapidly. Still, it wasn't until 1887 that a fully trained ornithologist made it to the Main Islands: a man named Scott Wilson, sponsored by the British Royal Geographic Society. He arrived full of enthusiasm "in the belief that [he] would be able to throw some light on the geographical distribution of the species which constitute the very peculiar Avifauna of this Archipelago."

Wilson never made it to the Northwestern Islands. But he did bring back to England specimens that included fourteen new species of bird, among them a stuffed flightless rail obtained from a shopkeeper in Hilo, who had collected five of the rails in the uplands of the Big Island thirty years earlier. The last sighting of a rail anywhere in the Main Islands had been the year before he arrived, Wilson was told.

At last, in 1891, the English financier and ornithologist Lord Rothschild, intrigued by Scott Wilson's specimens and earlier tales of landbirds sighted on Laysan, sponsored the first scientific collecting expedition to be led by Henry Palmer, the first trained ornithologist to do research in the Northwestern Islands. Palmer hired a vessel named the *Kaʻalokai*, captained by F. D. Walker, who would later gain fame by shipwrecking with his family on Midway Atoll.

The naturalists of the 1891 Rothschild expedition identified the flowering shrubs the captain of the *Gambia* had described thirty years earlier as a Hawaiian caper and a dwarfed sandalwood, a new species to science but related to the tree that had already been harvested to near-extinction in the Main Islands. But the sheer excitement of the discoveries made at Laysan come through only in a few brief notes Palmer made in his diary. The number of seabirds amazed the ornithologist, but what astounded him were the landbirds. Feeding on the nectar of the flowers were "honey eaters" that closely resembled the Hawaiian *ʻapapane*, a honeycreeper now uncommon in the Main Islands in all but a few areas of rainforest. "A most touching thing occurred," Palmer wrote, when he caught one in his net: "When I took it out the little thing began to sing in my hand."

From rails Palmer collected and sent back to England for comparison with the skins Scott Wilson had collected on Hawaiʻi Island, it was determined that the Laysan rail was a separate species. It was given the name *Porzanula palmeri*. No one at the time knew that it was the last existing species of Hawaiian rail.

Palmer was particularly taken with the rail. The birds were about four inches high and tailless, with tiny truncated wings. They had large feet like those of quail and bright red eyes, and they bowled fearlessly around the expedition camp, running right over the feet of humans who got in their way. They were mostly silent, but at dusk they joined together in a short and peculiar chorus. "I can only compare the sound," Palmer wrote, "to a handful or two of marbles being thrown on a glass roof, and then descending in a succession of bounds, striking and re-striking the glass at each ricochet."

According to Palmer, the rails made nests on the ground. They were opportunists, living on insects, seeds, meat picked from dead birds, and eggs broken open by finches or by a common winter migrant, the bristle-thighed curlew. Palmer saw a rail break and eat a noddy egg: "The egg being large and hard he was quite a long time before making a hole. The rail would jump high into the air and come down with all its force upon the egg."

The expedition found, as well, a bird that resembled an Old World warbler, which they named the Laysan millerbird because it fed on large moths resembling the miller moth. They also noted a finchlike bird and an unknown species of duck.

The Laysan finch still thrives on the island, perhaps because it too is a fearless opportunist. When we ate our supper outside, the birds landed on the edge of our plates, even on our raised forks. And a dangerously small population of Laysan ducks still survived on a diet of brine flies around Laysan's inland lagoon. But for the millerbird, the Laysan rail, and the "honeyeater," time was running out. As had happened in the Main Hawaiian Islands, the naturalists had arrived as part and parcel of the juggernaut.

FIVE

Song of the Honeyeater

In July, we entered a period of such intense heat on the all but shadeless Laysan that it brought all work to a halt in midday. My tent offered only slight refuge. I stretched out on my makeshift bed. We had no freshwater to spare for laundry, so the sheet, washed in saltwater, was damp and sticky. I had given up trying to kill the flies that entered whenever I zipped open the tent flap, and sometimes I no longer swatted at them when they landed on me. Hot light penetrated the white canvas roof of the tent, illuminating its burden of bird droppings, brown splotches that were raggedly oval, like islands.

In a sun-driven daze, I thought about the Peaceable Kingdom, that ideal place where we lie down comfortably with the animals. Here there was certainly no comfort—there was, in truth, no place for us here. Albatrosses, boobies, tropicbirds, shearwaters, petrels, terns, and noddies were nesting everywhere, burrowed into the sand, tucked into the sparse shade of grasses and shrubs, precariously perched on any available branch. Brown noddies made quarrelsome attempts to balance nesting materials on the ridgepole of my tent.

Such a wealth of wildlife made it easy to imagine I was catching at last a glimpse of Hawaiian wilderness as it would have been before the arrival of humans. That was probably an illusion, I knew. It was unlikely that the Polynesians who had sailed their great voyaging canoes to nearly every corner of the Pacific, settled the Main Islands to the south, and left behind tantalizingly mysterious archaeological sites on the two nearest Northwestern Islands had not also been here. The Polynesian rat that until recently infested Kure Atoll at the far end of the chain may have arrived on those canoes. Perhaps Polynesians visited but spent little time here, for the Laysan described by the earliest Western visitors bore a dense shrub-forest of endemic species and no sign of the plants Polynesians had introduced elsewhere. But by the time the first scientific expedition arrived, that world had begun to vanish.

The Rothschild expedition found Eden occupied when they landed at Laysan in June 1891, three months after the first shipment of guano, eighty tons, was sent to Honolulu to be used as fertilizer in the sugarcane fields. The guano operation was the idea of German sea captain–turned–plantation developer H. Hackfield, whose company would be confiscated during World War I, then would reemerge under new ownership as American Factors, one of the Big Five corporations whose heirs still control much of the land and wealth in Hawai'i.

Hackfield's Laysan manager, an Englishman named George Freeth, set up a guano mining camp that included clapboard quarters and storage sheds, a tramway to move carts down to the storage sheds, and a wharf where, in favorable weather, the guano could be loaded by chute into boats and ferried to a clipper ship anchored offshore.

In the state archives there is a photograph taken at Laysan

of Freeth, a round-faced, heavy-set man wearing what looks like striped pajamas, seated in a wooden chair on the sand in front of a dark wooden building with a long porch. Next to him is a Hawaiian woman in a long white dress, and four children are clustered around the couple. In front of this suburban tableau sit albatrosses on nests—giving the only clue as to where they are.

Sometime in 1892, a photographer named J. J. Williams arrived with an expedition sponsored by England's Royal Society and took the wonderful images that include this portrait of Freeth and family. Williams also documented the early days of guano mining. One photograph shows Japanese workers in straw hats, including a young boy who could not be older than ten, raking the dark guano soil into piles and shoveling it into wheelbarrows. Directly behind them is a primordial sea of albatrosses, stretching like flecks of white spume into the far distance.

A couple of Williams's photographs give a final glimpse of a fast-disappearing landscape. One photograph of the broad plain that is now bare sand shows a sea of albatrosses nesting so densely the ground is obscured. In another, the ghostly shapes of albatrosses sit on ground dark with guano, the accumulation of countless years, in the shade cast by the fan-shaped fronds of what may have been the island's last remaining loulu palms.

The palms were gone when German naturalist Hugo Schauinsland and his wife visited Laysan for three months in 1896 on his collecting expedition through Oceania, sponsored by the new museum for "natural history, ethnology and commerce" in the bustling port city of Bremen. A man of broad interests and a fascination with Darwin's theories about the formation of coral islands, Schauinsland gives us a feeling for what the still nearly wild island was like. He described the sandalwood, growing "luxuriantly on the northwest side," its bluish-red fruit eaten by birds. The Laysan sandalwood was an endemic variety, but closely related to the sandalwood found in the Main Islands, where it had been rendered all but extinct by becoming an article of trade shortly after Western discovery of the islands. Hawaiian chiefs got whole ships, guns, and adornments in exchange for cargoes of the fragrant wood that the conscripted labor of their subjects had cut, hauled, and measured in pits the size of a ship. By 1820, only four decades after Cook's arrival, the once-vast sandalwood forests were gone on the Main Islands, and only the pits still remain to tell of them.

On Laysan, Schauinsland commemorated in his notes the extinction of the Laysan loulu palm, one can only presume at the hands of the guano miners: "As the many rotten remnants of their stumps show," he wrote, "they were very numerous." But to him, Laysan was still a wild and thrilling place. "All the plants on Laysan," wrote Schauinsland, "even totally unpretentious ones, have a pleasant smell." He mused, "The island has very few insects, and we can assume that the color and odor of the flowers exist as extreme lures for the insects that the plant needs for fertilizing its flowers." King of these plants, noted Schauinsland, was the night-blooming Hawaiian caper, "with dark green leaves, and neatly built, large white flowers." In the evening, the petals opened and exuded a fragrance the phlegmatic naturalist found "intoxicating." Schauinsland's descriptions conjured up a vision that hovered like a fevered dream on the hottest afternoons in my tent: fragrant plants and nectar-feeding birds, and a dense rustling of deep-green leaves.

In the end it was the man who most wanted to possess the island who did the most damage.

Schauinsland's Laysan host was Maximilian "Max" Schlemmer, a German-born former Honolulu police captain who was made manager of the guano operations in the mid-1890s. By 1904 the guano deposits were depleted under Schlemmer's tenure. (It is not known how much guano was finally removed from the island, but at their height the mining operations were extracting and loading onto waiting ships nearly one hundred tons per day.) Schlemmer did not want to leave his tiny kingdom, though. He talked the company into selling him everything it had brought to the island for $1,750. Then he applied to the governor of Hawai'i for a ninety-nine-year lease of Laysan (he threw in French Frigate Shoals and Lisianski for good measure). Schlemmer offered as a condition that he would plant at least one thousand coconut trees per year, to build up a plantation.

Schlemmer also sought permission to sell a specified number of bird skins per year. As decorations on women's hats, bird plumage, even whole stuffed birds, had become hugely popular in Europe and America. Hardly a bird was safe. In the late 1880s an ornithologist walking down Manhattan's Fourteenth Street counted forty species of birds on the hats of women passing by him.

Vessels from Japan were documented poaching bird skins and plumage from the Northwestern Islands as early as 1904, when American captains reported thirty-nine poachers on Midway and seventy-five on Lisianski, where they had been set ashore to do their work. On Lisianski, the men were housed in thatch-roofed shacks, which also held several hundred bundles of dried birds' wings. The Hawaiian territorial government sent letters of protest to the US Secretary of the Interior and to the Japanese government. The secretary was already receiving letters from a group formed to protest the worldwide feather trade, a group that had named itself the Audubon Society.

In his petition to the governor, Schlemmer wrote: "Owing to the depredations of the Japanese, the birds are becoming scarce, and in a few years time, unless protected, will be driven entirely away." Schlemmer offered to "protect" the islands in return for permission to kill up to twenty thousand birds a year and sell their skins. Had he not asked permission to slaughter birds, obtaining the lease to Laysan, at least, might have been a simple matter.

The territorial government instead kept Schlemmer waiting, and in desperation to find a way to continue to live on Laysan, Schlemmer went to Tokyo in early 1909 and signed a lease for $150 in gold monthly, giving a Japanese shipping company the rights to remove and sell "phosphate, guano, and products of whatever nature in and from the islands of Laysan and Lisianski."

Six weeks later, the Hawaiian government granted him a fifteen-year lease to Laysan and Lisianski, which stipulated that no birds could be captured or destroyed. The lease was dated just six days after President Theodore Roosevelt issued an executive order setting aside all the Northwestern Hawaiian Islands, with the exception of Midway, as a federal bird reserve, but the news had not made it to Hawai'i.

Schlemmer was absent from Laysan for most of the following winter, so he was not on the island when the US revenue cutter *Thetis* arrived to find a Japanese crew at work slaughtering birds. Homer Dill, a zoologist who traveled to Laysan in 1911 along with zoologist William Bryan, described what the poachers left behind:

> Our first impression of Laysan was that the poachers had stripped the place of bird life. . . . In the old open guano shed were seen the remains of hundreds and possibly thousands of wings. . . . An old cistern back of one of the buildings tells

a story of cruelty that surpasses anything else done by these heartless, sanguinary pirates, not excepting the practice of cutting the wings from living birds and leaving them to die of hemorrhage. In this dry cistern the living birds were kept by hundreds to slowly starve to death. In this way the fatty tissue lying next to the skin was used up, and the skin was left quite free from grease, so that it required little or no cleaning during preparation.

Charges were filed against Schlemmer, but they were eventually dropped, since it could not be proved he knew the Japanese poachers were on Laysan. In any case, the havoc Schlemmer ultimately wreaked on Laysan had nothing to do with bird poaching.

Schlemmer told William Bryan that he brought domestic rabbits and Belgian hares to Laysan in 1903 as another survival scheme, intending to start a meat-canning business. In 1911, when Bryan came to the island, the two breeds "had crossed and produced some strange-looking animals." "They swarm over the island by thousands," he noted. "The amount of damage done by them can better be imagined than told. . . . Unless some drastic measures are resorted to within a very short time not a bush or spear of grass will be alive."

Schlemmer claimed that had he had the money to live full time on the island, he could have kept the rabbits under control by hunting them. Another expedition by the *Thetis* in 1912 killed five thousand rabbits before ammunition ran out. The *Thetis* returned again in 1915 to find that the rabbit population was again huge and that the feather poachers had returned, leaving behind up to two hundred thousand dead birds piled up in heaps. This time when Schlemmer asked to return to guard the island, the government agreed. But he encountered so many hardships in his stay that he soon abandoned his venture.

No one set foot on the island again until 1923, when the USS *Tanager* brought a scientific expedition led by Alexander Wetmore of the US Biological Survey. The scientists were stunned to find Laysan a virtual desert. Nearly all of the rabbits had starved to death; Wetmore and crew shot the few hundred that were left. Of the landbirds, the crew counted twenty ducks, three honeycreepers, two rails, and no millerbirds. "A few dozen Laysan finches," Wetmore wrote, "still sang their sprightly song."

Some days after the expedition landed, a storm hit, turning the place into a swirling, stinging sand hell. Three days later, when it stopped, the three honeyeaters had disappeared. Wetmore doesn't mention the two rails, so presumably they survived, though the next visitor to Laysan, thirteen years later, would find no rails.

At the Bishop Museum I had seen some filmed scenes of the island from 1923, shot by one of the members of the *Tanager* expedition. The film shows frigatebirds trying to balance their nests on the dead trunks of what were once small trees—perhaps the sandalwood. There is footage of the last two rails skittering across the sand, so quick they seem to roll like feathered golf balls, with a flap of tiny wings as they banked around the corner of a chunk of phosphate rock.

And there is a shot of one Laysan honeyeater—the bird that sang, unafraid, in Palmer's hand—perched on a piece of phosphate in lieu of a shrub, opening and shutting the curved beak that evolved to sip nectar from flowers, the life of an entire species reduced to one unheard phrase in a silent film.

Vanished Laysan, with the caper's white flowers and the red flash of the honeyeaters' wings, shadowed my thoughts during all my days on the island. The island had reached a full evolutionary flowering and was now diminished by the loss of these species. Yet the landscape that remained was potent in its harmony. At sundown one day as I stood at the water's edge I heard a snort and turned to see a young monk seal's head emerging close by. I backed up the bank a few feet. The seal, its coat the golden color of near-molt, humped half out of the water and gazed at me, where I hunched down, as still as a log. It caterpillared up the bank toward me, eyes a liquid black and coat burnished to a sheen in the glow of sunset. It dipped its nose in the sand and pushed forward a few more feet with its nose buried, then its whole head, neatly scooping out a wallow, and then looked up at me again, blinking through a mask of sand. Young seals in particular are unwary and seem to seek out company to bed down next to: other seals, preferably, but sometimes a turtle or a log, or even me, apparently. The seal was an arm's length from me now and gave me one more look, closed its eyes, and slept, its sandy face a mask of fading gold.

Out over the sea, a crescent moon had appeared, with Venus riding its horn. I inched away from the seal, scooting up the bank on my rear, smiling at my own awkward version of seal locomotion.

In the middle of the night I woke up in my tent and wondered if the seal was still there. I walked down to the beach. It was, sleeping soundly. The new moon was down, but Venus laid a gleaming track on the water nearly as bright as moonlight. In the bushes behind my tent, the roosting frigatebirds and black noddies were inky shadows. On the ground the large, downy albatross chicks slept with their heads turned and buried in the thick feathers on their backs, making shapes like dark inverted quotation marks against the starlit sand. As just one more shadowy animal form, I lingered for a moment in a Peaceable Kingdom.

SIX

Ducks near the Vortex

A newborn seal was being raised right in front of our Laysan camp. At first the pup's skin was loose and wrinkled, like a wetsuit several sizes too large, but in three weeks she ballooned on her milk diet, her pelt still glistening black but now stretched tight. I named her Momona—Hawaiian for "plump, bursting with ripeness." The mother seal, "Camp Mom," and Momona bunked down every night against an old driftwood log directly in front of Michele's tent. Michele had scared up a piece of plywood and placed it in front of her tent, a platform for her aerobic workout; and every night she donned her Walkman and sweated through a militant, arm-pumping routine. The seals took no notice.

In the mornings Camp Mom would lead Momona down to the water, to a place where the coral formed a shallow pool. The pup spent most of her time nose down to the coral, back flippers up in the air, getting acquainted with reef life. The mother rested her head on a shallow coral head and dozed. She was beginning to lose weight, her ribs showing under her pelt.

One evening Bill Gilmartin and I sat out watching the last light fade and storm clouds gather. The next day we would start building the pen to hold the seals we planned to capture. Down the beach a group of young albatrosses stood at water's edge and flapped their wings in the rising wind. "They're close to flying," Bill said. "That means the tiger sharks will be showing up. Keep that in mind next time you take a bath."

I asked him about the "hit list." "We're nearly done with compiling it, from information gathered from the last few years' observations of which seals tend to do the mobbing," he said. "We'll have a primary list and a secondary list. We hope to get all seals from the primary list, but we can't hope to find all our 'most wanted.'"

"Do you worry that you're not getting the right ones?" I asked.

"On our CRAM list?" asked Bill, widening his eyes in mock surprise at my doubtful tone. "That's what I've dubbed them: Convicted Rapists and Murderers." He laughed at my frown at such flagrant anthropomorphism. It was the kind of maverick humor that has not always been appreciated in the sober halls of marine science.

"It's been hard to collect data on mobbing, because it's only been witnessed a few times," Bill said, cradling tenderly what he said was his last beer. "But we've learned how to predict potential mobbers. Generally they're the subordinate males."

The daily patrols, Bill explained, helped to separate out the dominant males—"they're the ones you find on the beach near the mature females"—to make sure they didn't end up on the hit list. "Some biologists," he went on, "have been concerned that by taking some males we'll interfere with natural breeding variability. But generally it's a small number of dominant males that are doing the mating, so those are the genes being passed on. They don't stay dominant for long—maybe one to three years. It's a consuming job."

I thought about what another scientist had said to me in the NMFS warehouse as I was loading up my plastic buckets for the trip to Laysan. She had spent considerable time on Laysan and was very skeptical about removing male seals. "Other pinnipeds, such as elephant seals, exhibit mobbing behavior," she said, "so we can't say it's abnormal. It's been observed at French Frigate Shoals, where the population *isn't* skewed. We really don't know much about these animals—we don't have a clue what the optimum male-to-female ratio is."

"Are you convinced that removing some male seals will make a difference?" I asked Bill, who was tilting his head far back to drain the beer can. Alcohol was one way he self-medicated his back problem, and I wondered how he would do without his evening dose.

"Nope," he said. But he knew something of the perils of intervening too late: "Biologists trying to save the condor waited until there were only a few left, captive-bred those, and then released these clueless animals into a habitat where they had to deal with things like low aerial wires. That's what got the first couple of them. . . . Or, if you want an example closer to home, think of the *'alalā*, the Hawaiian crow."

I was familiar with the crow story, since the *'alalā* was Hawai'i Island's most endangered species. The fossil record showed other species of crow on other islands, but only the Big Island *'alalā* had survived into the twentieth century. It was never plentiful in number, but in 1940 small flocks could still be found in the remaining forests above Kona and in a couple of places on the east side of Mauna Loa. The surviving species of Hawaiian crow, *Corvus hawaiiensis*, looks much like the American crow but behaves with uncharacteristic shyness, and, unlike its cousin, is highly sensitive to disturbances near its nesting sites.

The 'alalā had been placed on the Hawaiian protected bird list as early as 1931. But the territorial administration, and after 1959 the state, had made little effort to protect it. Federal efforts to save the 'alalā had begun with the US Fish & Wildlife Service turning over to the state three fledglings captured in Kona. In 1980, when a federal 'alalā recovery team tried to take back the birds to establish a captive breeding program at the San Diego Zoo, state officials stalled, and the birds languished at a state facility on the Big Island.

In 1991, after the Audubon Society sued the Fish & Wildlife to push the agency into taking more aggressive action to save the 'alalā, the few eggs laid in the wild that year were collected and reared at a Big Island facility run by the Peregrine Fund. A few years later, some of the growing captive flock were released back into the wild. But they had not fared well. "The old story," Bill said. "If you raise an animal in captivity, it is never going to have the savvy of an animal reared in its natural state. It already has one big strike against it."

Bill was staring out at the horizon, his expression somber. "We're probably going to get a lot of shit for moving these seals," he said. "I expect, for one, to hear from fishermen if these seals show up at their boats and snag their catch. That's why I wanted to get it done this year."

Bill put his hands on top of his head and stretched gingerly up and back. "Look," he said, "these animals are going extinct, due to direct or indirect human impact. Maybe it's the numbers of seals killed in the past, maybe it's the disturbance to their pupping sites. Maybe it's more subtle: the state is still allowing commercial lobster fishing and bottom-fishing within these waters, so we could be competing with the seals for food.

"So with 'mobbing,'" he continued, "what might be natural—

and relatively harmless—behavior in a large population could spell doom for a highly endangered one. If you have a species like the monk seal that humans have interfered with so much it's no longer viable on its own, does the argument that wildlife biologists shouldn't 'interfere' make sense?"

That we would start building the pen for the seals was good news to me, since it meant release from the onerous task of weeding *Cenchrus* with Josh and Hannah and Cindy, the Fish & Wildlife biologist who had come along on the *Cromwell* to help the couple get set up. Someone had come up with the perfect outfit for protection against ticks: pantyhose. It was almost unbearably hot, and the nesting brown noddies dove at our heads; seeing Josh tackle platter-sized clumps of the sandbur, legs clad in Tawny Pink, was the only amusing thing about the job. Josh and Hannah couldn't afford to complain—this would be their main job as the lone custodians of Laysan for six months after the rest of us had left.

Josh and Hannah were also learning the ropes of the once-a-week Laysan duck census. I tagged along, since it was my only chance to venture inland—generally off-limits so as not to disturb the burrowing petrels and shearwaters, who had almost completely honeycombed the interior. And, though the ducks reportedly came down to the shore now and then, it might be my only chance to see one of the world's most endangered waterbirds.

The ducks mostly stayed around freshwater seeps at the edge of Laysan's interior lagoon, which produced an endless supply of their main food: a brine fly whose larvae grew to maturity in the hypersaline water. The ducks fed most actively at dawn and dusk, so the duck walk always started at 5 p.m. Cindy lined us up and gave us strict instructions to keep up with her, as she was supposed to keep the same pace every time she did the walk, to complete her circuit around the lagoon in one hour. We followed her single-file along a path marked with stakes that threaded through the bird burrows, coming up and over the highest point in the island. At the lofty height of forty feet I could see the whole island for the first time. The mile-long lagoon was rimmed by dried mud crusted with salt and colored a startling pink from the carcasses of brine shrimp. I could see, at the far end of the lagoon, the grove of coconut trees, and, across the island, waves splashing against the eastern shore.

As we walked toward the lagoon, we cut a transect through small mounds of the rare endemic herb *Nama sandwicensis*, interspersed with a low-growing naupaka, then bunchgrass. We were walking through a landscape I had never before seen whole—coastal strand vegetation as it had once been everywhere in the Hawaiian Islands. Nearly all the naupaka was colonized with nesting frigatebirds. The birds' sound swelled as though we had entered a stadium, and looking ahead, I could see young albatrosses clustered thickly among clumps of sedge that surrounded the edges of the saltpan.

We stepped across a thick green carpet of morning glory and puncture vine onto the salt-soaked ground around the edges of the lagoon, which gave way under our feet with the sponginess of an uncooked Pop-Tart. Not a duck was in sight. I recalled a photograph of a small brown teal-like creature with a distinctive white ring around the eye. The duck stood in an empty concrete wading pool in some zoo, and the white around its eye gave it a haunted, insomniac air. The wild population stood then at an estimated two to three hundred individuals on this tiny island, vulnerable to tropical storms, to an introduced disease or predator—rats, say, from a shipwrecked fishing vessel.

"Last year," Cindy said, "we found an alarming number of dead ducks and decided they died of starvation or of the freshwater seeps drying up. It was an El Niño year, and that produced a drought here. This year's count is also very low. It's a bit scary, but then there have been really low counts in the past. These ducks have made some miraculous recoveries."

Guano miners and feather hunters had fed on the ducks. An expedition in 1911 counted only six, but then Laysan ducks were never easy to count: the instinct to flush was no longer bred in their genes, and their cryptic colors were hard to spot. But in 1923, when Alexander Wetmore of the *Tanager* visited the island that had been turned into near-desert by rabbits, with little shrub to hide the ducks, he counted only twenty-five individuals. So the population had more than once been through a genetic bottleneck—a reduction of numbers so severe that what emerges at the other end is a population with greatly reduced genetic diversity.

It was only in the late 1980s that a working theory for how genetic bottlenecks occur emerged, aided by advances in genetics and in computer technology. By studying populations on the verge of extinction (such as the red wolf, the black-footed ferret, and the Florida panther), biologists can measure how a small population can spiral downward into what has been gloomily named an "extinction vortex." If no genes migrate into a small population through breeding with members of another population of the same species from elsewhere, the isolated group will inbreed and slowly lose genetic diversity. The possible negative results of inbreeding—deleterious genes that might have lain quietly recessive expressing themselves in the new generation—are so notorious that to protect from human inbreeding twenty-four US states still prohibit marriages between first cousins. But inbreeding also has other negative effects that in a small population may begin the spiral toward extinction. Inbred populations commonly begin to show reduced growth rates and decreased reproduction and survival. Less gene diversity often entails a narrower range of traits and behaviors, and less ability to adapt to changes in the environment. What would seem like relatively minor fluctuations in their environment can kill off such small groups.

A famous study of Darwin's finches done in the Galápagos Islands by evolutionary biologists Peter and Rosemary Grant illustrates clearly how one small variable in a population may be the adaptive key to survival. On rocky Daphne Major the Grants kept track of endemic populations of finches over a span of twenty years. In that time span they saw evolution actually happening through intense pressures of natural selection. A severe drought reduced the finches' food supply to primarily the hard mericarps of the puncture vine, *Tribulus cistoides*. Genetic diversity had produced a few birds with unusually large bills, and it was just those with bills large enough to crack the tough pods that survived and were able to breed a new, large-billed, generation.

There have been captive Laysan ducks in zoos since the 1920s. But captive populations inevitably show all the downsides of inbreeding. Even carefully selective breeding programs run into problems maintaining a healthy genetic mix: sexual selection is one of the key components of maintaining diversity, and humans will never be as good at selecting the right mate as ducks themselves are.

As we followed Cindy single-file around the edges of the lagoon, whose placid surface began to glaze over in an opaque silvery-gold under the late afternoon sun, and no ducks appeared, I thought of the German naturalist Hugo Schauinsland's amazed and puzzled speculations about the mystery of finding "on this tiny island in the middle of the endless ocean . . . five different land birds which do not live anywhere else on earth." It was 1896, sixty years after Charles Darwin felt the first little nudges of evolutionary theory, nearly forty years after the publication of *On the Origin of Species*, when Schauinsland savored the cool air of twilight on Laysan and watched a "neat little red bird," the Laysan ʻapapane, "searching for food in the local flower-cups." He noted that it especially favored the "large, frail white flowers of the Hawaiian caper" that bloomed in the evening and filled the air with its perfume. He watched the Laysan rail run between the sedge so fast its legs were a blur, and wrote: "The great specialization of the avifauna [of the Hawaiian Islands], which do not exist anywhere else to such a high degree, testifies either to the very great age of these islands or the proximity of a very old, now defunct landmass from which the fauna originated."

There was another possibility: that the Laysan duck had in fact evolved on one or more of the Main Hawaiian Islands, and found its way to Laysan at a later date, but was now extinct everywhere else. But the idea that major extinctions had occurred before Western arrival and the damaging introduction of cats and mongooses and disease-bearing mosquitoes was an idea that none of the early naturalists could get their minds around. "We could not think," Schauinsland mused, "that [Laysan's endemic landbirds] also occurred on [the Main Islands] in the past and died out there at present." When the naturalist spent his brief time on Oʻahu awaiting the boat to Laysan, he admired the rich fertile landscape, the cultivated fields that stretched all the way up to the foothills where forests began, and, like seventy years of scientists after him, never imagined that the Polynesians could have radically changed the Hawaiian environment.

That paradisiacal view was not challenged until 1971. In a conversation I had with him in 2002, zoologist Alan Ziegler remembered being in his office at the Bishop Museum, cataloging bones of various mammals from as far away as New Guinea, when a woman on the island of Moloka'i called. She'd been walking the windswept dunes of the island's west end and had come across bones sticking out of a bank recently eroded by storm waves. She knew enough about natural history to tell that the bones belonged to a bird, but it was a larger and stranger one than any she had ever seen.

"I tried to get the Smithsonian to send someone out," said Ziegler, "but finally ended up going over with my daughter, Marjorie, and digging the thing up. It was the size of a very large goose, but it had a very heavy skull. I had brought my goose skull collection with me when I moved to the Islands, and this wasn't like any of those. I dug it out in one big sand ball, encased the whole thing in plaster when I got home, and mailed it off to the Smithsonian."

In fact the bones were those of a duck—a very large, flightless duck—and radiocarbon dates yielded an age of around twenty-five thousand years ago. In 1976, the Smithsonian sent paleontologist Storrs L. Olson to Hawai'i to look for more fossils of the moa nalo ("lost fowl"), *Thambetochen chauliodus*.

Olson, soon joined by biologist Helen James, began to explore lava tubes and limestone sinkholes—the La Brea tar pits of this volcanic terrain—on several islands. What they found astonished them: forty-four previously undiscovered species of landbirds. Of these, twenty-two were either flightless or "nearly so," including flightless ibis, geese, and rails. The researchers found other remains of Ziegler's bird, which turned out to be a nearly four-foot-high gooselike duck with a massive beak (somewhat like that of the recently extinct moa of New Zealand). "It must have grazed like a herbivore," said Ziegler. "In a land with no ungulates, you could say it was the Hawaiian sheep."

Other finds included a goose that fed heavily on fern spores, a long-legged owl, a duck that resembled the New Zealand kiwi and was probably nocturnal, a sea eagle, two large species of crow, and several extinct species of honeycreeper. The seabirds were represented too. The Bonin petrel, which now nests only in the Northwestern Islands, was found in many of the sites, and the dark-rumped petrel, with only a few tiny populations still breeding on upland Hawai'i, Maui, and Kaua'i, was the most abundant fossil found in the sinkholes on O'ahu.

Hawai'i had once been a paradise of both land and sea birds. Where had they gone?

Evidence from sinkholes and middens suggests that most of them disappeared in the first few hundred years after humans arrived in the archipelago. Birds who had never known predators were a bountiful food source for early settlers. But Ziegler preferred to explain their demise in terms of what anthropologists call "transported landscapes." "People bring their environment with them into a new land," he told me. "They bring along rats, pigs, dogs; they clear forest and plant crops." Consciously or unconsciously, in other words, pioneers impose their own cultural landscape on new environments, usually to the detriment of endemic species.

I was interviewing Ziegler in his home when he told me this. Every surface was covered with objects from a richly eccentric life, a Museum of Ziegler of everything from beer-can hats to ancient bee smokers. They vied for space with rocks, bones, seeds, shells: a landscape transported indoors.

In the ensuing decade one man in particular would begin to solve the puzzle of where the birds went, assembling piece-meal the fossil record in his own excavations on remote islands throughout the .Pacific, and from bones sent by colleagues. David Steadman, a dark-bearded, intense man whose specialty is paleoecology—the study of fossil bones for clues to past envi-ronments—has searched for bird bones on many of the world's remotest islands. What he has found nearly everywhere is evi-dence that an extraordinary number of species disappeared after humans arrived. At many of the sites the bones are mixed in with cultural midden: bones of fish, chicken, dog, and shells of the marine mollusks the Polynesians favored as food. Humans, Steadman, says, delivered a "triple whammy," directly preying on birds that had no defenses against predators, introducing predators like the rat, and destroying habitat, all in the process of establishing their own transported landscape.

The rail is the signature bird for the fate of flightless birds throughout the Pacific. "There are around eight hundred 'major' islands in Oceania," Steadman says. "Each had at least one endemic species of rail, probably the descendants of birds blown there by storms. After they ended up on isolated islands with no predators, losing their flight muscles was not a huge evolution-ary step." The rails evolved into many species, including a giant swamp hen nearly a meter tall in New Ireland and a minuscule crake in the Cook Islands.

At a time when the work was still controversial, Steadman's mission was to bring birds back to "islands where they once occurred, or as close as we can get to that." "We can't afford to be real choosy," he stated at a conservation conference held in Hawai'i in 2001, "since we have to work with what we've got left, and only a few islands are free from rats or other predators." Like Bill Gilmartin, he was not interested in "waiting around for population viability analyses when a species is right on the brink of extinction."

"I recently translocated some megapode eggs to 'Eua Island, in the Tongan archipelago," Steadman told the conference audience. The small limestone island had lost at least twenty-three species of landbirds, including a tiny megapode, after humans had arrived about a thousand years ago. Steadman's eggs were from a closely related megapode. "A very low-tech operation," he said, "just me and four rugged Tongans who like birds."

Sheila Conant, the senior ornithologist when it comes to Northwestern Hawaiian landbirds, advocates a more cautious approach, partly based on her own experience with translocating the Laysan finch. "With species disappearing, we may be tempted to jump at any chance to translocate species, but we need to consider such moves with absolute care," she wrote in a seminal paper in 1995: "Saving Endangered Species by Translocation: Are We Tinkering with Evolution?" Translocation in the form of *reintroducing* endangered species into former habitats is a fairly accepted goal within the biological management community, though not without its problems, particularly with animals that may compete with humans for resources, such as grizzlies, wolves, even sea otters. But *introduction*—or, as Conant defines it, "establishing populations of an endangered species outside the species' known range"—is a different kettle of fish.

In 1981 Conant, immersed in her research on Necker and Nīhoa Islands, read with great interest about the work of Peter and Rosemary Grant in the Galápagos Islands. Conant put together a research proposal to measure the bills of a population of Laysan finches introduced from Laysan to Pearl and Hermes Atoll, eighty miles southeast of Midway, in 1967. The translocated finches had done well, and the population had nearly doubled in size when Conant, after measuring finch bills at Laysan, arrived at Pearl and Hermes in 1983.

On Laysan, the puncture vine *T. cistoides* is not common and makes up only a small portion of the finch diet, but on Pearl and Hermes it is abundant, and in the harsh conditions of this much smaller atoll, it became an important source of food for the finches. Conant found significant differences in shape and size between the bills of finches on Laysan and those of the introduced species of finches at Pearl and Hermes. "It appears," says Conant, "that the mericarps [of the puncture vine] are acting as an agent of natural selection." As the Grants had discovered in the Galápagos, only the birds with beaks large enough to crack the tough pods were surviving.

Conant had learned from the Grants' work in the Galápagos and from her own research on the introduced Laysan finches how rapidly evolutionary change can take place when intense environmental pressures are at work. "When we translocate a species," she wondered, "are we taking a chance that it may eventually become so distinct from the original type that biologists must call it a new race or species? Our aim may be to save a species, but what we may be doing is tinkering with evolution."

This was a long-term outcome that had to be considered. But for species in imminent danger of collapse the more immediate concerns were these: if introduced to a new environment, what opportunity did the species have for survival, and what effect might it have on the flora and fauna already there?

In the same year that she documented the changes in finch bill size, Conant found herself fighting against a Fish & Wildlife Service proposal to introduce the Nīhoa millerbird to Mokumanamana Island. The proposal, she commented, "failed to consider the potential impact of this insectivorous warbler on the terrestrial arthropod fauna of the island, which contains at least 15 endemic taxa, and no avian insectivores." In other words, the cost of translocating the millerbird might be the demise of several species of endemic Mokumanamana bugs. When her analysis also suggested the island could only support a maximum of seven pairs of millerbirds, the translocation idea was dropped.

The Laysan duck, though, was a bird of another feather. Alan Ziegler, on a field trip to dig for evidence of human settlement on Lisianski, found no such prehistoric evidence but came home with bones of the Laysan duck. A year after I left Laysan, the fossil remains of Laysan ducks would be identified from five of the Main Hawaiian Islands. The fossil bones were about three thousand years old, on average, making it likely the ducks were around when Polynesians arrived, and suggesting that the ducks may not have survived the self-propelled translocation, a thousand years or so years ago, of humans to the Hawaiian archipelago.

Software that could model the likely future of any endangered species suggested the Laysan duck stood perilously close to the "extinction vortex," even if its environment remained stable. And in truth their saline lake habitat on Laysan was a tiny lifeboat any rogue wave could swamp: prolonged drought, a severe storm, disease brought in by a migrant bird. It was time, Conant agreed, to act. The ducks could be reintroduced to Lisianski. But whatever freshwater seeps had once been available to them on that island must have filled in over time and would have to be dug out, and the logistics of transporting people and equipment there to do so were daunting. Surprisingly, it was thought that Midway, if current efforts to rid the atoll of rats were successful, and if the groundwater was not too polluted, might be the best option.

In 1994, from the viewpoint of Laysan, these ideas were only plans on paper, and the ducks themselves were one tiny flock on one small island, condemned by an evolutionary path toward flightlessness to stay where they were. On the duck walk that evening, we had reached the end of the lake where freshwater seeps supported rich stands of sedge along the edges of the salt flats. Cindy stopped abruptly. Out from the sedge and across the salt flats ran three small brown ducks. Neck to neck, they stampeded across the flat, raising a huge cloud of brine flies. They ran full bore and open-beaked through the flies, scooping up dinner, a behavior unexpected but perfectly tuned to this environment, an exhibit of Laysan-style duck pluck that converted us all immediately, irrevocably, to the cause of their survival.

Over a decade later it would be impossible to look back on that bright moment without a certain nostalgia for simpler times. The complex issues of restoring species to their former homes had become all the more complex in light of global climate change and rising sea levels.

Yet the emerging message of islands on a slow-motion roller-coaster ride over underwater risings and deeps toward a more northerly clime, in an archipelago that in its 70-million-year life has weathered global shifts in climate, warming and cooling seas, shifting currents, rising and receding sea levels, is that flux is the engine driving evolution.

Here was the Laysan duck, surviving on one small 20-million-year-old island. Holes have never been drilled at Laysan, but at Midway, three hundred miles northwest, deep probes to the drowned basaltic platform of the atoll brought up cores that tell of drastic change. From as far back as 16 million years, periods of coral growth are layered like a cake with long intervals when only sediment, no living corals, were laid down. There have been periods, the cores tell us, when conditions—rates of subsidence, ocean temperatures, sea levels—changed so dramatically that the lowest Hawaiian islands lost every living thing. For the most vulnerable islands, such events may not be buried deep in the geological past. Over the glacial and postglacial periods of the last several thousand years, sea levels have risen and fallen, possibly standing two meters higher in this region of the Pacific only twenty-four hundred years ago.

Islands, in their root sense of "isolate," play a crucial role in creating new species, but within a web of life that allows periodic renewal. The young, high islands of Hawai'i must have once served as repositories of species to reseed the fragile older islands. Now, with those once-vigorous ecosystems stripped of much endemic biota (such as the Laysan duck), the shoe is on the other foot: fish larvae drift down from the northwest to renew fish stocks among the overfished Main Islands, turtles return from their crèche at French Frigate Shoals, seabirds are slowly renewing nesting sites among the Main Islands wherever they can be protected from introduced predators. But with the Laysan ducks of the high islands now all gone, the on-the-edge survival of one small population on their namesake island reminds us that no island stands alone.

SEVEN

Transported Landscapes

Surely Polynesian voyaging canoes had come here to Laysan. I was so sure of it I would wake at night thinking I heard the scrape of a canoe against sandy shore. The wishful dream of the castaway? Yes, but it was also born of excitement over the recent accomplishments of the Polynesian Voyaging Society. In 1976, the *Hōkūle'a*, a sixty-two-foot replica of a Polynesian voyaging canoe, sailed from Hawai'i to Tahiti using only traditional navigation techniques under the tutelage of master navigator Mao Piailug, from the Caroline Islands. The lost art of wayfinding was reborn.

By the early eighties, Piailug's Hawaiian apprentice Nainoa Thompson had fully mastered his craft. Under Thompson's guidance the 1985–1986 journey of *Hōkūle'a* tracing likely ancestral migratory routes in a 16,000-mile circuit of the Polynesian Triangle (Hawai'i, Aotearoa [New Zealand], Rapa Nui [Easter Island]) was a triumph, reconnecting the people of Polynesia and proving that sailing canoes were capable of making crossings in all directions, with attention paid to prevailing wind patterns at different times of year. In 2004, ten years after the canoes entered my dreams on the shores of Laysan, the *Hōkūleʻa*, with Nainoa Thompson navigating using ocean swell, star position, the shapes of clouds, and the flights of seabirds, would sail from one Northwestern Island to the next—all the way to Kure, the last atoll.

Archaeological sites on the volcanic remnant islands of Nīhoa and Mokumanamana—130 miles and 290 miles, respectively, northwest of Kauaʻi—are testament that ancient canoes had sailed northwest, but no further physical evidence has been found in the ephemeral sands of the more distant low coralline islands. A few chants, though, such as those that relate the arrival in the archipelago of the volcano deity, Pele, do suggest knowledge of islands beyond Mokumanamana (Necker). As befitting a story of the island chain's sequential creation by volcanism, Pele's journey starts at the far northwestern end, home of the most ancient islands, and finishes at her present home in the actively erupting Kīlauea Volcano on Hawaiʻi Island. The chants give no specific names to the first low islands encountered by Pele, referring simply to "Mokupāpapa," or "low reef island." (Hawaiian elders have now given that name to Kure, the oldest and last island in the archipelago.)

The earliest Western visitors record a couple of hints that Hawaiians regularly visited at least one of the low coralline Northwestern Islands (most likely French Frigate Shoals, only 75 miles beyond Mokumanamana). There is, for example, this intriguing journal entry of Lt. James Burney, a member of Captain Cook's crew, dated March 15, 1779: "At 7 in the morning, weighed and sailed from Neehow [Niʻihau, the oldest and most northwesterly of the Main Hawaiian Islands]. Steered to the Westeward in search of a low flat island which the Indians told us lay to the west. . . . They call it Tomogoopapappa [Mokupāpapa]. It is uninhabited and abounds in Turtle."

According to another journal entry from Cook's last voyage, Hawaiians said they sailed in search of "red birds," most likely a reference to the red-tailed tropicbird (once resident throughout the archipelago but now rarely found among the Main Islands), whose tail feathers were highly valued.

In the decades following the arrival of Europeans, whatever connection Hawaiians had to the Northwestern Islands seems to have been severed. In 1822 the Hawaiian regent queen Ka'ahumanu, hearing the name of Nīhoa in an ancient chant, decided to sail with an American captain to search for the island and annex it to the Hawaiian Kingdom. Some of the crew managed to land on Nīhoa, but apparently not the queen herself.

In 1885 an "excursion party" organized by Hawaiian princess Lili'uokalani landed on Nīhoa and, according to one member of the party, the Reverend Sereno Bishop, "ransacked" the island for "birds, skins, eggs, and feathers." One of the party accidentally started a brush fire, and in the precipitous departure most of the loot was lost.

Nine years later, representatives of the provisional Hawaiian government, American businessmen who had colluded in the overthrow of Hawaiian Queen Lili'uokalani the year before, visited Mokumanamana to claim the island. A photograph shows the party standing on a rocky outcrop reading the proclamation: six men looking self-important, with an inquisitive frigatebird hovering overhead.

At the top of the island, a place they named Annexation Peak, the men found several structures that were clearly *heiau*—religious sites. One temple platform, more elaborate than the others, was a two-tiered structure, walled on three sides, and paved with small water-worn stones. On the paving stood several stone human figures nearly a foot high, with flat faces and wide mouths, protruding eyes, jug-handle ears, and erect penises. The annexation party brought back seven of these "curios."

In 1923 the Tanager Expedition arrived, with archaeologist Kenneth Emory aboard, to spend several days doing a survey of both 170-acre Nīhoa and 45-acre Mokumanamana. On Nīhoa, Emory was astounded to find signs of ancient human habitation everywhere. Terraced areas on every portion of the steep island that could hold them still showed through the shrub. In a gulch filled with native loulu palms, drywall masonry had been carefully laid, built up into impressive stone platforms that Emory guessed were house sites. This had been no temporary occupation—clearly there had been a settlement of some duration.

In five days Emory managed to survey most of the island, identifying eighty-eight archaeological sites. He found bones of men, women, and children in burial sites, confirming the idea of settlement. There were three small freshwater seeps (perhaps adequate, Emory thought, though the guano-tinted water, laced with nitrogen, must have been hard on the kidneys). Loulu nearby could be used for thatched roofs and some—very little!—firewood. For food, there were the birds and their eggs; sea turtles; an occasional seal; and abundant fish.

After estimating the amount of sweet potato that could have been grown on the narrow terraces, Emory thought the island could support up to one hundred people. But who would choose to live here under such harsh conditions? Had they chosen to, or had they been shipwrecked on this far shore?

On Mokumanamana Emory documented a total of thirty-three rectangular religious sites, some crowned with upright slabs. Besides the stone figures, Emory found some artifacts that, though decidedly Polynesian, were unusual, including an adze and fishhook of rare design, found only in a couple of very early sites in the Main Islands, and carved stone vessels. Nor were the religious sites typical—they reminded the anthropologist of shrines found over 2,500 miles south of the Hawaiian Islands, at Tuamotu Archipelago in French Polynesia.

All of these things suggested to Emory that a population of some of the earliest Polynesians to find the Hawaiian archipelago had settled or been marooned at Nīhoa and Mokumanamana. But archaeologist Paul Cleghorn, who conducted extensive fieldwork on the two islands in 1984, theorized that Nīhoa and Mokumanamana were occupied seasonally to harvest birds, eggs, and feathers and that the religious shrines might be evidence of a bird cult such as that found on Rapa Nui (Easter Island). At Rapa Nui, complex rituals surrounded the return of the sooty terns to nest, with a ceremonial competition to gather the first egg. Emory had also hinted at a connection with the early Marquesan culture that may have sailed to two distant points of the Polynesian triangle to settle both the Hawaiian Islands and Rapa Nui. The Easter Island temple platforms and huge stone figures, he noted, could be thought of as "exaggerated, glorified" versions of the platforms and small human figures of Mokumanamana.

The Easter Island story is one of the more dramatic versions of a tragedy that befell numerous small Pacific islands. Rapa Nui, as it is now known, is a windy island with a more temperate climate than the Hawaiian archipelago. Pollen counts reveal that Rapa Nui was once covered with lush subtropical forest. Its trees included an endemic palm that grew more than sixty-five feet high, with trunks exceeding seven feet in diameter. This forest disappeared over a puzzlingly short period of time—latest pollen analyses point to between 1200 and 1550 AD. Very small Pacific islands like Nīhoa and Laysan may provide clues to explain why.

In *Collapse* (2005) Jared Diamond, influenced by his friend David Steadman's work, dramatized the ecological devastation of Rapa Nui as the classic ur-tale of human exploitation outstripping a land's productivity. Diamond argued that purposeful deforestation, and the accompanying loss of soil cover, turned Rapa Nui into an arid savannah.

Here's where conditions on ratfree Nīhoa and Laysan, and formerly rat-infested Kure, provide an interesting context. At Rapa Nui, as throughout Polynesia, rats and humans appear to have arrived in tandem. Whether brought purposely or accidentally, rats are a part of the "transported landscape" of Polynesian settlement. Diamond notes that most palm nuts found on Rapa Nui showed evidence of being gnawed by rats.

University of Hawai'i archaeologist Terry Hunt began excavations at Rapa Nui in 2004 at a sandy cove called Anakena, a likely place for early colonizers to settle. He expected to confirm Diamond's theory that humans wreaked "ecocide" on the Rapa Nui environment by destroying the forest. Instead he found evidence that rats were the primary villains.

Diamond's calculations were based on an early settlement date (around 900 AD) and a rapidly growing population. Hunt's dating of carbon fragments suggested a later date for human (and accompanying rat) arrival—around 1200 AD. Could humans have been the primary cause of such rapid destruction of Rapa Nui's forests?

Hunt considered what was known about the introduction of the Polynesian rat in the Hawaiian Islands:

On Kure Atoll in the Hawaiian Islands, at a latitude similar to Rapa Nui but with a smaller supply of food, the population density of the Polynesian rat was reported in the 1970s to have reached 45 per acre. On Rapa Nui, that would equate to a rat population of more than 1.9 million. At a density of 75 per acre, which would not be unreasonable given the past abundance of food, the rat population could have exceeded 3.1 million.

Hunt notes that excavations of sinkholes in the Ewa plain west of Honolulu demonstrate the devastation rats can do even on a large island, in an environment with no predators and endemic plants that have evolved without defenses. Rats spread into the plains a couple of hundred years before humans occupied the area, gnawing the seeds and devastating native forest dominated by loulu palms. Tiny Nīhoa sustained some form of human settlement over centuries but, ratfree, managed to retain thriving groves of loulu. Laysan too, in the records of its earliest Western visitors, gives us a rare picture of an endemic Hawaiian coastal ecosystem where rats were never introduced.

In *Collapse*, Diamond described Rapa Nui as "the clearest example of a society that destroyed itself by overexploiting its own resources." But Hunt's exploration of the role rats have played in destruction of native habitat on several Pacific islands led him to a different conclusion. The damage rats do to seabird colonies—eating eggs, even attacking birds—has been graphically illustrated at Kure and Midway. Rat control on Kure started in 1993, on the eve of the closing of the coast guard LORAN station there. The joint effort of the coast guard and Hawai'i State Department of Land and Natural Resources took about five years to eliminate the rat population completely. Seabird populations subsequently rebounded dramatically, particularly those of the burrowing birds: Christmas and wedge-tailed shearwaters, and the Bonin petrels. Fish & Wildlife–sponsored efforts on Midway produced even more dramatic results, with burrowing bird populations showing a nearly 100 percent increase every year since the last rat sighting in 1995.

Interesting to contemplate, from the microcosm of a small island, is the potential significance of a secondary effect of losing seabirds: the loss of guano. Hunt's version of Rapa Nui's ecosystem "collapse" points to a much more complex interaction with the environment than Diamond proposed—one where humans and their transported landscapes affect new environments in unforeseen ways, pulling at the skein of life till it unravels in a way that no one can fully predict. But it is a particular virtue of small remote islands that we can sometimes see into this process.

On Laysan in 1896, Schauinsland had been surprised to find that parts of the low, sandy, windswept island were green gardens of blooming plants and shrubs. It was not until long after he had returned to Bremen to write up his accounts and compare his Laysan plant specimens to similar species collected along the coast of the Main Islands that he realized how much "larger and more robust" the Laysan plants were than those others. Oddly, he does not make the connection to a soil constantly enriched by bird droppings.

It is hard to imagine in a twenty-first-century world fed mainly on crops grown with synthetic fertilizers how important guano was to food production in the past. Whole societies, such as the Inca who settled along the coast of what is now Peru, were built on the fertility of crops liberally fed with guano. During the nineteenth century Peru became one of the richest countries in the world based on its guano sales. In 1860, 43 percent of American crops were fertilized with seabird guano, mostly bought at a premium from Peru. America was hoping the Guano Act of 1856 would result in a substantial US supply, as well as helping the nation acquire new territory. It did lead to annexation of a total of fifty-nine Pacific islands, though only a handful were ever actually mined for guano. Photographs taken on Laysan during the guano mining show workers scraping off the dark soil and loading it into carts lined up on a tram. Today the island has no dark soil, only the nutrient-poor sandy substrata. The vanished forest of Laysan had been nourished by a very lengthy accumulation of bird poop.

The fossil record of Rapa Nui has shown that the island once supported huge numbers of at least thirty species of seabird, more than any other Pacific Island. In what Hunt calls a "synergy of impacts," Rapa Nui lost its major nutrient addition to otherwise poor soils as well when, through human predation but probably more heavily through rat predation, ground-nesting birds, particularly seabirds, were wiped out.

Both Diamond's and Hunt's accounts of Rapa Nui's environmental collapse tell a sad tale of unforeseen consequences. The Hunt version is the more hopeful, because it leaves open the possibility that, had humans arrived sans rats, they just might have learned to live in harmony with their new home.

EIGHT

Capture

In less than two weeks the *Cromwell* was due to pick us up from Laysan: time to prepare for the seal captures. I repeated to Michele, whose mood had improved little, Cynthia's comment that Bill had a lucky star. "Right now, Bill doesn't need luck," she grumbled. "He needs a fucking miracle." We were leaving camp, heading south on a seal patrol. She was wearing a bathing suit top that showed off a buff torso, and a pair of men's boxer shorts that featured a pattern of squares filled with crossed tennis rackets.

As we walked up the beach, skirting the tarp-covered equipment for the seal capture, I asked why she was so dubious about Bill's plan. "Well, have you looked at what we have to work with?" she asked, pulling back a tarp. Under it was something like a horse cart, with big inflatable tires. Lying next to the cart was a long wooden pallet with handles along the side.

"We'll capture a seal with this hoop net, then roll it onto this pallet. Okay, that part's not easy, but it's doable.

"But here's the thing. We have to go wherever we find these seals. We may find a seal at the other end of the island. Now, we have the Boston Whaler, and it's going to tow this." She pulled back another tarp to reveal a small dinghy with the back cut low and the bottom padded with a flat wood platform.

"But we can't go outside the reef area, in open ocean, because we don't have a backup vessel. We can't risk getting engine trouble and being blown out to sea.

"So we can only get a little ways north and south of here with this boat, towing the dinghy. We have to get the seal from wherever we catch it to wherever we can get the boat. The males aren't as heavy as the females, but still they can weigh up to five hundred pounds. Even with six of us, there's no way we can carry that pallet through up to a mile of sand. So that's where this big wheel thing comes in." She pointed to the cart with the inflatable tires. "Is that contraption really going to work? We'll have to pull it like carthorses. Nobody has thought this thing through," she added, yanking the tarp flap down. "Here we are, four women, two men, one with a bad back. Bill's the only one who can administer the drugs to the seals. What if his back goes out?"

At age twenty-six, Michele was only a couple of years older than my daughter. She had joined the officer's corps of NOAA right out of college. "If I'd been a man I would've gone into the Navy Seals," she had told me. Her boyfriend was a Navy Seal. They weren't getting along.

"We don't really know what effect we're having by removing these males," she went on. "Do we really know we're not getting some of the dominant males? We're going partly by the list made up from last year's observations. But dominance shifts all the time. In any case, there's no proof that equalizing the ratio of males to females will stop the mobbing. I don't think any of this is good science."

The day we started work on the pen coincided with the first sighting of a tiger shark. I was standing at the water's edge, finishing my coffee, enjoying the last coolness of early morning and watching a young albatross floating on the water a hundred feet out. I turned to go, then turned back at the sound of splashing water. I saw a dark flash of fin and tail. The bird had disappeared, and an oily slick spread in the spot where it had been.

The morning turned very humid, and flies massed as the wind died down. We dug holes for the pen on the beach, and then anchored the whaler waist-deep so that it could hold a pump to force a flow through hollow pipe, scouring a hole in the sand. We took turns holding the pipe, our delight in the cool water lessened considerably by the shark sighting.

The enclosure would be made of strong wire mesh a hundred feet square, divided into three pens that each could hold up to four males. It would extend far enough into the water that the seals could immerse themselves even at low tide.

We did a trial run, taking out the dinghy, with pallet and cart loaded, towed behind the Boston Whaler with Michele piloting. "We have to stay really close to shore," she said. "That means we get out and walk over all the stretches of shallow coral."

I got in the barge along with Lucy—we weren't nearly as heavy as the seal would be, but it would give some idea of how the dinghy would handle pulling a load. Michele steered around the coral heads. The stop and start made the engine die, and we drifted. Chad leaped out to fend the whaler off the reef, but the next wave caught him between boat and coral. I heard him grunt as the wind went out of him. If Chad, our main muscle, was disabled, our chances of success were slim. He leaned against the boat side for a moment while we all watched him anxiously, then straightened up and pushed the boat away from the coral.

Off a lovely crescent of beach we could inch our way no further, so we beached the barge and unloaded the cart. The plan was to meet early the next morning with all gear ready and wait while Bill, Cynthia, and Lucy went out on patrol. If they found a seal on the hit list, they would radio back to camp. There would be six of us, with Cindy, who had agreed to help us in return for our toiling in the *Cenchrus* fields.

I woke up long before dawn, disoriented. I realized I was hearing a finch sing for the first time, a beautiful melodious trill just outside my tent. The sound was otherworldly: Ariel's song floating on the wind. The green ghost of a vanished landscape hovered, for a brief second, over the grueling day that lay ahead.

By 7:30 we had assembled by the boat with our gear, which included long pants, kneepads, and sneakers for protection in the rough-and-tumble of the capture. Cynthia, Lucy, and Bill headed south, taking a radio, to look for seals on the list. Soon they radioed in: they were witnessing a mobbing. Four males surrounded a female on the beach. While the dominant male fought one of them, the other two herded the female toward the water. Then they were all in the water, the female pinned under the fighting males. Cynthia feared she would be drowned, but all the seals disappeared out toward open ocean. The search team continued to the south end of the island, but found no male seals from the list.

After lunch the search team headed out again. The radio squawked alive: a seal on the list found a quarter-mile south. We pushed the boat out and piled in, Chad riding the dinghy, Cindy up front guiding Michele, me in the middle. The dinghy lurched behind us, slamming into coral in the stiff wind. We got out and walked the boat over the reef, wondering whether the seal would still be on the beach by the time we got there.

When we arrived the seal was still sleeping, with its head down toward the water. Chad and Bill crept toward it from two points up the bank, Bill cradling the hoop net. As Bill looped the net over its head, the seal woke with a startled roar, twisting to escape. Chad was astride, trying to pin the seal on his belly, as Lucy and Cynthia pulled the hoop net down his body. Michele piled on behind him, then Cindy, and together they wrestled him around until his head was pointing up the beach, away from the water.

I crouched behind Bill with the medical kit, trying to keep out of the way of the flailing seal while I readied a Valium syringe. Bill grabbed the syringe, pinning one hind flipper under his knee while Cynthia and Lucy pinned the other. He probed for a vein as I readied another vial for a blood sample. Unable to locate the vein, he shot the drug into the muscle and helped Chad hold the seal down. I watched the seal's body go limp as the Valium reached his bloodstream.

Lucy doused the seal's head and flippers with seawater to keep him cool; then she and Cynthia did flipper tags and pit tags. The tiny plug of flesh from one flipper tag was passed to me to slip into a special insulated vial. Kept frozen in our propane freezer, it would be transported back to the lab for the DNA database. We rolled the seal, shrouded in the net, onto the wooden pallet and strapped him down. The boat was beached only a hundred yards away, so we carried the pallet, teetering under the weight of the

seal. The barge turned out to be easier to tow with the weight of
the seal in the back. Bill rode on the barge, tight-lipped, which
meant his back must be hurting. I walked back to camp with
Cynthia and Lucy to open the gate at the pen. We unhooked the
barge when the others arrived and pushed it through the gate
backward, in a quick shove, after loosening the seal's straps. The
Valium had long since worn off, and he came off fast and mad,
thrashing back and forth against the pen, looking for a way out.

The second seal was a relatively easy catch, right next to the
pen, that same afternoon. But the next day was a different story.
The only "hit list" seal to be found was asleep on the sand over
a mile and a half from camp. We slogged down to where we had
left the cart and pushed it to where the seal was sleeping; even
with the cart unloaded, its wheels were sluggish in the soft sand.

The seal, a very large male, wrenched one flipper loose in the
melee and knocked Chad head over heels. He was still struggling ten minutes after the Valium went in, so Bill gave him a
second dose. Finally we rolled him onto the pallet and strapped
him down.

We slid the pallet onto the cart. The boat was nearly two-thirds
of a mile from us, and the cart almost impossible to move in the
soft sand. Straining, we got the wheels rolling, but we hadn't
gone fifty feet when a tire blew—one of the smaller balloon tires
in the rear. We all stood looking at Bill, who was oddly silent. He
gave something between a grimace and a grin and said, "Another
of those little items we should have packed—spare tires."

Then he was down on his knees next to the tire, using a pock-
etknife to enlarge the place where the tire had ripped along one
seam. Struggling to pull apart the rubber, he started filling the
tire with sand. We all watched him. Cynthia said, "Bill, I think

we should release this seal. Even if we manage to get him back to the pen, the stress will kill him. "

"I'll take that chance," Bill said. Cynthia looked at him. She knew that in Bill's scheme, the seal was expendable. Michele broke the impasse, kneeling down to help Bill pack sand into the tire.

When the tire was packed tight we started pushing, with Chad and Michele pulling in the traces, and five of us behind. The tire, weighted with sand, carved a deep rut. After twenty yards we stood, winded, with the tires mired in soft sand. Cynthia scouted inland and came back with an old board. We pushed it under the bad tire and heaved the cart forward, positioned the board and pushed again. A hundred yards farther we stopped and drank the last of our water.

The seal was awake, thrashing inside his net shroud, and it snapped at Michele as she leaned down to position the board under the tire again. Bill pulled the medical kit from the cart and prepared another dose of Valium. Cynthia looked away.

There was no energy left to question what we were doing. It took us three hours to cover less than a mile. The seal was awake but lay still when we reached the dinghy, watching us with red, glazed eyes. After all this, I thought, he's going to die on us.

The whaler was still a quarter-mile away, beached where the water was calmer. Squalls had been coming through all afternoon. We loaded the seal on the dinghy and strapped him down; Lucy, Cynthia, and I waited with him while the others went for the boat.

I watched an albatross chick caught up in waves breaking against the coral ledge. I was too drained to even think of trying to save it. I saw Cynthia watching it too, with a defeated look in her eyes.

Another squall hit and we were engulfed in wind and rain. Michele and the others returned with the boat, but were unable to maneuver it over the shallows through the wind-blown waves. Cynthia tied the dinghy rope around her waist and swam it out to the boat, through water where Lucy had seen a tiger shark the day before. We pushed off the dinghy. Minutes later it was wedged sideways in the coral, with the whaler motor dead. They brought the boat into the shallows and we all stumbled over the shallow reef, pushing boat and dinghy.

Five hours after we captured the seal, we released him into the pen. Miraculously, he was alert and seemed unharmed. It was already dusk. I staggered to my tent, peeled off soggy clothes, and climbed under my sheet.

The next day, Cynthia was sporting a bandage of duct tape around her big toe, Bill was wearing his back brace, and I had a knee that had swollen up like a blowfish. We were all sunburned and haggard.

This time there was a seal on the list just a quarter-mile south of camp. It was Cynthia's favorite, Five-ten. He dodged the net and charged us open-mouthed and roaring, rolling and snapping at us when we moved in again, then breaking for the water. We flailed our arms and got him turned, and Bill pitched the net at his head again. Our exhaustion was showing. The seal struggled free of the net, and it was several minutes before Bill and Chad had him wrapped in it and pinned down.

We got the seal to the pen in a record hour and twenty minutes. He was still immobile when we slid him off the dinghy into the pen. Bill stood watching the seal with concern. "Sometimes they go into shock from the adrenaline, and there's nothing we can do. There's other species that react the same. We used to catch dolphins with a net somewhat like a hoop net. We'd come up in the boat and put it over them, and some would lie still after they realized they were trapped. But one species would be dead by the time we turned the boat around to pick them up."

"When it takes that long to get the seal in the net, is there some point you stop and let it go?" I asked.

"Not in this case," said Bill. "We are *taking* these seals, which means we've already taken into account some may die." He was looking at Cynthia, who turned away.

All of us except Cynthia headed back to camp to get some lunch. At the cook tent I looked back and saw that she sat just outside the fence, watching the comatose seal.

In midafternoon we emerged from our tents for another round of seal capture. I looked down toward the pen. Cynthia still sat watching the seal, who was lying in the same position. Bill sat up on the berm, looking toward Cynthia. He stood up, glanced back at camp, and walked toward her. He laid his hand on her shoulder. She stood up, and he put his arms around her.

Chad had located another seal on the hit list, nearly all the way back to the cart. The cart was permanently mired now, its tire split wide open, so we decided to turn over the pallet to use as a sled for the seal. Our improvised sled kept digging in so much that we had to stop every few feet to free it. We pushed the pallet onto the barge and walked it, scraping across the shallow reef, to the boat.

An hour later we were back at the pen, to find Five-ten very much alive, trying to slip by us as we backed the barge into the pen. Only Cynthia had the energy to stop and watch him and celebrate his recovery. I fought the desire to crawl the last hundred feet to my tent. I lay down in my wet clothes, covered with sand, in a swarm of flies.

It seemed mad, all of it. I wanted to get off the island and leave these animals in peace. But later Bill came to the door of my tent and asked, "Want to see the results of a mobbing?"

Lucy and Chad joined us, Chad carrying the kit I knew held instruments for doing a necropsy so pathologists could study the samples. The seal was lying with its face in the water, on the coral ledge just north of camp, near the shark pool. It was a subadult male. His eyes were half open, and his muzzle tinged green with algae. Most of his back was laid open, the blubber hanging in white shreds.

"The wound looks older than a day," said Bill, "but the body is still pretty fresh. He must have stayed alive like that for a while, half flayed."

Bill rolled the seal over and made a cut from neck to lower belly. He incised small samples from the lung, kidney, spleen, and pancreas. He studied the adrenal glands: "They're swollen, probably from infection setting in."

"I'll have to take the head too," he said, "so the lab can make skull measurements. I'll bury it, and the crabs will have it cleaned in a couple of weeks."

I chose not to watch, but went with Lucy to dig a shallow grave for the body.

It was harder to question what we were doing after seeing the dead seal. And our luck seemed to change. We had a fairly easy catch that afternoon, close to camp. As we released that seal into the pen, another seal hauled out on the other side, up against the fence, curious about the boys in the pen. He was on the list.

Lucy and I climbed inside the fence at the top, crouching down and moving slowly. We took wire cutters and snipped an opening. The others crawled on their stomachs toward the seal, pulling large squares of plywood. At a signal they stood up and rushed the seal using the plywood to block his frightened rush toward the water and turn him in to the fence. In a minute he was floundering through the hole, and Lucy and I hurried to lace the square of chicken wire back in place. We stood looking at our captive with stunned delight—the five-minute capture!

Bill walked around camp hunched over with back pain. Seals kept hauling up along the fence to look at our captives. We caught the last four in the same way, unlacing the holes we had cut in the fence. Cynthia stood shaking her head in disbelief as we counted twelve seals. "Bill's lucky star," she said.

Now there was little left to do but wait for the *Townsend Cromwell*. I went out the next morning to finish weeding the *Cenchrus* patch. A brown booby was feeding a chick larger than itself under a clump of sedge grass. The chick crouched coyly and made tiny *peep-peep* sounds, and the parent's large yellow bill nearly disappeared down its craw, transferring something that made a large lump in the chick's throat. Nearby, a brown noddy pair were courting. The male nodded his head, made a rattling coo, and showed off his bright orange tongue.

The young albatrosses were all down by the water, most of their down gone, flapping their wings and becoming briefly airborne every time the wind picked up. A mother seal with a fat pup slumbered nearby. I smelled the guano as I chopped out large clumps of the sandbur. It reminded me of all the places I'd liked as a kid—attics and old toolsheds, hidden places under hedges, the crotches of trees. The bright and empty horizon supported that feeling of being back in a childhood emptied of the weight of past and future.

A few days later the *Cromwell* was sloshing and battering its way through water stirred up by a hurricane east of us, making our ministrations to the seals in their wooden cages on the wet front deck difficult. We slipped thawed herring into their cages, but they ignored the food, perhaps as seasick as some of us, their eyes red and dull. But they gave the rolling bubble sound of warning when we came close, and raised their heads to the water when we doused them with the hose. We worked in shifts, each half-hour of the day and night, keeping them cool and wet, hauling the hose and clutching at whatever was handy when the ship pitched and rolled.

We woke on the fourth morning to a world suddenly rearranged on the vertical: the towering cliffs of the Nāpali coast of Kaua'i dark green and ruddy brown and folded into each other like stage curtains, an apparition as huge and incomprehensible as an undiscovered continent. We cut the engines, loosed a seal from his cage, and, holding up big squares of plywood like shields, herded him to the side of the ship. The seal hesitated at the edge, looking down at the water fifteen feet below. We shoved him off unceremoniously. He surfaced and circled the ship, the only thing familiar to him, and we saw him still watching us, head reared in the waves, as the ship moved on.

"None of this ultimately leads anywhere," Bill was saying one evening to us as we continued down the island chain, dropping off seals as we went, "if you're not working to ensure enough habitat to sustain a population in the wild. Every other measure of wildlife management is glorified zookeeping.

"Who knows, maybe these boys we're dropping off will help build up the seal population around the Main Islands," Bill continued. "And then won't we at NMFS hear about it, from irate fishermen getting their fish snatched, or from the hotel manager at the Royal Hawaiian when the first seal pup gets born right in front and a passel of NMFS volunteers are trying to keep the tourists from sunbathing next to it."

The thought that monk seals would recolonize beaches in the Main Islands, however unlikely, was appealing. But we knew it would be a population always at risk, from human activity and diseases carried by other animals, both wild and domestic.

"People tend to think these seals have the whole northwestern end of the archipelago," Bill added. "But what is that? It's a hell of a lot of coral reef, potentially a huge feeding ground for them, but only six square miles of land, total, and out of that only a small amount of good beach area with protected water to raise pups."

"That's why it's important to gain some control at Midway," he went on. "Midway has some great beaches and shallow reef; it should be able to support a good number of seals. We could do another head-start program for undernourished seal pups there like we did at Kure, if we know the place is clean enough. But that's a big 'if.'"

As we dropped off our last seal opposite the verdant sea cliffs of the Big Island's Hamakua Coast, I thought of Laysan and Midway. Living on Laysan had been no picnic, but now, far from the heat and flies, the beauty of the island hovered in my mind as something irreducible and sustaining. Laysan had offered a palpable dream of restoration, one in which I could join, if only to weed out a small patch of *Cenchrus*.

But Midway, with its long history of less-than-tender care from the US Navy, had begun to intrigue me. At Midway, I imagined, the sad history of damage I had witnessed at Kahoʻolawe would be compressed into a smaller space, with no refuge from the sight of a world that had been dismantled. Yet at Kahoʻolawe, I knew, there were those who could see beyond the stripped landscape to a greener future. Midway too could be a testing of vision.

PART III

Midway

NINE

Island of Dancing Birds

SOSUS, an undersea cable and hydrophone system for detecting submarines, closed its Midway post in the late 1980s, the
last of the Cold War operations. Since then, the atoll, about 350
miles northwest of Laysan, has been a sleepy outpost at the
back of beyond, with a handful of navy personnel and a host of
imported Asian laborers maintaining a military ghost town. In
1993, Midway Naval Facility was chosen for closure under the
Base Realignment and Closure Act (BRAC). Because Midway
was a National Wildlife Refuge, the Environmental Protection
Agency (EPA) and navy BRAC cleanup team was augmented
by Fish & Wildlife and National Marine Fisheries Service personnel, Bill Gilmartin included. The first step in remediation
was an environmental baseline survey, performed by a private
contractor named Ogden Environmental Services, to determine
the extent of environmental damage. Congress appropriated $43
million to clean up Midway, but that was clearly not enough to
do an effective job. The atoll was rated so seriously polluted that
it qualified for the Superfund, a huge appropriation already set

aside for the nation's most polluted sites. With its "small and transient" human population, however, Midway could not compete for funding with sites close to towns and cities.

The physical work of the cleanup had begun in early 1994, and I wrote to the Midway Naval Facility commanding officer asking permission to visit as a journalist. Permission was not granted. "It's his call," Ken McDermond told me from Fish & Wildlife's Honolulu office. "And they do have a hell of a cleanup operation going on. The only way I can get you out there is to wait until this CO is transferred out, and then try to put you on as a research volunteer. If you're willing to go for at least six weeks, I'll see what I can do."

What needed cleaning up? "You'll find that out from our BRAC workers when you get out there," McDermond said. "We have three employees working full time, trying to keep the impact of this cleanup on the wildlife as minimal as possible. But let's put it this way. Guess you haven't been in the military. Or to Subic Bay. Or Guam. Or Johnston Atoll? Well, the military has been out at Midway since well before World War II. It's a very small place. . . . Go figure."

On January 12, 1995, I climbed inside the cavernous belly of an Air Force C-141 making its weekly flight to Midway. My fellow passengers included twelve men on the cleanup crew and a few civilian workers. There was one other woman, a navy yeoman. Removable seats had been set up for us, facing toward the back of the plane. Exposed pipes and air ducts veined the windowless cavity. A hundred feet from us toward the tail, a pyramid of cargo pallets was wrapped and tied down—a monolith we faced from our rows, like worshippers at an industrial altar.

Talk was impossible over the engine noise reverberating

through the metal capsule. We all jammed in air force–issue ear-plugs. I had time to think about my strange trajectory through these islands, heading deeper into the Pacific to a destination that sounded like it had all the makings of an environmental nightmare. Laysan, despite its troubled past, had felt wild and whole, but now I found myself pulled back into a tangled web of human history, one that wove the world's remotest islands into a pattern of military lines of power.

My friends were puzzled when I said where I was going. "But that's not a Hawaiian island, is it?" they asked. "Isn't that near Guam? They burn chemical weapons there, right? They had that big battle during World War II?" It was as though human history had lifted Midway from its position in the Hawaiian chain and set it down in some parallel world: Mondo Military.

The atoll seemed to have no reality outside its use as a strategic location, a place where one could anchor and, from that anchorage, rule the northern Pacific. I had tried to find information on Midway's natural environment. But with issues of the Smithsonian's *Atoll Research Bulletin* devoted to every Northwestern Hawaiian Island except Midway, contemporary information was hard to come by. With history of the human encounters, however, there was some better luck.

Midway was the first noncontiguous territory to be annexed by the United States, under the Guano Act of 1856. When Captain Brooks of the seal-hunting *Gambia* came across the atoll in 1859, he became the last discoverer of a Pacific island. It didn't matter, in the end, that there never was a commercially viable amount of guano at the atoll.

The bird poachers did their dirty work at Midway, though, and in 1903 President Theodore Roosevelt placed the atoll under navy control, ostensibly to provide some form of law enforcement and protection for the cable company facilities, but certainly with future military uses in mind.

Since the 1960s it has been mandatory for every military installation that hosts endangered species to work with the US Fish & Wildlife Service to develop a conservation management plan. But the navy was not eager to have Fish & Wildlife out at Midway during the Cold War years. The Endangered Species Act of 1973, under which protection of the Hawaiian monk seal was mandated, was the tiny portal through which Fish & Wildlife squeezed, opening an office on the atoll in 1988 and establishing an "overlay national wildlife refuge" ("overlay" meaning that wildlife interests took a backseat to navy operations).

Don Williamson, a mild-mannered biologist, became the sole staff of that new refuge. He ran wildlife displays and a tiny museum. He gently suggested ways the navy could do things that would kill fewer birds and tried to educate people about why seals needed undisturbed time on the beaches. He lasted only a year, but Fish & Wildlife managed to expand their foothold there in the ensuing years, as the naval facility became moribund, and the human population shrank to a couple hundred caretakers.

Before I left for Midway, I had talked to Bill Gilmartin, who was thinking about retiring at the end of the year. It had been nearly fifteen years since Bill joined NMFS to head the monk seal[1] recovery team. During that time he had watched the seal population at French Frigate Shoals increase after the departure of the coast guard in 1979, and then enter into a decline, with young seals showing signs of emaciation, many not surviving into adulthood. He had asserted what power he could within the confines of the National Oceanographic and Atmospheric Administration's bureaucracy to bring an end to lobster fishing in the Northwestern Islands. But NOAA's commerce-supporting Western Pacific Fisheries Management Council (WESPAC) contested the research that indicated lobster populations were in steep decline, and denied that the fishery could be taking food that was important to monk seals.

With the head-start program no longer funded, and the money redirected into research programs that seemed to mainly buttress what Bill characterized as the "NMFS do-nothing approach," he felt that time was running out for the monk seal and that there was little more he could do from the inside. He was now putting all the energy he could into Midway.

"Midway could make a big difference," he said, "if we can restore seal habitat there, build up the population. But it's going to be real tricky. We've had one bad experience with introducing seals into Midway."

These were the seals Tim Ragen had told me about: eighteen underweight juvenile female seals from French Frigate Shoals, fostered on Oʻahu and released at Midway in 1992. Within seven months all but two had died or disappeared. "We only managed to retrieve a few for necropsies," Bill said, "and they were already far too decomposed for us to be able to tell much. But I suspect there may be something polluting the water. It'll be interesting to see what they find during this cleanup. Midway could be a great place to do research and foster seals, if they really can clean up whatever is there, and if Fish & Wildlife can hold onto the place."

Even before the navy announced it would close Midway, various interests began eyeing the atoll. In 1990, the House Armed Services Committee proposed turning Midway into a penal colony. Now, on the eve of its closure, a private company submitted a proposal to run Midway as a nuclear waste dump. Commercial fishing interests lobbied the state to claim the atoll, whose official status was "unincorporated US possession," as Hawaiian territory and boost the state's fishing industry by subsidizing a fish-packing plant there.

Ken McDermond agreed with Gilmartin that Midway, which has a larger area (about sixteen hundred acres) of dry land than any of the other Northwestern Islands, could be crucial habitat in a refuge system made up mostly of coral reef. In addition, Midway offered what didn't exist anywhere else in the Northwestern Islands—a harbor, an airport, and enough infrastructure, if there was a way to maintain it, to allow for all sorts of refuge-related activities: research, head-start facilities for monk seals and other endangered species, even a limited visitor program.

The problem would be convincing his bosses that taking Midway on was worthwhile. McDermond was young, smart, and combative; he was willing to fight for refuge interests at Midway. But he faced long odds. Midway's natural world had been seriously disrupted—infested by rats and overrun by alien plants that were crowding out bird nesting areas, for example. Other than a rat eradication program already under way, the navy was not committed to any habitat restoration beyond removing buildings and cleaning up the large number of rusting fuel tanks. And it was not clear yet what responsibility the military would take for any toxic waste buried on land or dumped in the lagoon that might be left like a ticking time bomb after the navy was gone.

It would take time, work, and money to make Midway a healthy place for wildlife again. But the Department of the Interior had already passed the word along—no extra funding available for managing refuge lands that needed a lot of TLC. The National Wildlife Refuge System, which by 1994 comprised more than 95 million acres, teetered along on less money than was spent annually on the three top military bands in the country. The western regional office of Fish & Wildlife in Portland, Oregon, put it this way: "There's no money in the refuge system to run Midway. It's too remote. You'd have to keep the harbor in repair, the airport operational. It's too damn far from anything."

Ken McDermond knew that the service had been under pressure since the Reagan Administration days to bolster its revenues using private partnerships. It thus came as no surprise to him when the regional office pushed to find a partner in the private sector who was interested in operating an ecotourism business at Midway. Like many managers who were first and foremost biologists, he worried that the service, in catering to private interests, might be in danger of "selling the farm." But he was a realist about what it would cost to maintain even the most basic infrastructure at Midway.

The navy liked the idea of handing Midway over to another federal agency—perhaps, suggested McDermond, "because they could always get it back if they needed the place." (Another benefit would become clear as the cleanup progressed: lands passed from one public agency to another were subject to less stringent cleanup standards.)

By 1994 it had been agreed that Fish & Wildlife would take over at the end of the cleanup, tentatively set for June 1997. In December 1994 Fish & Wildlife advertised for a partner in the federal government's *Commerce Business Daily*. The agency got only two bites. One was from a billionaire who thought ecotourism should include casino gambling and feeding sharks from cages. The other was from a corporation called Phoenix Air.

"They're a private aviation firm out of Georgia," McDermond explained. "They do a lot of contract flying for the military.

They've been landing at Midway now and then for years. That's the thing—you gotta have the planes to pull this off."

"Do they do anything in tourism?" I asked.

"No, but they say they're really interested in, um, 'getting a start.'" He paused. "I believe they're our best bet. In fact, they're our *only* bet." Fish & Wildlife said yes to the airline company.

Phoenix Air, it turned out, was owned by an ex–army helicopter pilot named Mark Thompson, who raced cars on the Winston Cup circuit in his spare time. His airline, the world's largest private fleet of Gulfstreams and Learjets at the time, specialized in what it termed "threat representative electronic warfare training for air-to-air and surface-to-air operators." In 1992, the company had won a five-year $72 million contract with the air force for flight services that included target towing and exercises in electronic evasion and communication jamming.

It sounded like Phoenix Air didn't have an ecological bone anywhere in its corporate body. This was going to be an interesting partnership.

In true military fashion, we weren't told until we were airborne that we would not be going directly to Midway but would instead be making a big detour to deliver cargo to a chemical weapons disposal facility at Johnston Atoll.

Johnston, 750 miles southwest of O'ahu, about halfway to the Marshall Islands, was the nearest land to the Hawaiian archipelago. This ancient remnant of a chain of volcanic islands was, at 85 million years old, the oldest atoll in the world. Discovery of the atoll is usually attributed to Captain Johnston of *HMS Cornwallis* in 1807, though a British captain published a report of grounding on reefs that could only have been this atoll's in 1796.

In 1852 William Parker, captain of an American trading vessel, sailed through the area and claimed to have seen the atoll, though his description seems to fit nothing that was actually there. Even so, years later he thought it a good idea to claim possession under the Guano Act of 1856. His business partner submitted an analysis of Johnston guano as being of "extraordinarily good quality," though there is no evidence that Parker had managed to take any actual samples.

The atoll's history followed the pattern of Laysan and numerous other Pacific islands: a period of guano mining and feather poaching, then some years left blessedly alone, until the Tanager scientific expedition arrived to take stock of the place in 1923.

The expedition cataloged great quantities of birds, which led President Calvin Coolidge to declare Johnston a Federal Bird Refuge in 1926. But Johnston was soon a target of America's rush to fortify their interests in the Pacific, and in 1934 President Franklin Roosevelt placed the atoll under navy control. Dredging and blasting to form a sub and seaplane base would soon follow.

We landed at Johnston in late afternoon, after a steep descent in our windowless capsule toward a place I had never imagined I would go. We were told we would be there for an hour. As we stepped onto the tarmac, our welcome committee sat in an armored vehicle behind a machine gun trained on the last rung of the ladder.

A military police officer marched us into a low building with windows that opened onto concrete seawall fronting the lagoon. The officer allowed us to walk outside to the seawall, warning us to stay within a marked area and take no photographs.

I looked around at what could be seen of Johnston Atoll Wildlife Refuge. A few coconut trees cast feathery shadows on an expanse of sparse lawn. Two rows of buildings that resembled

1960s housing projects rose from the island's midsection. The island looked to be about two-thirds the size of 1,023-acre Laysan, dredged and built up from a 43-acre island. There were no natural shorelines in sight, only long stretches of seawall. To the east stood row upon row of low cylindrical bunkers, which one of my fellow passengers said were storage for chemical weapons. At the west end, downwind, loomed the burn towers of the disposal plant. A Pacific golden plover ran across the meager grass, and a lone tropicbird wheeled in the sky.

After World War II the atoll passed to the Air Force to become a command center for nuclear testing. In 1958 Operation Hardtack began with the detonation of two thermonuclear bombs in the stratosphere over the atoll. Other atmospheric nuclear tests followed. In a concession to the atoll's status as a bird refuge, a peculiarly military effort was made to protect the birds nesting on the few undisturbed acres: smoke pots were placed upwind as a shade screen and aerial flares fired to divert the birds' attention from the blinding flashes of the blasts. In 1962, two missile launches from the atoll misfired and another had to be aborted on the pad, contaminating about twenty-five acres of land with radioactive plutonium.

Beginning in 1958, the US military had also used the atoll for disposal of weapons. Disposing of obsolete weapons prior to the advent of environmentalism had been simple: burn them, bury them, dump them. Most horrifying, in retrospect, was the 1960s effort called Operation CHASE, acronym for "Cut Holes and Sink 'Em," in which entire ships filled with chemical weapons were sunk off the Atlantic Coast.

In the late 1960s the favored disposal method at Johnston was to burn the stuff on rafts in the middle of the lagoon. To already enormous stockpiles from World War II had been added the notorious defoliant Agent Orange, used in the Vietnam War. Agent Orange was laced with the world's deadliest toxic by-product, dioxin, released when the chemical was burned.

Environmental pressures finally induced the army to come up with safer methods of incinerating chemical weapons. In 1981, the army began building JACADS—Johnston Atoll Chemical Agent Disposal System—the monstrous incinerator plant that occupied the western end of the island. By 1985 Johnston was host to over two thousand tons of chemical weapons (about 6 percent of the total US stockpile at the time, it was said): mustard gas and two nerve agents, sarin and VX gas, a substance so deadly that one drop on your skin can kill you. By the time of my visit in 1994, Fish & Wildlife had stationed a refuge manager at Johnston in anticipation that the atoll would revert to wildlife refuge once the chemical weapons disposal was done and all facilities dismantled. That would end up happening a lot later, in an environment that was still very compromised.

As day turned to dusk and we waited to get back on our plane, a steady trickle of joggers dressed in bright outfits went by, a sight that seemed to belong in some other universe. I wondered whether the refuge manager was one. Maybe it was he who called out to us, "Last stop before the twilight zone."

Seeing Johnston Atoll produced in me a feeling of deep disquiet, not least at my own ignorance about military activities both inside and outside the Hawaiian chain. Midway, it seemed, might have suffered Johnston's fate were it not for the former's strategic importance *midway* between East and West in the island-barren northern Pacific.

The history of US military activities elsewhere in the Pacific no longer seemed something far away and in another universe.

I remembered a recent news article about the hundred or so former residents of Bikini Island, in the southwest Pacific, who since 1946 had been waiting in exile for the time they could return to a home still contaminated by radiation from American nuclear tests conducted there between 1946 and 1954. Their small island, in an atoll (also named Bikini) four times the size of French Frigate Shoals, had been a green oasis rich in birds and turtles. The photograph that accompanied the news article haunted me. It must have been taken by a remote camera set just inland from the shore to record the blast. The camera eye peered out from a grove of coconut trees, past a palm-thatched canoe shed, toward a beach fringed by gentle surf. At the horizon, midlagoon, the cloud-blast blossomed, a stupendous tree of death. One of those blasts had completely vaporized an island the size of Laysan.

Bikini had undergone what has been called the ultimate military occupation. Such nearly incomprehensible destruction was not all in the past: at uninhabited Moruroa and Fangataufa Atolls, in French Polynesia, the French military had continued nuclear tests until the government imposed a moratorium in 1991. (Six months after my arrival at Midway they would resume testing again.) But Johnston and Midway were still, technically, wildlife refuges, still places where, I wanted to believe, the clock could be turned back, their land and inland waters brought back to health.

Midway did not have the sinister aura of Johnston, but it was strange enough. I stepped off the plane ladder onto tarmac under a night sky and headed toward an enormous lighted terminal surrounded by blackness. Its entryway was cordoned with rope and flanked by huge anchors, like gates of Purgatory if that place were run by sailors. To the side was a sign that read "Welcome to Midway Naval Air Facility" featuring an ostrich-sized cartoon albatross standing on tiptoe and pointing his bill toward the dark sky. A crowd was gathered, mostly men and, it appeared, mostly drunk. Midway's cleanup crew was celebrating Saturday night.

Torpedoes painted in Easter-egg colors lined the central hall of the terminal. We were briefed—with handouts passed out and various warnings shouted above the noise from drunken revelers—and then disgorged on the other side of the building onto another vast stretch of tarmac.

Ken Niethammer, Midway refuge manager, a burly man whose fair skin should never have been exposed to tropical sun, loaded my bags into a golf cart and whisked me through streets lined with trees, showing me downtown Midway. Bowling alley, mess hall, All Hands Club, Fish & Wildlife office, abandoned theater. I wasn't paying attention. I was looking at the birds.

My sojourn among the albatrosses at Laysan hadn't prepared me for this. That was in early summer, when the overworked albatross parents returned to the island only to feed their chicks and rest briefly before their next long journey in search of food. Here in January the whole colony of adult Laysan albatrosses, the world's largest congregation, over a million total, were in residence, and at the height of their social season. Paired-off birds nested every three feet or so. Their nests were built of sand and dirt and bits of grass, rounded like tiny cinder cones, and many held large white eggs that gleamed in the golf cart's headlights.

The birds who were not employed brooding eggs were performing elaborate courtship dances, flickering in the headlights like a frothing sea. They bobbed and wheeled, whinnying, whistling, mooing, rattling their bills—filling the night with a lunatic mix of sound: drunken pennywhistlers jamming with stoned gamelan orchestras.

We were now weaving down a potholed road, dodging albatrosses standing transfixed in our headlights. Derelict buildings loomed along the road: enlisted men's two-story barracks, an A-frame chapel, a school. The golf cart carried us quietly past old wooden houses, still in use, with neatly mowed lawns. A few shadowy figures passed on bicycles. Beyond the buildings and streets, impenetrable darkness pressed in on all sides, making the place feel as insubstantial as a stage setting for a play that had had too long a run.

I woke up early to the sound of thousands of albatrosses clattering their bills. I pulled back the decrepit drapes and looked out from my officers' suite room on the top floor of Charlie, an old cinderblock Bachelor Officers Quarters (BOQ) building. On the lawn that stretched between this building and another set at right angles, dozens of birds were taking off and landing among nests spaced a few feet apart. Tall ironwoods and power lines blocked their lines of flight seaward. I watched albatrosses wing into position a hundred feet up, then drop steeply with big webbed feet angled up as brakes. One came down too steeply, crashed and tumbled, picked himself up, pointed his bill at the sky, and gave a long, sighing moo, perhaps the albatross version of an insouciant shrug.

To the left, beyond dunes and ironwood trees, I glimpsed the lagoon, a band of water the purest azure I'd ever seen, as though its color had condensed under the pressure of a sky the dull pewter of a skillet lid. To the right, the lawn ended in a huge expanse of black plastic, an orange net fence, and mounds of excavated sand spiced with pieces of rusty metal. A crane, an earth mover, and a dump truck were parked along the edge of the sand. Albatrosses, both Laysan and black-foot, stood on the sand mounds. Now and then one would lean into the wind, spread its wings, and be lifted effortlessly into flight. Could one even guess at the number of albatrosses that must have inhabited this island before the tarmac and concrete? They were clinging stubbornly to what they had left, and fully exploiting the added bonus of mowed lawns.

I watched the human day begin, in its grudging accommodations to the birds. Figures emerged from the barracks and houses, mounting bicycles, pedaling a slalom course around the birds on the road. A truck moving slowly down the road came to a halt; the driver got out and herded a stubborn albatross off to the side before continuing on. A man on a tractor-mower appeared around the side of the barracks and began working his machine around the nesting birds, who sat tight even when mower blades passed inches from them, showering them with grass clippings.

Midway Atoll is a lagoon about five miles across at its widest point, encircled by coral reef. Two small islands—Sand, where we were, and Eastern, an unpopulated refuge since 1978—and a tiny islet named Spit make up the total land area of about two square miles. Sand Island, at 1,128 acres, was just slightly larger than Laysan, but the dense ironwood forest that now blanketed much of the island made it seem bigger. The island had looked much different to the early-nineteenth-century explorers, who described Sand as a mostly barren, wind-blown expanse of sand dunes, while Eastern, by contrast, was noted as much lusher, densely vegetated with naupaka and sedge and morning glory.

What Midway did offer was a harbor inside its lagoon, through a natural break in the reef large enough to admit a good-sized ship. But it was hardly a safe harbor: a strong storm would kick up waves in the lagoon that could drive a ship onto the reef. This was what happened in 1886, when the shark-fishing schooner *General Siegel* went down, marooning eight men at Midway. The sailors lived on seabird eggs and brackish water from the seeps on the islands. Relations among the crew deteriorated quickly, however. One man lost a hand while trying to fish using dynamite. His screams of pain were hard to bear, and the captain gave him something he said was medicine. The wounded man died shortly thereafter.

One seaman suggested that the captain had poisoned the maimed sailor. That seaman went off one day with the captain, paddling the ship's boat over to Eastern Island. The captain returned alone: Brown, he said, had shot himself by accident, and the captain had buried him where he fell. Another seaman, Jorgensen, later claimed he went over to Eastern, dug up the body, and found a bullet hole in the back of the head. But his testimony was open to suspicion too: he took a trip to Eastern with the captain and came back alone. A shark had gotten the captain, he said. The remaining men, now mistrustful of Jorgensen, managed to construct a sampan with wreckage. They sailed off one day, leaving Jorgensen behind.

Jorgensen was alone at Midway for six months before a ship appeared, the *Wandering Minstrel*, with a Captain Walker, his wife, two sons, and a small crew. Jorgensen thought he was saved. That night a storm came up, and the *Wandering Minstrel* joined the *General Siegel* at the bottom of the lagoon. Everyone moved into the shack Jorgensen had put together. It was fourteen months before a passing schooner caught sight of their bonfire and put off a boat to rescue them.

Jorgensen was already gone, though. He and a member of Walker's crew had patched together a boat a few months before and sailed for Honolulu. They fetched up at the Marshall Islands, more than fifteen hundred miles south.

Jorgensen's shack had once stood in the dunes back of the north beach. The dunes were now partly covered with ironwood, but I could see segments of them from my window. I walked out of Charlie BOQ in that direction. The road followed the curve of the island a hundred yards inland, past the adjacent Bravo barracks and a satellite dish, and up a sandy stretch shaded by a few towering ironwoods.

At the top of the dune a pavilion had been erected on what looked like a concrete bunker. Beyond it stretched the widest, most dazzling beach I had ever seen. To my left nothing was visible but the forest fringe of ironwoods, small dunes with stands of naupaka, and that astounding beach, perhaps a hundred yards wide, lapped by jeweled water. A seal lounged near water's edge; a green sea turtle cruised near shore. Above me, hugging the tree line, albatrosses glided by, barely moving their wings, somehow avoiding head-on collisions. In all the talk of Midway no one had mentioned a beach with sand like white sugar. Perhaps the irony was too much. The spell was broken when I glanced to my right at a corroded iron seawall and the orange fencing that edged an enormous fuel farm.

I would realize later why the beach had a perfect beauty even the beaches of Laysan lacked. There were people here who picked up the trash and the dead birds. Not the navy, but labor brought in from Thailand, Sri Lanka, and the Philippines by the private contractor the military paid to keep Midway running. The navy called them TCNs, or Third Country Nationals. Fish & Wildlife carefully referred to them as "Foreign Nationals." (As the atoll's official status is "unincorporated insular US possession," not all federal labor laws apply.) A small green pickup driven by one of these workers was the first vehicle out on the roads in the morning. It was the bird hearse.

I turned from the glare of white sand back into the shade of the ironwoods. A hundred feet inland the trees gave way to a riotous mix of shrubs and vines, all entangled in columns of roots from huge, spreading banyans. Nearly hidden among the dense vegetation was an old building that stopped me in my tracks. It was a large two-story structure with the hip roof, deep eaves, and encircling veranda of Pacific colonial architecture. A wrought iron railing with rusty filigree decorated the veranda. It was a setting worthy of Somerset Maugham.

Pushing through the shrubs I came close enough to see that the building was made of concrete with metal girders, explaining why it could have survived this long. (Termites were one of the bugs that arrived with early shipments to the island.) An identical building lay beyond it, and a third to the side of it. I pushed farther into rankly growing oleander and rosebushes run wild, and found myself at the base of a circle of concrete that once supported a flagpole.

It had never occurred to me that any remains of that period of Midway history could still exist, but these elegant structures must have once housed the cable company. The first permanent settlement on Midway was established a century ago by American Telegraph, ancestor to AT&T. The race was on between the British, Germans, and Americans to build the first around-the-world cable system. Midway was chosen as a relay station in the San Francisco–Honolulu–(Midway)–Wake–Guam–Philippines linkup.

After the first supply ship for American Telegraph wrecked on Midway's reef, temporary buildings were thrown up so they'd be ready in time for the system's inauguration. In Washington, President Teddy Roosevelt tapped out the first message on July 4, 1903. On that day Ben Colley, the first Midway cable station superintendent, hovered anxiously over his assistant at the keys. The message came through faint but audible: "Happy Independence Day to America, her territories, and possessions." They tapped it on to Wake Island. It took nine minutes to circle the globe.

Four cable buildings were completed in 1904, placed in a square, centered around flower beds and the flagpole. Ben Colley's journal describes interiors lit by acetylene lamps, with furnishings from Wanamaker's of New York. Outside was nothing but sand and birds, so Colley set to work planting trees and gardens. Ship supplies included tons of topsoil—termites included, it seems. Colley thought the local bird life needed augmentation with at least one good singer, so he brought in canaries.

Some of the plants he brought in would escape their gardens and spread aggressively. Mixed in with the soil were seeds of grasses and weeds, parasites, plant diseases, and various species of bugs. The alien species colonization of Midway began in earnest.

Ben Colley would have applauded the way, eighty years later, the skeleton crew of navy personnel were keeping up their ghost facility. Meals were served up at military hours in the mess hall. The cooks, however, were all Sri Lankan, and the food was a strange mix of military meat and potatoes and spicy dishes catering to Midway's largest population—over 150 Asian men hired at wages as low as ninety cents an hour, with six weeks off to go home once a year. The private contractor who ran Midway was Piquniq Management Corporation (PMC), a company owned by a group of Alaskan Native Americans that got its start in that state's oil fields. For my first meal I sat at a long table divided from the rest of the mess hall by a bank of food machines lined up with a salad bar, flanked by two PMC managers. I had passed up roast beef and glutinous scalloped potatoes for a three-alarm chicken curry.

Groups segregated themselves in the mess hall. I could see two tables of Filipinos, two of Sri Lankans, one of Thai men. Four tables held workers for OHM, the contractors doing the remediation work. I asked Leonard, the harbor master sitting across from me, what OHM stood for. "Stands for one hell of a mess," he said, and winked one guileless blue eye in a battered face.

Fish & Wildlife staff filled the rest of our table, their brown uniforms mixed in with naval whites. Midway had continued its downgrading, with the last OIC, or Officer in Charge, a commander, recently replaced by twenty-six-year-old Lieutenant David Black. His word was as much law here as it would be if he commanded a ship. He was tall and lanky and blushed easily.

Over the next hour I heard many speculations, some more informed than others, about what had gone on at Midway:

"In the sixties they had some kind of ET secret stuff going on over on Eastern. They had these big antennas, and the place was lit up like a sports stadium."

"You know Area Seven, where they're storing hazardous materials now? There's a building there where they assembled nuclear-tipped torpedoes. Whole place was fenced off—double fence and guard dogs. You can still see the guard house."

"The navy was flying all kinds of surveillance out of here in the sixties. Probably even U-2 planes, like that one they shot down over Russia."

"I was in the navy here in the fifties. We used to just shoot the gooneys that got on the runway, or run over them. But doesn't seem like there was so many of them then."

"Fish & Wildlife blames everything on the navy. Like saying the navy brought in the rats. Hell, it was probably some scientist. I heard it was some scientist brought in the termites so they could run an experiment."

"Some Fish & Wildlife guy brought in the canaries."

"You're nuts. The canaries were here before people ever got here."

"Oh, come on. Canaries don't live out in the middle of nowhere."

"This cleanup business is just spending taxpayer money. If they think this is bad, they oughta see Subic Bay. All this fuel cleanup is unnecessary. They used to just spread this stuff on the roads to keep down the dust."

The navy was getting a lot of mileage out of the Midway cleanup. "An unprecedented cooperative effort between the US Fish & Wildlife Service and the navy" was the oft-repeated line. My first day coincided with a visit by the navy captain in charge of the cleanup, an open-faced man named Steve who held an engineering degree and worked out of Pearl Harbor. He had a few minutes before he climbed back on board the C-141. We walked out to the orange fencing overlooking the fuel farm.

Heavy equipment operators were clearing sand to expose a huge rusted-metal fuel tank. "They cut an opening in the top, then drop in sampling kits to test for gases," said Steve. "Then they break the ceiling with a pile driver. Any remaining fuel residue is pumped out and stored to ship on the next barge to Honolulu, where it can be reprocessed into useable fuel.

"In the last year ninety-six underground fuel tanks have been removed from Sand Island and eleven from Eastern. The pipeline also has to be broken into, flushed, and removed. So far we've removed some thirty-five thousand feet, and we still have a long way to go."

It was becoming clear that a whole lot more had gone on out at Midway than I had imagined. The rows of abandoned barracks in classic 1950s military architecture testified to that. And clearly the cleanup involved more than fuel tanks.

"The original estimate for cleanup costs was very high," said the captain, "so we have to be sure all work we do is essential. We plan to be done by the scheduled date—June of '97. The cleanup, like all base closures, must meet EPA standards. Those standards are applied according to the site—obviously an urban site with a large human population might need to meet different criteria."

"Different?" I asked.

"More stringent, if there are more people impacted," Steve said.

After talking to the captain I returned to my room, pulled on hiking boots, put a water bottle in my fanny pack, and set off to explore. I took a road that went past the abandoned school and then turned north. More banyans and large trees nearly obscured two more cable buildings—the other two corners of the quadrangle. The road angled west, past a playground overgrown with weeds and a sprawling yellow-flowered shrub that seemed to have taken over nearly everything in the unmowed areas. A baseball diamond was ankle-deep in grass and dense with nesting birds. A large, low abandoned building with a gaping doorway stood between the road and the dunes, and through it I could see a huge brick fireplace black with soot. I peered in. One end of the cavernous interior held a curved bar with shredding moss-green tuck-and-roll upholstery that evoked a sudden memory of the backseat of my first boyfriend's Chevy, covered with a similar material that I had gotten to know up close and from many different angles.

The building, which I later learned had been the Chief Petty Officers' clubhouse, opened onto a huge patio coated with some kind of crumbling once-green tarmac. I walked through the patio and into the ironwoods covering the dunes. There seemed to be several trails, though I couldn't imagine what purpose they served. From the top of the dune, one trail descended among naupaka shrubs and opened out onto the beach. The sand was so patterned with albatross footprints that it looked like a textile design. I sat down in a spot with a view of the water.

I was thinking about my conversation with the captain about the extent of the cleanup and remembering the "dead zone" on Laysan. Along the north shore of that island, beyond the shark pool, was a forty-foot square of sand marked off with stakes and nylon twine. "Biologists have observed that the sand there is always scattered with dead crabs and insects," Cynthia had told me, "as though something was poisoning them. The speculation is that something very toxic was buried there, maybe in oil drums, and is now leaking out." The period from World War II through the Cold War had left few Pacific islands untouched by the legacy of military activities.

Midway's World War II buildings, if salvageable, qualified

for historic preservation, but most of the Cold War structures, it appeared, were slated for demolition. No one seemed concerned that the visible record of that period would be disappearing in the year or so of the cleanup. A lot had gone on out here, a lot the public would probably never know about. It made me wonder about the cleanup. If you couldn't uncover the history, how could you determine what needed to be cleaned up?

I heard a slapping noise behind me. An albatross walked up the path from somewhere deep in the ironwoods, each foot pulled up high and dropped with a slap at each step, its body rocking in a sailor's gait. The bird paused next to me, gave me a goofy look of surprise, and then continued a few feet. It stood for a minute, then spread its wings and galloped toward the beach. The wind gusting across the open sand lifted the bird into a wide arc out to the lagoon, where it turned to skim along the shallows, the tip of one wing nearly cleaving the water. I watched several glides and turns until it disappeared out toward the reef. Another albatross walked past me and broke out into a gallop, and another. It appeared I was sitting in the middle of an albatross runway. I stood up. Two white terns swooped down to hover in front of my nose, chattering. Their wings would have inspired Botticelli.

I slipped out of the wind between two dunes, where brown ironwood needles carpeted the sand and dimmed the light. The volcano-shaped albatross nests were sparsely strewn about. The white bodies of a few nesting adult birds looked eerie in the gloom of thick forest. Were they old enough, I wondered, to have started nesting here before the trees grew up? Albatrosses live a long time—the oldest banded albatross on Midway was over fifty and still producing young—so some of these birds could be older than the forest and still returning to old nest sites, though now they had to struggle through woods to get to them. Everywhere, white against the pine needles, lay bird bones: long, delicate leg bones, hollow and amazingly light, and intricate vertebrae that looked like scattered pieces of a Chinese puzzle. Many bones, and a few dead birds, here where the cleanup crews didn't make their rounds. I wondered if the dead ones were birds who tried to fly to their nests through the trees, instead of making the long walk in from the beach.

The forest ended abruptly in the cracked surface of an old runway, which, to my left, cut through the middle of the island and joined with the active runway in the distance. To my right it ran out to the shore, giving way to heaped-up broken concrete and rusting metal—the military method of beach erosion control. On the runway's pitted surface, huge piles of dirty sand had been dumped neatly in several rows, each covered with black plastic.

Across the runway, beyond a thin strip of ironwoods, a narrow beach faced the west. Albatrosses were gliding along the tree line. In an open sandy area black-footed albatrosses nested, and some were dancing. I lay down in the bunch grass and trailing morning glory to watch one pair, with the late afternoon sun backlighting their heads. They moved in a stately fandango, half opening their wings and bowing. Their ancestors had been doing this, perhaps, as long as the life of this island, on the beaches when its young, high volcanoes loomed toward the sky. Would they prevail long after sand buried the evidence of human history here?

I saw the skull-and-crossbones sign only when I stood up: Danger—Asbestos Dump.

TEN

The Steam-Cleaned Island

The US Fish & Wildlife Service had its office in the Midway Mall,
a cluster of World War II–era buildings in varying states of decay
next to the Midway Memorial. The Memorial itself featured two
mounted five-inch guns relocated from batteries in the center of
the island after World War II. A flagpole flew the American flag
and the navy insignia in front of a large mural depicting Dauntless bombers diving on a Japanese aircraft carrier. In center position stood a twelve-foot- high plaster statue of a Laysan albatross,
painted realistically, sporting a metal band on a leg as thick as a
fire hydrant. A live albatross sat on a nest between its legs.

In the Fish & Wildlife office a crowded warren of desks shared
space with seashells, the long-boned skull of a spinner dolphin,
and Midway memorabilia, including a model of the iconic Zero,
the Japanese fighter plane featured in the Battle of Midway. I
had been assigned a desk facing the windows, looking out past
ragged tennis courts to a dilapidated enlisted men's barracks
that now housed Foreign Nationals.

As a volunteer research assistant I was assigned to the Midway
Refuge biologist, a small-boned young woman with long black

hair named Nanette. Raised in Honolulu, she was the daughter of Chinese immigrants. She had done her master's work partly at Midway, on Bonin petrels, and got the Midway job and her degree at about the same time.

Jon, Nanette's boyfriend, was the biologist assigned to work with the cleanup. He had brown hair that flopped forward boyishly and a brusque manner; he wore regulation khaki shirt and shorts that looked as though they had been starched. He was talking with the navy chief petty officer (CPO) about representatives from Phoenix Air, scheduled to arrive the next day along with various Fish & Wildlife bigwigs. The plan was to hammer out an agreement on their partnership, and both parties were bringing their lawyers. The CPO was wondering "how the hell Fish & Wildlife could pick guys like Phoenix Air to run an ecotourism business."

Jon reminded him that a bid had gone out, but few had responded: "There was some billionaire who wanted to open up a casino. He submitted a proposal that had something like eight hundred people out here, doing things like shark fishing."

"Lots of parties want to see the airfield and harbor kept up," said the CPO. "Navy, coast guard, FAA—they all want that. But nobody wants to put up any money. Nobody but crazy billionaires and these southern dark horses."

"These guys are actually real familiar with Midway," Jon said. "They do contract flying for the military—towing targets, I think. They've been refueling here for years."

"They sound kinda dubious . . . probably CIA-funded," the CPO suggested.

When I asked for information on the cleanup, Jon handed me a thick volume titled *Preliminary Site Inspection Work Plan*, dated

1992. I asked if he had anything more recent. He dug out a second enormous ring-bound volume, saying, "Here's the *CLEAN*." I looked at the cover: *Comprehensive Long-Term Environmental Action Navy (CLEAN): Site Inspection (SI) Work Plan 1994.* The first five pages were a list of acronyms. At the end of the day I lugged both tomes back to the barracks, crammed into the rusty metal basket attached to the vintage Schwinn bicycle Nanette had presented to me.

A few days later I headed over to Eastern Island with Nanette to spend the day baiting rat traps. Both Sand and Eastern were infested with *Rattus rattus,* the common roof rat, descended from stowaways on cargo ships during World War II. Nearly all of the burrowing birds—the shearwaters and petrels—had been wiped out by rats preying on eggs and young. The year before, Fish & Wildlife had employed cleanup funds to launch a major campaign against the rats, starting with ninety days of intensive trapping and poisoning. Now the rat-bait stations had to be replenished once a month.

We left at dawn, the sun just beginning to redden the sky behind Eastern Island, which lay a mile across the lagoon. Nanette and I loaded our gear onto the military surplus landing craft the remediation company had brought to Midway to transport cleanup equipment and personnel back and forth. In the bay of the craft were two ATVs rigged with flatbeds for hauling supplies.

Next to me on the iron deck in front of the cockpit stood Terry, a retired radio technician who looked like a well-salted Tugboat Annie. After a stint as a Fish & Wildlife volunteer she had been hired to help Jon monitor the cleanup.

"I worked in communications in Honolulu," Terry told me when I asked how she had ended up at Midway. "Then I got a job working as an electronics technician at Midway in 1986."

Terry was in her early sixties, I guessed. She had leathery skin, a set jaw, short hair that was gray at the roots but dyed a peculiar rust color, and sea-green eyes that focused somewhere just beyond me. Heavy in the shoulders and short-legged, with a forward tilt to her stance, feet planted square, a bit bulldoggy. A thick Connecticut accent. "My husband lives in Tucson," she told me. "I tried to live there after they closed down the communications work here in '88. Couldn't stand the place. Nothin' there but red dirt."

"What was the work here?" I asked.

"Spy stuff," she said. "You aren't supposed to talk about it, but us technicians didn't know anything anyway. We just kept it all running. I worked out at the south end of Sand Island—bunch of buildings still there, though they'll be gone by next year. NAV-FAC, they call it, short for 'naval facility.' Sound surveillance system. All the information from cables strung all over the damn Pacific seafloor came in there. You can still see the cables. They had hydrophones on them. We were listening for subs. Mostly what we heard was a hell of a lot of whale talk. We didn't do any decoding—just sent everything on to Pearl Harbor."

Terry looked sideways at me, pressing her weight into the wall of the cockpit as we pulled out of the harbor into the chop of the dredged channel. "The real heavy-duty spy stuff happened on Eastern, earlier on," she continued. "You shoulda seen the antenna system, before they pulled it down last year. In the sixties the place must have been lit up like a stadium at night. The buildings are all still there, but they're getting ready to take those down too. If you want to see any of that before it all disappears, you got here just in time."

Talking about spying on this tiny, way-beyond-backwater place made me feel like I'd stepped through the looking glass. "Tell it to the birds," I wanted to say. A dozen spinner dolphins leapt and spun in our bow wave. We motored into the lee of Eastern Island, its low profile broken by a few patches of ironwood trees, heading for an old pier.

In 1891, naturalist George Munro of the Rothschild expedition described Eastern Island as "the most green of any that we have seen, being almost all covered with bright green scrub. . . . The scrub is mostly a large leaved pithy plant [naupaka] of which we have seen a little on Laysan."

Since Munro's visit nearly every inch of land on Eastern has been dug up, moved, or paved over, and invaded with alien plants. After being left on its own, the island had become overrun with thickets of *Verbesina*, the same golden-flowered weed that infested Sand Island. Still, as we pulled up to a narrow beach beside a crumbling concrete pier, I could see that patches of naupaka and bunchgrass had regenerated.

The landing craft lowered its front like a dump truck, and we stormed the island, nearly under the barrel of a rusty antiaircraft gun pointed across the lagoon toward Sand Island harbor. In the gloom of a grove of ironwoods were numerous buildings, some made of concrete and some of wood. Eastern Island had been uninhabited since 1978. Oddly, it was where Midway's military history began. Though smaller than Sand, it was long, allowing for two full runways, laid out across each other like open scissors, and another short runway across the open end of the scissors. Construction of Midway Naval Air Station began on Eastern Island in 1940, by a construction battalion of Navy Seabees living in tents.

We waded through a dense crowd of nesting albatrosses to the old runway. These birds had not learned to live with constant human disturbance, and some not guarding chicks or eggs fled in panic, galloping over the backs of their neighbors to get airborne.

A dozen Thai and Filipino workers on the cleanup crew went by, packed into one of the ATVs, smiling and waving as though headed off to a game of golf. Others were employed near the dock, cutting up huge piles of coiled, rusted wire that resembled bedsprings from the mattresses of giants. "Submarine netting," Terry informed me, stomping along at my side. "That stuff used to be strung along the entrance to the lagoon and between the lagoon and reef on both these islands. These beaches were covered with all the old antennas—they were just knocked down and left where the seals and turtles could get trapped in them. Old rusting fuel drums, the whole works."

At the shell of a concrete building that served for storage, we loaded up with buckets of wax-covered squares of a rodenticide called Vengeance. Nanette handed me protective gloves, extra plastic bait houses, marking tape, and a clipboard with checklist.

I walked out to the cracked, weed-filled tarmac of the old runway and consulted the map she had given me. I was to bait the traps placed at hundred-foot intervals from the middle to the northern end of the half-mile-wide island. That was the theory, at least; in reality the traps had been laid in meandering lines through patches of *Verbesina* and naupaka, and stands of ironwood, and around abandoned buildings, with each trap marked by flagging tape tied to whatever was handy, often some now-missing twig. Identification numbers on the boxes were faded, and some boxes had disappeared, blown into the brush by one of the winter gales.

Although the *Verbesina* was dying back at the end of its season, finding the bait boxes was still a nightmare of a scavenger hunt. I bushwhacked back and forth across the island, leaving a swath of upset birds behind me. The nesting birds with young chicks tried to cover them as I approached, lifting their chests up to push their offspring under their brood patches. Older chicks, left alone while their parents foraged at sea, sat upright like downy bowling pins, clattering their beaks at me as fiercely as adults.

That any birds nested here at all seemed a miracle. I had seen war photos of Eastern Island. By November 1941 the runways made a peculiar triangular hieroglyph from the air. From the pier down to where the runways crossed at the northern end was solid tarmac and buildings, or bare sand; only the fringes of the island were still green with shrubs.

Sand Island had already been fully developed into a seaplane base by that time. The facilities originally built for Pan Am clipper ships had been taken over by the military. Sand Island also supported officers' quarters, shops, and administration buildings, but no airstrip. The island was far from battle ready when it faced its first threat.

On the evening of December 7, 1941, hours after the early-morning attack on Pearl Harbor, two Japanese destroyers paid a visit to Midway, shelling Sand Island from a mile off its south end. The destroyers soon sailed on, but not before the power plant/command post received a direct hit that killed four soldiers.

Five months later, in early May 1942, Naval Intelligence officers at Pearl Harbor broke the Japanese secret code and listened in to plans to attack a place called AF. They suspected that AF was Midway, so they sent a bogus message that the water system on Midway had failed. On May 22 they overheard a Japanese coded message reporting that "AF was out of water."

Pearl Harbor's two seaworthy carriers, the *Enterprise* and the

Hornet, were sent steaming toward a point 390 miles northeast of Midway. They would rendezvous there with the battered *Yorktown,* readied for battle by fifteen hundred Pearl Harbor yard workers in three days.

At Midway, a few weeks of frantic scrambling began to fortify the atoll against a full invasion. Little of the native vegetation and few nesting birds could have survived this period, as Marines hastily excavated dugouts and slit trenches all over Sand and Eastern islands.

At 9:25 a.m. on June 3 the Japanese attack force was spotted by Midway's search planes. Nine B-17 Flying Fortresses from Midway were initially dispatched from the island to drop their bombs on the fleet of eighty-eight ships, including five battleships. There were no hits.

At 5:45 a.m. the next morning many enemy planes were sighted heading for Midway. The first wave dropped their bombs on Sand Island, demolishing the laundry, the dispensary, and the brig. The seaplane hangar and three fuel tanks were set ablaze. The second wave of Japanese Zeros dove at Eastern Island, scoring hits on several buildings but sparing the runway, perhaps so that Japanese aircraft could land once Midway's defenses were subdued. The attack on Midway was over in thirty-one minutes.

The real battle would happen at sea. Midway's bombers were already launched again toward the Japanese fleet. The air combat above the battleships would leave fourteen of Midway's twenty-six pilots dead and only two planes fit to fly again.

But now the *Yorktown's* scouts had located the Japanese fleet, and the heavily outnumbered American fleet launched their fighters. In what would later be called "a miracle," the American bombers caught the Japanese carriers with most of their planes on deck, refueling from their Midway attack. Three Japanese carriers were set ablaze. A fourth carrier fled (aircraft from the *Enterprise* would later deal it a killing blow), but not before it launched several planes whose torpedoes would find the *Yorktown*. The next day, as the crippled carrier was being towed toward Honolulu, a Japanese sub finished it off.

Somehow, the American fleet had vanquished the hugely superior Japanese force. The balance of sea power in the Pacific, which had swung heavily toward the Japanese after the devastating attack on Pearl Harbor, began to swing the other way.

I was threading my way down the runway from which Midway's bombers had taken off, thinking of a time that would soon pass from the memories of the living. Only a few signs of that history remained. ARMCO huts (tin-roofed weapons magazines camouflaged with mounded soil and vegetation), bunkers, and a couple of rusty tank turrets that had been used as instant pillboxes sat among birds and yellow flowers. A thin concrete ring encased in chicken wire surrounded an area about eight feet in diameter that had served as a gun battery. The sand that once buttressed its walls had blown away, and the whole assemblage looked as insubstantial as a stage prop. In the center of the island, within the triangle formed by the runways, steep-sided dunes, now a favored spot for the nests of burrowing birds, were the remains of revetments hastily pushed up to provide partial shelter for aircraft.

These few shards of World War II history were eclipsed by the visible history of the second, more secretive battle that had been fought here: the battle for information. In 1949, the Soviet Union exploded its first nuclear weapon, and soon it matched America's arsenal of long-range bombers with nuclear capability. By 1953 the fear of Soviet attack on the continental United States from across Canada had resulted in DEW, the "distant early warning" line of radar stations strung out over ten thousand North Arctic kilometers, from Baffin Island to Alaska. But from Midway to the Aleutian Islands, the empty, unwatched North Pacific offered a clear route for enemy bombers to ride the jet stream to the West Coast.

Or so the reasoning went. In 1957 radar stations were extended down through the Aleutians. A second extension was added linking Greenland, Iceland, and the United Kingdom. The third, the Pacific Seaward Barrier, would provide a radar line from Midway to Adak Island in the Aleutians, some thousand miles north. It was done with ships at sea and with planes on a staggered schedule, flights leaving Midway every one and a half hours. The radar-equipped planes flew for six hours north toward Adak, then followed a parallel track back to Midway.

In 1957 a huge construction program began to prepare Midway to house over six thousand people involved in DEW and other Cold War activities. Sand Island had a runway by then, but to accommodate the newest planes, it had to be lengthened. Over a hundred acres of dredged sand and coral held together with sheet piling were added to the island as a result. Sand Island was full to bursting—ready to sink, some thought—under the weight of its small city. Eastern Island was abandoned.

But not for long. In 1958 transformation of Eastern into a spy station began. As I walked the transects at the northeastern end of the island, I came upon the buildings incongruously squatting among the yellow-flowered weeds and birds: monolithic, flat-roofed concrete structures surrounded by derelict fuel tanks. Knobs and metal ventilator shafts and tie-bolts that once held antennas of all shapes and sizes sprouted from their roofs, and through a couple of empty doorways I saw huge, rusting generators. The two largest buildings were ringed with yellow tape and posted with a sign: Danger—Hazardous Materials.

The bulky cleanup document Jon had given me listed these buildings as part of the Naval Communication Unit (NCU). My rat baiting next took me up to the building housing the Army Pacific Scatter System (part of a Pacific-wide long-distance signaling system), then past the Naval Security Group Activity building, dedicated to cryptology and intelligence gathering. These were the heart of Midway's spy station and listening post, a vital link in a network that spanned over 7,800 miles.

The Soviet launch of Sputnik in 1957, announcing the advent of satellite communication, was, in President Lyndon Johnson's later words, "a technological Pearl Harbor"; the launching of satellite after satellite soon rendered most traditional long-distance communications systems obsolete. By 1970 Eastern was abandoned for good, and the rats inherited the island. The ironwood forest was spreading, still pushing against the few patches of native shrub left.

But at the northern end a small patch of naupaka had survived or regenerated, and it was festooned with birds—red-footed boobies, black noddies, frigatebirds. A pair of masked boobies stood in the shade of one large shrub. The immature red-foots took to the air and came swooping over me. On the narrow strand at the very tip of the island lay a monk seal, one of the few I had seen at Midway. For a moment I could imagine how this island might once have looked. Out over the lagoon appeared one of those magical apparitions that atolls sometimes offer: low-hanging cumulus clouds with their bellies painted a luminous green by light reflected off the water, hovering like some vestigial image of a green paradise.

I made my way back to the pier along the second runway, past concrete pylons that once supported huge antennas, and debris sorted into heaps: rusty metal, coils of wire, ceramic insulators, batteries. The shells of buildings, the piled wreckage of the past, gave the place an after-the-holocaust feeling.

In a year these buildings would all be gone, parts of them placed on barges and taken to Honolulu to be recycled, much of the material buried in a new landfill in the middle of Sand Island. How much, if any, of Midway's Cold War period would be documented, preserved, interpreted, I wondered. And what would we learn about the hidden costs of that period, of which the kind of pollution you can't see was only a part?

Back on Sand Island I looked through the material Jon had loaned me for information on the buildings cordoned off with yellow tape. The NCU was built in 1958 for communication with other bases in the Pacific. A photo showed a towering grid of microwave antenna sprouting in an upside-down U from the roof of the larger windowless building.

After an inspection found a leaking oil-filled transformer amid piles of oil-filled switches, batteries, and other debris inside the smaller building, along with seven leaking fifty-five-gallon drums with unknown contents outside, the buildings were listed in a 1991 preliminary assessment, prepared for the navy by Ogden Environmental Energy Services, one of the nation's largest remediation contractors. Besides the NCU buildings, the assessment had identified five other potential contaminant sources on Eastern Island and "at least seven" on Sand Island. But the Draft Site Inspection Work Plan dated September 1992 identified only three of the thirteen sites. It did not include the NCU buildings as an area of concern for contaminants.

This was probably not an oversight on Ogden's part, but a reflection that any large-scale environmental cleanup is a receding target: there is simply not enough funding available to completely clean up a Superfund-sized mess. (In fact, ten years on, the Pentagon would be seeking amendments to the Superfund Law and other regulations because none of its thirty-four military bases on the Superfund list since 1988 had been "completely" cleaned up.) The navy was committed to removing its enormous system of rusted, leaking fuel tanks and pipelines, and doing what it could to remediate the petroleum that now floated atop the groundwater lens under much of Sand Island. And it was committed to taking down and disposing of what would finally tally as over one hundred buildings. But it was not interested in looking for other pollutants.

Ogden's mission was to identify what needed to be cleaned up at Midway according to Environmental Protection Agency (EPA) requirements. But these were subject to interpretation, depending on the type of risk pollution might pose to specific "ecological receptors." As Captain Steve had pointed out, the most stringent requirements would apply not to a place like Midway, but only where contaminants endangered a permanent human population of appreciable size.

As both a national wildlife refuge (and one that included an endangered species—the monk seal) and a military facility, Midway was blessed with an unusually strong BRAC (Base Remediation and Closure) team; in addition, NMFS and Fish & Wildlife were able to bolster the EPA with on-the-ground knowledge. Comments on Ogden's work plan from the watchdog team ran to fifty-one pages. Fish & Wildlife spent three weeks doing field reconnaissance and a week reviewing navy files at Midway. The files were full of gaps, making it impossible to piece together an environmental history of the years when Midway had been an isolated military fiefdom. The final maps for the cleanup would code gray all areas of possible environmental contamination. Every inch of land on both Sand and Eastern fell in this category.

The agency comments made it clear that some basic issues were not addressed in Ogden's work plan. Background sampling, for example: samples from suspected contaminated areas need to be compared to samples from the general area in order to establish a baseline for any contaminants that may be ubiquitous in the environment—that can't be pinned, in other words, on the polluter in question. Ogden's plan called for background sampling in various locations that were hardly likely to show pre-navy conditions, such as the artificial shoreline of the extended runway.

Of the contaminants to be monitored, some particularly potent ones—mercury, asbestos, pesticides, dioxins, dibenzo-furans—had been left out. The comments from Fish & Wildlife and the other agencies called for investigations of all areas where navy activities might have left persistent contaminants. Searches through records and maps had turned up at least forty-five such sites on Sand Island, not counting nine raw sewage outfalls. At least ten sites left out of the Ogden plan were identified on Eastern Island, including a drum disposal area with "unknown contaminants, possibly toluene and other solvents"; an asbestos disposal area; a quarry pond with "shallow water curiously devoid of aquatic fauna"; and a bulky-waste landfill likely contaminated with POLs (petroleum, oil, and lubricants), battery acid, pesticides, and polychlorinated biphenyls, or PCBs. Compounds used ubiquitously as lubricants from their creation in the late 1930s (by Dow Chemical) until they were banned in 1976, PCBs are among the most dangerous pollutants over the long term. Insoluble in water and extremely slow to break down, they persist in the environment and accumulate in the tissues of organisms, working their way up the food chain in increasing concentrations. Evidence was beginning to indicate that even at relatively low levels they could disrupt animals' endocrine, reproductive, and immune systems.

The day after I went over to Eastern, a brisk but sunny Sunday, I talked Jon into taking me on what I privately dubbed "the Toxics Tour."

While we drank coffee at the duplex he shared with Nanette, Jon mentioned that he was also investigating the "dead zone" at Laysan. "We haven't gotten the final analysis, but we think it's Carbo-Furan [a highly toxic pesticide]. Could have been a barrel washed up. But we found crabs that had come to the surface and died. Flies would land and twitch and die. We dug down and found dead insects and crabs. That would suggest something seeping out that was buried."

Who would have buried pesticides on Laysan, and what were they doing there? Jon had gotten up to fiddle with the knobs on a small espresso machine. "Maybe the military brought something over at some point—to control flies or something while they were on the island," he said over his shoulder. "What were they doing there? God knows . . . A lot went on out here that we'll never know about. I try not to think too much about that."

He sat back down and peered into his coffee cup. "They may have been more cavalier in the past, because they knew less about the effects of some of these contaminants," he said. "But you have to think they would have dealt with major spills and things. . . . If not, how can you get to some comfort level about living out here?"

That was a good question. The draft work plan had also listed an "Area 7," now used as a place to store hazardous materials, but formerly a "special weapons storage area." Now *there* was a term to make you pause: "special weapons" is navy-speak for chemical, biological, or nuclear weapons.

Jon's driving made me wish the golf cart had seat belts. We careened through the old "industrial section," passing the abandoned power plant that still displayed bullet holes from the Japanese ships that shelled Midway on their way back from the attack on Pearl Harbor, down a rutted road that ran past the historic electric-powered torpedo shop, with its tower for untangling and repacking parachutes, and then the air-powered torpedo shop, both buildings now used for maintenance. We drove past fields dense with albatrosses and out through a patch of ironwood forest to the runway, turning down the side of the runway toward the east end of the island. The east end was all artificial island dredged up to allow enclosure of the harbor and extension of the runway. The landfill was in the middle of scrub ironwood forest. Mynah birds picked at garbage, and a burning pile of cardboard boxes, plastic bags, and other rubbish sent acrid smoke inland. The waste was piled into long trenches, and sand was bulldozed over the residue after burning. Fish & Wildlife comments had noted rusted-out drums and containers and other evidence of potential contamination scattered throughout the forest. The navy had no records of their landfill use.

We walked through some oily-looking mud to the edge of a small stagnant pond in a depression where sand had once been quarried. "You would expect to find more life in a freshwater pond," said Jon. "We don't know if this connects directly with the groundwater, the basal lens of freshwater that underlies the entire island." (Midway's actual drinking water is rainwater collected in shallow concrete basins and stored.) What shape was the groundwater in? There had been "containment failures" in numerous fuel tanks, Jon said. Most of the tanks had been installed in the war years, then left to rust in later years with the fuel still in them.

"So the groundwater is contaminated?" I asked.

"In some areas, yes. There's a lot of free product—fuel, that is—floating on the surface in areas like under the fuel farm. They're doing a feasibility study to see if it can be cleaned up. OHM has a system they've used elsewhere, though not for anything this size. It's called vacuum extraction—you steam-heat the spilled fuel, I think, and then siphon it off. Then you can separate the oil out of the vapor somehow."

"Sounds like a giant carpet cleaner," I said.

The next stop was the bulky-waste landfill, a thousand-foot-long thumb protruding from the south side of the island. Since the 1940s, the navy had been dumping metal wastes and scrap material here, creating an artificial peninsula now 300 feet wide and 23 feet deep, filled with nearly 2 million cubic feet of debris. Sand and coral rubble had been bulldozed over the heaps of rusting scrap metal, aluminum siding, old appliances, motors, and steel pipe to make a road of sorts, and the edges of the landfill had been shored up with concrete slabs. At the far end was a rusty metal water tank with its top removed, which served as an incinerator. A couple of years earlier, the tank had leaked its accumulated sludge into the ground.

"Possible contaminants?" said Jon. "A long list: in the landfill itself, heavy metals, battery acids, oil, paint, brake and transmission fluids; in the tank, oil and solvents."

Records since 1981, the date when the first private contractor was brought in to manage Midway, seemed to indicate that at least since that time no lubricants, hydraulic fluids, or other possible sources of PCBs had been burned in the steel tank. But sludge from fuel storage tanks had burned, along with waste oil, kerosene, and some cleaning solvents. The open incineration of these materials potentially produces hazardous by-products, including dioxins and dibenzofurans, some of the most toxic chemicals on earth.

Final stop on the Toxics Tour was the "new" asbestos dump, a hill covered with sand, near the decaying seawall of the east end. "The old dump was being compromised by burrowing seabirds," said Jon. "Material in this dump was, according to the navy, first sealed in plastic, and then covered with soil. It will be immensely costly to replace this seawall. But if it's not replaced, all this has the potential of being washed into the sea."

The navy had kept Midway essentially free from civilian scrutiny until the late 1980s. Tugboat Terry was here, keeping the hydrophone system running, from 1986 to 1988. We talked one night in her suite on the second floor of Charlie. A stack of videos— *Wackiest Ship in the Army*, *Midway*, *Operation Petticoat*, and the like—occupied the shelf next to the tattered orange plaid couch where I sat.

Terry had on orange overalls that matched the couch. The hard hat she had worn all day had made the rust-colored ends of her hair clump together like a rooster crest. "Sometimes this job we're doing seems a joke," she said. "I was asking myself today out there. Here I'm moving these tropicbird chicks so they won't get crushed. Meanwhile I'm walking around in there crushing shearwater burrows at the same time. If we really care about making it nice for birds we oughta just get outta here."

She handed me a Dr. Pepper and popped the top on another. I steered the conversation around to her surveillance work.

"All that Eastern Island spook stuff had stopped a long time before I got out here," she said. "Area 7—that still had the ten-foot double fence, with barbed wire at the top. The rumor was they built bombs and torpedoes in there. Nuke-u-lar bombs? I dunno. But why else would they need all that security on an island like this?

"When I got here they had this program called the Pony Express, which was to monitor Soviet missile tests. There were planes taking off round the clock when they were doing that. Right up to 1988, then they didn't have to worry about the Russians anymore.

"But that earlier period, that's when things were hopping all over the Pacific. But nobody's gonna talk to you about that stuff. I don't talk about the work I did, and it wasn't much, just relaying messages."

In the 1950s and 1960s, the US military occupied the Pacific more thoroughly than it ever had in World War II. The most visible aspect was the cultural legacy, what a sociologist friend summed up as "the spread of canned Spam." But it was more of a literal colonizing. The military brought an economy that displaced local economies; at bases they established what amounted to feudal states. They brought hitchhikers, animal and vegetable, that established beachheads on islands throughout the Pacific.

On Oʻahu, I had grown up just outside the feudal walls of a huge military base. Here I was inside, and outside was nowhere in sight.

ELEVEN

Map Sense

By the third week of January on Midway, the eggs of both Laysan and black-footed albatrosses had begun to hatch, and bedraggled chicks with outsized bills emerged, just in time for a winter gale. I woke in the middle of one night to the boom of waves pounding the atoll, the noise reverberating inward from the entire circumference of reef, putting us in the eye of a storm of sound. It echoed through the cinderblock walls, a potent reminder that only a coral membrane protected us from that wind-stirred fury of ocean and certain catastrophe. The bird cries grew loud and then dimmed, whipped by the wind, like cries from a ship going down.

The following morning it was calm. Out over the lagoon, the disk of a waning moon floated in the clearing sky like an unmoored atoll in its own blue sea. A cleanup crew was already at work nearby, using a chainsaw to clear the huge limbs of an ironwood that had fallen onto the road. Narrowly sandwiched between two limbs, an arm's length from the ripping chainsaw, a Laysan albatross still sat on its nest. A few other albatrosses attempted to brood eggs immersed in a puddle, while one tried to nestle a drowned chick under its feathers. But wind and rain were nothing new to these birds, and most chicks, tucked under parents in their little cinder-cone-shaped nests, had weathered the storm.

It was Sunday. A day off, with the promise of sun. I climbed on my bike to explore the rest of the island. I was hoping to see the golden gooney.

"Go look for her by the end of the runway, near Frigate Point," said Silva, the Sri Lankan who headed the grounds maintenance crew. "She has been gone a long time but she just came back."

I thought he was pulling my leg, but I asked Nanette about this mythical bird. It was indeed real, she told me: a short-tailed albatross, also known as a "golden gooney" because it sports a gold-colored crown of feathers when mature. "The birds are highly endangered—the only breeding colony left is on an island off Japan—but one or two have been showing up here for years. It would be great if a colony got going here—maybe it would help us get some more money!"

I followed an old road that ran through a thick forest of ironwood, coming to a tiny cemetery surrounded by a low picket fence. The grass had been mowed fairly recently, but it was hummocked with bird burrows. I threaded my way over to five headstones guarded by nesting albatrosses. Four of the names on the graves bore the title MD, with the earliest date of death May 11, 1906, and the latest August 1, 1950. Only the earliest, James Miller of Georgia, had a birth date on his headstone: October 11, 1875, which made him thirty-one when he died. One early account told of a Midway doctor who had died trying to take out his own appendix. Maybe it was poor James.

The old road led me to the abandoned runway, and I crossed

its cracked surface and cycled the smooth tarmac along the edge of the working runway toward Frigate Point. On the right a dirt road led back into the woods, and a sign next to it read HAZMAT—Authorized Personnel Only. This had to be Area 7, the site marked on a navy map from the 1960s as the "Advanced Underwater Weapons Complex," now being used by the remediation contractors as a staging area for hazardous materials before their removal by barge to Pearl Harbor. I hesitated a moment, parked my bike, then stepped past the sign and along a rutted dirt road shaded by a dense grove of sea grape trees with leathery bronze leaves.

The woods opened abruptly to the left, revealing the broken-windowed shell of a two-story guard tower, the upper walls pierced with slots for guns. A clearing beyond the guardhouse was divided by an enormous concrete wall at least twenty feet high, a good eight feet wide at the base but narrower at the top.

To the right of the wall was a long, low building, divided into cubicles like a series of garages, each with a number over the door. To the left stood a heavily reinforced concrete block building with two sets of giant steel doors. I walked between the building and the wall until I stood outside the second set of doors. On the ground were the fallen girders of what appeared to have been an overhead tramway.

The steel doors stood slightly apart. I squeezed through and stood in a huge room dimly lit by high, barred windows. Twenty feet above, the ceiling was crisscrossed with ventilation pipes, a fire sprinkler system, thick-wired electric circuitry, and tram rails bearing the sign LIMIT 500 LBS. The walls were painted military green and festooned with circuit boxes and stencils that read DANGER—HIGH EXPLOSIVES.

I walked outside and around the end of the huge concrete

berm. The overhead tram had probably skirted this end of the berm and extended to the garage-like structures, which had to be weapons bays. Heavy metal doors were still attached to a few of the cubicles, all of them ajar. The metal posts of a tram that had once run the length of all twelve bays still remained, and inside each dark rectangle I could see tram rails on the ceiling. The end cubicle closest to the guard tower had a metal door heavily reinforced with concrete. The floor was a steel grid over a square cistern filled with dark, oily water. I walked around the end of the building and discovered it was double-sided, with twelve more bays, some filled with steel drums marked with a hazardous waste symbol.

What would be the point of a weapons complex of this magnitude, built in 1960 in the middle of nowhere? The search through Midway naval documents undertaken as part of the cleanup plan had turned up no information on the weapons complex, and the navy had not been willing to provide any information about the site, other than to state that it had "never been used for 'special weapons.'" The buildings were not old enough to qualify as historic; they would be taken down, and all signs of what had been here obliterated. This part of Midway history would be literally buried, another missing piece of the puzzle that was Cold War history in the Pacific.

The empty menace of these buildings, a weapons complex in a hidden war, weighed on me as I walked back toward the runway. On the tarmac again, I cycled toward Frigate Point to pick up the road that led past the buildings where Tugboat Terry once sat, listening to hydrophones strung along the Pacific floor.

The golden gooney stood in the midst of a patch of sweet alyssum near a black-footed albatross. She was very big, dwarfing the black-foot. Her glorious honker of a beak—she was indeed making a deep-throated honking sound—was twice the size of his, bright pink with a blue tip. Her head was crowned by dark feathers edged with gold, a color that someday would spread to form a solid golden cap. She bobbed her head and cakewalked ponderously toward the black-foot. The object of her affections fled in alarm.

This place, so perilously close to the runway, was where she and an older male short-tail had spent time the year before. The older bird had disappeared, and this one produced an egg that she incubated for a month before she abandoned it. The egg was found to be infertile, causing great sorrow at Fish & Wildlife. To have such a rare bird establish a breeding colony in the Northwestern Hawaiian Islands would contribute to the stature of the region, and might just save the short-tail from extinction.

The huge birds were once one of the most populous species in the North Pacific, but millions were wiped out by feather hunters early in the twentieth century, and by the late 1930s the only breeding colony left was at Torishima, a tiny volcanic cone among the southern Izu Islands of Japan. In 1933, when the Japanese declared Torishima a wildlife sanctuary, it was estimated that fewer than a hundred birds remained anywhere in the world.

The Torishima volcano was a dangerous guardian of their fragile sanctuary. In 1939 an eruption overran the main albatross breeding area. Then in 1941 another eruption filled in the cove where boats could moor, making it very difficult to land on the island. Even so, Torishima was occupied during World War II by a garrison of soldiers who saw only one albatross during their tenure. It was thought the birds had gone extinct. But albatrosses spend several years at sea before they breed, and as the young ones grew old enough they returned, and the colony grew again, very slowly. By the mid-1990s there were around four hundred short-tails, but still no breeding colonies anywhere but Torishima, at the mercy of the volcano.

I followed the runway to its eastern end before circling back along the harbor toward "downtown." That end of the runway was all artificial fill, buttressed on one side by the sheet piling of the boat harbor, on the other by concrete riprap. A two-story-high cross marked the place where Easter sunrise service was held every year. Midway being just forty miles east of the international dateline, it was the last sunrise over land on Easter Day.

The international dateline was originally drawn to be 180 degrees from the Greenwich meridian. It handily divided the Eastern Hemisphere from the Western. But like most human trajectories marking the globe, it was subject to the lines of empire. When the US purchased Alaska in 1867, a huge portion of the dateline was moved west.

For half a century, from pre–World War II days to the closing in the late 1980s of the last Cold War operation, the SOSUS (Sound Surveillance System) hydrophone post, Midway anchored the lines of American empire in the largest empty space on earth—the northern Pacific. Here, on this edge of empire, the nation may have stored our ultimate weapons of destruction. From this point ran invisible lines of power: patrol flights around the clock, miles of cabled listening devices along the ocean floor, information lines leading to other islands in the Pacific—a cat's cradle of military occupation.

The Polynesian seafarers fashioned maps out of split bamboo and shells, weaving into them their knowledge of the ocean, the circling of stars, the movements of birds along multitudinous skyways. They followed the migratory birds just as the aborigines followed the "songlines" of animals over the ancient topography of Australia. The aborigines too imposed a conceptual order on the world, but it was a recognition of the earth's great wheels and cycles.

Migrations of truly pelagic seabirds like the albatross are in effect prolonged nomadic wanderings in the wilderness of the Pacific Ocean. The birds could never live year-round in their overcrowded breeding colonies; as soon as their breeding and nesting duties are over, they're off to more solitary pursuits. Location of food sources and the pattern of prevailing winds determine their migration patterns. For the large-bodied albatross, exploiting the movements of wind is crucial, and its flight requires precision that even the most carefully engineered glider can't duplicate. (This absolute reliance on wind explains why Northern albatrosses rarely show up south of the equator: they would have to cross a several-degrees-wide region of unreliable winds called the equatorial doldrums.) Although their normal migrations may follow a fairly regular geographic path (in the case of resident Hawaiian birds, foraging near the Aleutians, in the south Bering Sea, and off Japan in the warmer months, moving closer to the Northwestern Islands as the weather cools), Laysan albatrosses have been proven to have remarkable homing abilities. The navy briefly considered relocating Laysan albatrosses nesting near the Midway airstrip. As an experiment, biologists working for the navy took one albatross to the Philippines. It homed easily to Midway, covering a distance of 6,600 kilometers in thirty-two days. An impressive feat, but the speed record belongs to an albatross released along the coast of Washington State, who showed up at Midway ten days later, having averaged over 500 kilometers per day.

Then there's the story of a Laysan albatross named Munch. In 1979 he was banded by the International Bird Rescue Center in Berkeley after someone found him, with his wings clipped, walking around in San Francisco. He got his name from the number of fingers he munched during attempts to feed him. It was decided that waiting nearly a year for his wing feathers to grow back was not an option, so feathers from a dead albatross found in Hawai'i were flown over and spliced onto the broken shafts of his old feathers. The bird was flown to Midway, since it was assumed he had originally come from the Northwestern Islands.

Munch had not been sighted again after his Midway release, and those who helped him wondered how he had fared. In 1986, scientists investigating a recently established colony of Laysan albatrosses nesting on Guadalupe Island off the coast of Mexico traced the band number of one of the birds—only to find it was Munch, the great traveler.

Albatrosses and green sea turtles alike navigate hundreds of miles of open ocean. In both cases, the source of their homing abilities is a mystery that scientists have yet to unravel. Certainly these very different animals rely on different senses for their information. Although sea turtles are sensitive to light sources, they are much too myopic to make use of star constellations to orient themselves, as some evidence suggests birds may do. Wave and wind patterns may provide information to both animals; odors might likewise aid both.

But animals such as Munch display homing abilities that transcend a compass sense based on instinctive knowledge of an ancestral route or even on sophisticated tracking skills. They seem to exhibit a "map sense," an ability to orient themselves globally even when taken far from the areas they know. How does the albatross transported by plane to the unfamiliar waters of the Philippines, more than 50 degrees in longitude west of

Midway, position himself on the globe and fly what must be a fairly direct course to a tiny atoll 6,600 kilometers away?

Recent studies have suggested that the earth's magnetic fields may provide orienting information for a number of species, including whales and sharks as well as birds and turtles. The magnetic field is generated at the earth's core by fluid iron, which moves with the earth's rotation. Electromagnetic energy radiates out from the earth in hoops aligned north to south, returning to intersect the earth at increasingly steep angles as you move toward the poles. Many animal cells, including those of humans, contain magnetite, which may act as minute receivers to detect variations in the field. We too may have once "known in our bones" where we were.

The movements of migratory animals are strong strands in the web that unites Pacific islands into a vast ecosystem. This is a truth the Western world has not been eager to grasp, since it is easier to rationalize the plunder of islands viewed as isolated, haphazard treasure, strewn in a waste of ocean. Certainly it has not been in the interest of the military to look deeply at the ecosystems of the islands they exploit. This reluctance has produced devastation. It has also on occasion produced black comedy: the war between military and albatross, for example.

Albatross attachment to nest—what biologists call "site fidelity"—is an attachment, in fact, to place. An albatross will likely never land on any other island, on any other patch of land in its life, than its birthplace. Not only does the Midway albatross return to its home island, but the bird gets as close as possible to the exact spot of the nest where it was raised.

You could call these birds the ultimate conservatives. The albatross returns to the nesting spot even if it has changed for the worst, in fact even if it has lost nearly all the qualities that made it attractive in the first place. Species who evolve in isolation over long periods of time, without major predators, are deeply conservative—rather, they are slow to adapt.

On Sand Island, you soon notice the peculiar pattern of albatross nests: the Laysans nest thickly near some of the buildings, where the birds must have faced much disturbance. In the ironwood forests one comes across Laysans laboriously waddling through the woods to nesting sites deep among the trees. Yet in open, easily accessible areas around the southern end of the main runway, the population is a lot less dense. These were the landfilled additions to the island created during World War II, and the albatrosses have still not fully claimed it. Though Blackfoots nearly always nest along shore areas, where they can find easy takeoff and landing spots (they are heavier, and less agile flyers than Laysans), one finds a long band of them inland of the main runway. Their nesting traces the original shore of the island.

At the height of the war, when Sand Island may have garrisoned as many as six thousand men, there was little room left for the albatross. Those who were concerned about Midway bird populations were a long way away, as this recollection from the time attests: "Washington had sent word that the goonies must not be hurt, so for a while Gallagher had to detail an extra man to walk in front of every vehicle, awkwardly requesting the birds to step aside, setting the young out of harm's way one at a time. Gallagher protested that too much time was being lost; with Ventres's permission, he gave orders to run over the creatures."

Midway's current population of over 1.5 million albatrosses may be close to the atoll's carrying capacity, and may reflect the numbers of birds resident before humans arrived. By the time the Cable Company set up shop in 1903, feather poachers had killed possibly as much as 90 percent of the albatross population.

Once the feather poaching ceased, the colonies grew even through the activities of the war years. But directly after the war, the change from seaplanes to land planes and the consequent construction of the large runways on Sand Island spelled big trouble for the albatrosses. Worried that the birds were large enough to cause possibly fatal plane crashes, the navy ordered extermination of birds nesting near the runway. Marines and the construction crew, armed with two-by-fours, did the job.

With heavy use of Midway as a refueling station for planes and ships during the Korean War, the battle against the albatrosses escalated. The air force brought in two wildlife biologists, who tried firing bazookas over the heads of nesting birds. They set rubber tires ablaze, along with smoke flares. Finally they resorted to taking the eggs along with the nests, but the birds simply built new ones. "Invitation to leave ignored by gooney birds," declared a *Honolulu Advertiser* headline. Midway's albatrosses were, the reporter said, "stubbornness held together by feathers."

Then came attempts to relocate birds, giving biologists their first knowledge of the amazing migration skills of the albatross. In 1957, a $40 million building program prepared Midway for its role as surveillance post in the Cold War and base for planes flying the DEW line. With planes now taking off and landing around the clock, the number of bird strikes climbed to 538 in the first year. The navy tried once more to rid the atoll of albatrosses. They cleared long swaths through vegetation at nearby Kure Atoll, with the idea that the birds chased from Midway might find their way there. To loudspeaker noise and smoke and sulfur flares were added huge scarecrows.

Fish & Wildlife took over management of the Northwestern

Islands from the state in 1962, but Midway was excluded, which left the navy still in charge. In 1964 the navy settled on paving huge areas on either side of the runway as a solution to keeping nesting birds at bay. Birds who attempted to nest on the pavement soon found that the nesting material went airborne in the first gust of wind. But those birds unable to nest didn't move elsewhere—they simply became "unemployed birds," according to the navy director of natural resources, and a bigger hazard to planes than ever. Permission was given to kill twenty thousand birds if a "humane" method could be figured out. Ultimately the birds were loaded fifty at a time into the sealed back of a large truck, where they were gassed with carbon monoxide.

By 1965, with the advent of other methods of spying, such as satellite technology, DEW line patrol missions dwindled. Air flights in and out of Midway were hugely reduced, and large-scale attempts to control the albatross population on Midway came to an end. Earlier methods had attracted some very unfavorable publicity. Rachel Carson's classic work, *Silent Spring* (1965), with its urgent message about dangerous synthetic chemicals spreading through the environment and accumulating in the food chain, was perhaps the single most important contribution to an awakening awareness that environmental threats transcended local boundaries. The Endangered Species Act and the National Environmental Policy Act of 1969, which mandated that all federal agencies, including the Department of Defense, prepare an environmental impact statement for "major federal actions," meant that military lands were no longer entirely exempt from environmental laws—at least in principle.

TWELVE

Unincorporated Possession

As the cleanup at Midway was demonstrating, enforcing environmental laws in practice is no easy matter. Even though the atoll was home to a critically endangered species, the monk seal, the navy effectively ignored environmental laws and kept few records of its activities until the late 1980s, when it ended active use of the atoll. Now Fish & Wildlife was trying to hold the navy's feet to the fire, extracting the best cleanup it could from the limited funding available, with the least damage to wildlife. I wanted to see how things played out over time, so when I returned to the Big Island at the end of January 1995, I arranged to volunteer again for the following fall. I arrived back at Midway in mid-October, a week before the first albatrosses were expected to return for the nesting season.

Without the albatrosses Midway's human settlement felt like the military ghost town that it was. But the Bonin petrels—the "nightbirds"—were back already and courting, whipping wraith-like through the dark, their raspy growls reminding me of the sound boots make walking over volcanic cinder. Nanette, who met me at the air terminal in her golf cart and drove me to my room, told me that on Eastern, the rats were now nearly gone, and Bonins were nesting on the island for the first time in decades.

When I reported for work the next morning, Nanette sent me out to count the number of white-tailed tropicbird chicks nesting in the big old ironwoods around the enlisted men's housing. Midway is the site of the only white-tail nests in the Northwestern Islands, and nearly all of the nests were, ironically, in these introduced trees. The housing, along with the school and chapel, was soon to be torn down, and the surrounding land had been bulldozed and covered with black plastic to keep the albatrosses from nesting. OHM Remediation Corporation's crews would remove asbestos from the buildings, storing the toxic debris in a newly created bulldozed pit at the end of the runway landfill, wrapped in black plastic and covered in four feet of soil. In an area only twenty feet above the sea and inhabited by birds who dig burrows, you had to wonder how long it would stay put.

The two-story barracks, doors and windows gutted, sat like a bombed village on a black sea of plastic. Faded paint showed they were once color-coded—pink, yellow, blue, green—perhaps to aid the children in identifying their homes. I walked inside one. A kitchen drawer lay on the concrete floor, lined with shelf paper in a yellow sunflower pattern I remembered from my childhood. I looked out to where there once must have been neatly mowed lawns, swing sets, walkways—an almost normal suburban scene, it might seem, in the months the albatrosses were gone.

The island was now swarming with cleanup crews, though. The main effort seemed to be going into cleaning up fuel. Or, in *CLEAN* lingo: POL (petroleum, oil, lubricant), which releases toxic VOCs (volatile organic compounds), had been leaking from over a hundred USTs (underground storage tanks) and more than five miles of rusted pipe. Most of the tanks had been dug out, pumped out, and demolished. Contaminated soil had been removed and was stored on an abandoned runway in huge black plastic-wrapped berms that suggested postmodern burial mounds. There was discussion of mixing the soil with concrete and reburying it.

Up and down the streets of the "superblock"—as the cleanup crew called the area still housing the old World War II torpedo shops and the shell-damaged power plant—and throughout several acres of the "fuel farm" had been laid an intricate grid of PVC piping, connected at intervals to rectangular white boxes. The boxes capped injection wells and pumps and extracting wells and would be hooked up to a piece of machinery that was apparently the world's largest vacuum and steam cleaner. This monster of a system, called the FIVE (fluid injection vacuum extraction), was designed by OHM to inject heated water and steam to loosen the spilled fuel from the soil and groundwater, where it apparently floated in a scummy layer, and then extract these contaminants.

Across the hall from my room bunked a middle-aged Canadian woman named Susan, employed by OHM to oversee underground storage tank removal. She was skeptical about the need for some of the cleanup work, particularly the removal of PCB-contaminated soil. "I know electrical workers that have waded in that stuff," she said, "and they haven't got cancer."

Scientific studies, however, had already suggested that PCBs were as potentially toxic as dioxins, accumulating in the same way in the fat of animals. Years earlier, research had shown that tiny amounts—as low as 5 parts per million (ppm)—were potentially fatal to small animals. In one oft-cited study done in the 1960s on ranch mink fed on a diet of Great Lakes fish contaminated with 5 ppm of PCBs, all of the female minks failed to reproduce. (Much of this information would be presented as a compelling argument for much stricter regulation of these contaminants in Theo Colborn's *Our Stolen Future*, in 1996.) And there was mounting evidence that PCBs and dioxins and other such toxins could have devastatingly disruptive effects on the endocrine systems of large mammals, affecting reproduction or development.

According to the *CLEAN* manual, the navy had performed a "basewide remedial program" in 1984 "to remove or retrofill . . . PCB-contaminated transformers and electrical components." But the additional site inspections the Fish & Wildlife Service insisted upon had turned up PCB transformers and oil-filled equipment at several locations. Some equipment had PCBs in concentrations higher than 500 ppm, one hundred times what had proved lethal to some of those small animals. Two sites held leaking equipment.

Additional funding was required to clean up these sites. Were the place not critical habitat for an endangered species—monk seals—this part of the cleanup wouldn't be happening. Even so, the fundamental issue wasn't being addressed: as Colborn's book compellingly documents, some types of pollution were uniquely likely to spread far and wide. Contaminants such as PCBs, which don't break down but persist in the environment, accumulate in living tissue in increasing amounts as they work their way up the food chain, especially in a marine environment. Colborn traces the journey of such bioaccumulation: zooplankton feeding on PCB-contaminated sediment become food for tiny crustaceans who are, in turn, fed upon by fish, and so on, each animal further up the chain receiving a more concentrated dose of toxins.

The previous winter I had met a visiting biologist, Cheryl Summer, who with the help of her assistant Heidi Auman was doing research to help determine the global spread of toxic chemicals such as DDT, PCBs, and dioxin. They worked for a private research group called SERE (Science, Ecological Research, and Education) on a grant from the World Wildlife Fund. I joined them one afternoon at the harbor. The two women, both young and long-haired, sat on upturned buckets along the seawall, in the shade of ironwood trees. Between them, resting on a carpet of brown needles shed by the trees, were shallow blue bowls piled with albatross eggs that gleamed like slightly soiled treasure.

Approaching as I did, upwind, the scene had a fairy-tale quality: the deep blue of the harbor shining through the dark slats of tree trunks, the two women bending over the luminous eggs. But Heidi turned as I came up, and her face had a comically pinched look, as though an invisible clothespin pressed on the bridge of her nose. The smell hit me when Cheryl rapped one egg against the edge of an enamel basin, dropping a mass of yellow and black into the bowl. These were definitely not fresh eggs but, as I soon learned, harvested from abandoned nests.

With one surgical-gloved hand Cheryl separated the embryo from the remains of the yolk sac. I saw sprouting black feathers and tiny wing appendages, a stubby bill and sealed embryo eyes. Cheryl said, "We look first for a crossed beak, often a sign of DDT exposure." Heidi was marking a chart clamped to a brown clipboard. Cheryl picked up a scalpel and made a slit through the scalp. "I'm checking for edema," she said. "A swelling just under the scalp is usually the first sign of toxic-caused defects and seems to be specifically related to PCB or related chemicals poisoning." In places of serious pollution in the Great Lakes area, Cheryl commented, "I sometimes found edemas the size of cherries on cormorant embryos."

The SERE project's goal was to establish a baseline for monitoring global marine contamination. "We're establishing a picture of the world in 1995," said Cheryl. "We want to make a loop globally every seven years. Midway would be one stop, but it would also be a model. This is the only place outside the Arctic where you can live and work among a species like the albatross, animals near the top of the food chain, who are relatively cooperative."

Cheryl and Heidi were monitoring plots mapped out in various sections of Sand Island, tracking eggs hatched and chick survival in over five thousand nests. They examined the chicks for visible birth defects and took blood samples from the adult birds.

I found them in front of Charlie the next morning, banding albatrosses and taking samples. Cheryl was playing bird catcher, lunging and grabbing a bird around the neck, lifting it off the ground, reaching across its chest to imprison both legs with her other hand. The Laysan's slender wings dangled to the ground, snowy white in the middle, edged with strong black flight feathers. Its webbed feet looked like large pink maple leaves. Thin bones showed through the webbing, ending in tiny claws.

Cheryl adroitly flipped the bird around, tucking its head between her legs. The view from behind was comical—just below the researcher's rump extruded the rumple-feathered bird head with surprised eyes and long bill. She held the legs in one hand and fitted a metal band on one leg. Size 7B: I had used those to band boobies at French Frigate Shoals, and had needed both hands to squeeze the metal into a circle. Cheryl used one hand, and it took a second. The next bird was already banded, so Cheryl checked the number and passed the animal to Heidi. Heidi had a portable lab set up: a picnic cooler with blood sample vials and syringes, and a restraining device that looked like a metal papoose carrier. She placed the bird on its back in the frame and slipped the beak through a hole in the wire netting. Then she pulled one wing out from the netting and inserted the needle between chest and wing, "at the point where the brachialis vein crosses the ulna." The bird looked as resigned as a patient prepped for the operating room. A second albatross—perhaps its mate?—walked up and started to preen the feathers on the top of its head. "You can see why these birds are ideal for this kind of research," said Heidi. "They can take a lot of handling with little sign of stress." She released the albatross. It gave its tailfeathers a shake and walked away.

The blood samples would be spun in a centrifuge to separate the sera, then divided into subsamples, then centrifuged and split again. The splits would go to various laboratories. Some would be analyzed for biomarkers: high or low levels of certain natural elements that signal the body's reaction to a toxin. A high level of thyroxine, for example, is one indicator of dioxin presence, when correlated with several other indicators.

"By not only attempting to measure actual contaminant levels in the blood but also assessing immune response and other indications of toxic reaction," Heidi pointed out, "you are trying to determine not only the presence of poison but the actual effect."

For some tests you need actual tissue. To collect tissue you need a freshly killed bird. This would be a problem in most bird refuges, but for this, too, Midway in an unfortunate way was ideal. There was a small but steady supply of albatrosses who were injured on the wing navigating trees, buildings, and telephone wires. These birds were brought in by the work crews.

Heidi and Cheryl worked on the back porch of the CPO's house. A sign over the door said Heidi's Bird Guttin' Lab. With one brutal but mercifully swift motion, using a pair of pruning shears, Heidi decapitated a Laysan albatross that had been brought in with a broken wing. The two women worked fast: the abdominal cavity must be opened, the liver removed, and samples taken and put in the freezer within three minutes of death. The air was sweet and acrid with the smell of blood and bile as Heidi quickly removed the liver, slicing off some small pieces that Cheryl sealed in tiny jars and labeled, rushing them to the freezer. Heidi pointed out the ovaries, with eggs and one ruptured follicle—the bird had probably been sitting on an egg. In the gizzard were a few bits of green plastic and two small black squid beaks.

What had been found so far had shocked all of the scientists involved in the project. It had been expected that oceanic birds in one of the remotest corners of the globe, feeding over vast stretches of the North Pacific far from continental sources of pollution, would have had little exposure to toxins. But tests so far indicated an elevated level of contaminants in both Laysan and black-footed albatrosses. The contaminant level in black-foots, who fed somewhat higher on the food chain than Laysans, was slightly higher—indeed, nearly as high as levels at the time for bald eagles from the highly polluted Great Lakes Region. According to Cheryl, the contaminant level in black-foots was high enough that "adverse effects on population growth" should begin to. show up. "The black-foots are showing a decrease in reproductive success," she explained. "There is some indication that might be due to eggshell thinning. We saw some eggshell thinning in the fall. We were puzzled, because this particular pattern of thinning is related to DDT, and DDT levels in the ocean actually have gone down since Rachel Carson blew the whistle in the 1960s. But DDT is still being used by a number of Asian countries.... In fact, our government still sells old stockpiles of DDT to these countries, so these birds may be feeding in ocean currents transporting these chemicals from these countries far into the open ocean."

Studies over the next few years would show increased levels of organochlorines—PCBs and DDE—in both Laysan and black-foots, with corollary eggshell thinning in both species. Albatross feeding patterns, it appears, trace ocean currents, some of the great circulatory patterns of the globe. If one considers the earth as a total dynamic system, some aspects of its health can be measured at any point on the globe, even in the most remote places. Just as the circulation of the blood nourishes and sustains the body, so do the oceans sustain life on earth. But the flow of blood, like the circulation of oceans and atmosphere, carries agents of sickness as well as health. Ultimately there is no barrier to toxins—in humans, birds, fish, or any living thing on our planet. Albatrosses, indicator species for the health of the ocean, were delivering a very serious message.

It was near the third week of October, time for the black-footed albatrosses to return (Laysan albatrosses come back around the first week of November), but none had shown up yet. Each day their absence began to seem more ominous to me than the last. I gazed out from Midway's shore at an empty expanse of sea with a vague sense of dread. What I felt must have been a fraction of the anxiety ancient Polynesians felt as they awaited the albatrosses' return. The Tahitians called the albatross the "shadow of

Ta'aroa," the sea god on whose abundance their lives depended. Along with awaiting the rising of the Pleiades, the Hawaiians may have kept vigil for the albatross to mark the return of Lono, god of agriculture and of the fertilizing rains of winter. Albatross skins were hung on the cross-barred image of the god during the island-circling ceremony that opened the Makahiki, the four-month season of Lono.

But as the settlements of the Hawaiians spread along the shores, the albatrosses that came back must have been fewer and fewer. I thought of the stone figures found on Necker, and wondered if they had been erected to keep watch for the return of the albatrosses, harbinger of winter winds and rain. Lines from Coleridge's poem started coming back to me. The mariner has slain the albatross, the ship is becalmed beneath a merciless sun, and "the water, like a witch's oils, / Burnt green, and blue, and white."

A few days later Phoenix Air owner Mark Thompson arrived in his Learjet, bringing with him the western regional director for Fish & Wildlife, Mike Spear; assistant regional director John Doebel; and Pacific Islands Ecoregion Project Leader Robert Smith, as well as Ken McDermond and a lawyer who was helping Fish & Wildlife draw up a "cooperative agreement."

Mark Thompson was slim, with a face that looked boyish until he took off his sunglasses, which he rarely did. He wore a leather flight jacket. With him was Atlanta lawyer Ned Neely. The word was that Neely was a high-powered contract lawyer, well connected in DC. (He would be in the limelight a year later, defending an airlines called Valujet charged with unsafe practices after a fatal crash in Florida.) Besides working out the agreement with the service, Thompson was here to decide which buildings Phoe-

nix Air would be using, since Fish & Wildlife was eager to hold
the navy to their mandate to tear down any buildings that either
could not be used or did not have historic significance. (Like
many of the decisions that were being made at that time, this
question of which buildings should remain was one Fish & Wildlife worried over, and one that would come back to bite them. In
order to accommodate Phoenix Air, numerous buildings were
left standing that in hindsight should have been removed while
the navy was there to do the job. Unused and unrepaired, they
would remain an eyesore and a hazard, most seriously in the
peeling lead paint they shed. A significant number of albatross
chicks nesting near the buildings and nibbling at the dirt were
poisoned by lead ingestion each year.)

I went to the All Hands Club at the rear of the Midway Mall that
night, hoping to get a chance to talk more with one of the Phoenix Air people. Bicycles crowded the entrance. One long room
with a low ceiling was strung with Christmas lights, a bar along
one wall and booths along the other, with tables in the middle.
The end of the room, mostly taken up by a wooden stage, opened
into a wing occupied by pool tables and shuffleboard. The bar
was padded with red Naugahyde; a poster on the wall behind
it showed a young Raquel Welch in a yellow bikini straddling a
giant bottle of Heineken. The opposite wall held scenic posters
of Thailand. The ambiance was timewarp 1950s, at the edge of
American empire somewhere in the East.

The Asians drank at the tables, mostly in their segregated
groups. The OHM workers crowded the bar, along with a few
navy and Piquniq Management Corporation folks. Harbormaster
Leonard anchored down one corner, with an air of belonging that
suggested it was his nightly berth. He offered to buy me a drink.

A young Thai man came up to him and stuck out his hand. "I like to thank you," he said to Leonard. "You been good to us."

"My pleasure," said Leonard.

Leonard watched him go back to a table of Thai men in the farthest corner of the bar. "I threw a Christmas party," he said. "Had a pig flown in and we had a barbecue. I invited the whole island. They all came, but they all sat at separate tables in their own little groups. Broke my heart."

A group of Thai men had formed a band, calling themselves "The Bali Bad Boys." The PMC accounting manager, a life-of-the-party woman from Texas, was singing with them. The song, "You Are the Wind beneath My Wings," seemed appropriate for Midway, but the singing was way off-key. "One step below karaoke," Leonard muttered.

Ken McDermond was talking about the navy's reaction to remarks he had made at the morning's briefing. "They got mad when I said the navy introduced rats to Midway. But it's a fact. They're hoping to get out of here smelling like a rose. The fact is they're leaving a whole legacy of environmental problems out here."

The Phoenix Air pilot was sitting at a table. I went over and joined him. He was heavyset, with a mustache and a smooth southern-accented baritone. He had flown helicopters toward the end of the Vietnam War and had recently been hired by Phoenix after not flying for twenty-seven years. Now he was flying all over the world. Mostly contract flying for the military, he said—usually war exercises with the Phoenix Air planes rigged to simulate enemy combatants.

"Why doesn't the navy use its own planes?" I asked.

"We're a lot cheaper. For one thing, we don't have to adhere to military regs on maintenance, and other things."

"What else does Phoenix Air do?"

"You name it. Just finished a job—delivering for the Thai military."

"What were you delivering?"

He grinned, "If I told you, I would have to kill you." He signaled the bartender to make us each another drink without asking whether I wanted one.

"What does Phoenix Air want with Midway?" I asked. "Is it mainly the airstrip?"

"Sure we want use of the airstrip, but it's not necessary. We can fly out of Alaska. It's kind of an entry into the Pacific."

"For tourism?"

Long pause. "Uh, right. Besides Mark just kind of fell in love with this place."

"What does he love about it?"

"Birds." He grinned again. "He loves these goddamn birds."

Later that evening I asked Mike Spear if there were any precedents within the national refuge system for this kind of cooperative agreement with a private corporation such as Phoenix Air. "It's a very different kind of place, of course," he said, "but we're trying to do something at Matagorda Refuge, in the Gulf of Mexico off Texas."

I had never heard about Matagorda, but I would read about it a year later, in a *New York Times* article by John Cushman that also mentioned Midway. The article said a historic ranch on the remote barrier island was to have been turned into "an unusual resort, which would have solar power and other earth-friendly features." The enterprise was supposed to be "a prototype for a new wave of developments in other refuges."

But some conservation groups opposed the project, apparently not agreeing that the refuge's fifty-seven thousand acres of beaches, dunes, and wetlands, home to various rare birds and plants, were the place to offer birding tours, hiking, biking, swimming, and windsurfing, and the refuge system managers decided to abandon the project. The article called the Midway plan for ecotourism "a fledgling venture offering holidays at an abandoned naval station halfway across the Pacific." It quoted Robert Shallenberger, Washington chief of the division of refuges, the man to whom it fell to reconcile conservation goals with the government's push to make refuges pay for themselves. The problem, Shallenberger said, was that there was no consistent policy that made sure conservation was considered first. A few months later, Robert Shallenberger would be refuge manager at Midway, and promoting "conservation first" would become a daily battle.

Late in the afternoon of the next day I bicycled down the lane that led past the roaring generators of the power plant, and south through fields toward a stand of ironwoods. Where the lane ran in to the trees, an enormous bird came soaring like some great heraldic figure, its wings nearly spanning the road—or so it seemed in the moment before I recognized the first returning albatross, a black-foot. It skimmed across the field, looking for its mates, and then vanished across the lagoon. I knew it would be back. Tomorrow there would be a handful, and then dozens, each day a quantum leap in their numbers, until both Sand and Eastern Island were once again blanketed with birds, and all would seem right with the world.

Four weeks later, Silva, the Sri Lankan head of the landscaping crew, said that the female short-tailed albatross was sitting on an egg, though there had been no sign of the adult male. I remembered the egg she had produced two years before that never matured. Ken felt it must have been infertile and that this one was too, "though there's a remote chance she could have mated with the male, if he's out there somewhere," he said. "Or it's not impossible she could have mated with a Laysan or a black-foot."

Without a partner, she would not be able to incubate the egg for the whole time, much less raise a chick. Silva urged Ken to switch the egg, giving the short-tailed egg to a black-foot couple to raise. Ken said, "I'm tempted to do it. From a biological viewpoint it doesn't make sense. It's unlikely black-foots could successfully raise a short-tail, and if they did, then what? It would probably be too confused a bird to ever mate with its own. But we get into these gray areas in terms of management. We want the people here to care about the wildlife, get involved."

Nanette was against it, since it meant sacrificing a black-foot egg.

"How are you going to explain your position to Silva?" asked Ken.

Finally Nanette agreed that if a black-foot could be found incubating an egg that was cracked or obviously nonviable, she would do the switch. I was sent out to pry a few hundred black-foots off their nests in search of an egg for the sacrifice. I made a lot of birds very angry, and all I found was healthy eggs. The switch didn't happen. The short-tail egg never hatched.

It was on my days off that I felt both the incongruity and the odd appeal of semi–ghost town Midway. Even in its derelict state what remained of the settlement retained a 1950s air of bland comfort. I bicycled everywhere, sometimes late at night, enjoying moving from the lighted lanes and lawns into dark forest filled with the sounds of birds, and back again. There was something seductive in the sense of an Eden so domestic and so wild at the same time. One night I walked the lane through the restless, electric energy of the albatross colony to the lit-up bowling alley, where with a handful of others I tried out all twelve lanes. On another evening I visited the ceramics shop.

Military bases and mental institutions of a certain vintage have ceramics shops in common. Some prominent psychologist during the fifties must have done a study showing that working with clay had a soporific effect. The Midway ceramics shop was located in a compound that housed a weight room full of rusty equipment and a tiny library with magazines like *Asia-Pacific Defense Forum* and *Artillery Review,* and a surprisingly large collection of Harlequin romances.

The main room of the ceramics shop was lined with shelves holding glazes and supplies, and furnished with a long table where a single burly OHM worker sat carefully sanding the lip of a dainty teapot. The other end of the long table held rows of Laysan albatross figurines, bills pointing skyward, feet glazed pink, and the bases under their feet covered with a green glaze that I supposed was meant to look like a clump of grass. A thin Sri Lankan man with a round Indian face and curly wisps of gray hair was carefully painting black teardrop-shaped eyes on the clay gooneybirds.

He introduced himself as Mr. Nama and offered to show me around. He had worked at the Midway firehouse for eleven years. In Sri Lanka he had a large family—"very many grandchildren"—whom he got to visit once a year.

Mr. Nama had taken the night job running the shop to help with homesickness and to add to the money he sent back home. He had created the mold for the clay albatrosses. The job now required that he produce a certain number of gooneybirds per week. They were sold at the store managed by PMC at $3.50

each. It seemed that everyone who visited Midway took several of them home. The money all went to PMC. Mr. Nama's salary was ninety cents an hour plus room and board.

Mr. Nama led me past the kilns, which gave off a smell of something cooking that shouldn't be, into a third room, where shelves piled to the ceiling held thousands of ceramic molds. "Many nice things to make," he said. "These are very popular," he added, pointing out molds for a beer-stein with huge handles, and for a tiny cup with a skull-and-crossbones motif. Also visible: a large pot with a matching cover and a bas-relief of sprouting mushrooms; a standing Jesus with a heart on his chest; and a mermaid whose head was topped by a cylinder meant for a lamp socket.

The thousands of molds had random numbers on them. "Once these were all arranged," said Mr. Nama, "But now they put things everywhere and I cannot find them." He held out the beer-stein. "This has another piece to it—a nice decoration you can put on the side. Adam and Eve. But they are lost."

November 26, the day before I returned to Honolulu, strong winds and rain squalls swept in from the north. Waves frothed in the lagoon, and the reef boomed in a solid line of white spray. To the east the cloud bellies were the color of the blue lagoon, and a rainbow arched through them, folded into itself, then arched again. Albatross weather. The Laysans were back in full force now, and there had been a frenetic period of dancing and mating—a sometime free-for-all with any unattached females constantly harassed. Motor and bicycle traffic had been brought nearly to a standstill amid the sex-driven hullabaloo, but now things had settled down. The couples were doing some desultory nest building, the roosting birds stretching to pick up bits of grass and twig and strewing them untidily around their bodies. Mostly they sat and preened each other with careful maneuvering of their long bills. I watched one male dancing in front of his roosting partner, the female ignoring her still-charged-up mate.

Mr. Nama was on the plane back to Honolulu with me. I had heard that he was leaving Midway for good after fourteen years, having gotten into a fistfight with another man from Sri Lanka. His thin body was clad in brown pants that were too short. He climbed aboard carrying several large plastic shopping bags and a fake-leather satchel. In the sealed belly of the C-130, he took one of the backward-facing seats next to me, and I tried to ask him how he felt about leaving, but I couldn't understand his staccato version of English above the noise of the plane. After takeoff he took a wax-paper-wrapped bundle out of the satchel, spread an ironed white handkerchief on his lap, and unwrapped a sandwich. I closed my eyes and napped. When I woke up he was sitting, staring ahead, with the sandwich untouched on his lap.

Out in the night, Midway receded from us, a place neither he nor I had ever seen from the air. Fourteen years earlier he had left his own troubled island, in the same ocean over three thousand miles away, climbed aboard one of these windowless planes in Honolulu, and stepped out among the albatrosses. He had spent many of the lonely hours making clay castings and painting clay figurines of the birds.

I closed my eyes and tried to picture a photograph of the atoll taken by NASA satellite that hung on the wall at Midway's Fish & Wildlife office. It showed the atoll floating in the seamless blue of the Pacific, an irregular oval as delicate as a jellyfish, the thin white line of reef-spume like a membrane surrounding the mitochondria of a cell, its insides veiled and luminous.

THIRTEEN

Arrivals and Departures

I had hoped to witness the last phase of the navy cleanup, and the transition of Midway Atoll from navy base to a wildlife refuge linked to a dubious partner. Although a skeleton crew of navy personnel stayed on to oversee the end of the cleanup, Phoenix's ecotourism venture was now purportedly up and running, with the company providing commercial flights out of Līhu'e, Kaua'i. I got the opportunity to check out the new regime in October 1996, when the Honolulu Fish & Wildlife office offered me work for a few weeks as a tour guide at the atoll. The Phoenix plane was a nineteen-passenger Gulfstream turbo-prop. With a window to look out of rather than being sealed inside a navy cargo jet, I watched the endless tract of open water and then for the first time saw Laysan from the air—a blue-green mirage shimmering on the horizon, just as the sun was beginning to set. Later the lit-up hieroglyph of Midway's runways appeared out of a black abyss of oceanic night.

There was no room for me that night in staff housing, Charlie BOQ, so I was given one of the officers' rooms redone as a hotel room in Bravo. The new decor was back-street Waikiki, with

large flowers on the curtains, a startling striped couch and, inexplicably, a terrible reproduction of a painting depicting a canal in
Venice. The bath was still paved with barracks-green tiles, just
as the hallway still sported squares of green and black linoleum.

The next morning I moved into my old room in Charlie, which
had gone even more to seed since my last visit: black mildew was
swallowing the paint on one wall, and stuffing emerged from the
orange plaid couch. I left my luggage packed, cycled down the
forested road behind the old cable buildings, and walked through
the ironwoods to the beach to see what had changed. The FIVE
system generators could be heard far down the beach, and the
smell of fuel was in the air, but among the dunes and ironwoods
the place felt the same, though once again eerily empty without
the albatrosses. A few migrant shorebirds had already returned
to their winter residence, and the calls of a bristle-thighed curlew
echoed through the woods. Here and there young white terns
were perched motionless on low branches, waiting for their wings
to grow strong enough to fly. A few of last season's albatross eggs
gleamed in the shadows, in abandoned nests. Through gaps in
the trees I could see the white beach and the electric glow of the
lagoon and, far beyond, the white splash of breakers on the reef.

I climbed to the top of the highest dune, where I had looked
inland the year before at rows of abandoned housing encased in
a sea of black plastic. The whole area had been emptied of buildings and trees and bulldozed into a sea of sand. Below me, the
humped concrete back of an old bunker now sat exposed, and just
beyond it the new landfill began: piles of debris, partly covered
with sand, with smoke rising at the end. The old road that crosses
the island bisected the landfill; ruins of the World War II radar
building stuck up from the sand beyond it. Just to the west, sand
was being quarried for landfill cover; beyond that gouged-out area

I could see across the runway to the edge of the island, a vista that was an unsettling reminder of how little land there was.

I rode my bike along the dirt road that skirted the south end of the island, parallel to the runway, past banks of morning glory and clumps of sweet-smelling alyssum that would soon be a hubbub of mating and nesting albatrosses. The buildings where Tugboat Terry had listened in on whale song were gone, and the area that had been dug up to remove PCB-contaminated soil was now filled in. I wondered what had been done with the soil.

At the bulky-waste landfill the entire peninsula, built entirely of waste materials, had been bulldozed completely flat and covered with a huge, smooth expanse of white sand, betraying its contents only along the sides, above the riprap, where rusted pipe and twisted metal protruded. Someone had spray-painted a happy face on an orange metal buoy and set it at the entrance.

I cycled back around the end of the runway and into the road still marked HAZMAT—NO ENTRY. At the weapons complex the guard tower was gone. The main building looked nearly the same, but the inside tram system had been taken apart and piled in pieces outside. All the doors had been taken off the weapons bays as well, and the mysterious water-filled pit inside the most heavily fortified bay was now packed with sand.

At the Fish & Wildlife office I found Jon on the phone, talking to the Honolulu office. I heard him say, "It's valid to rethink earlier concern about erosion at the landfill. I think we could go to as little as two, two and a half feet fill."

Ken Niethammer was slumped in his chair. His sun-reddened face seemed to have taken on an even deeper hue. "I've decided to step down from being manager out here," he said. "There's just too many basic issues that haven't been addressed."

I had already seen the 1996 Draft Environmental Assessment, which laid out the agreement between the service and its "co-operator." Some essential protections were in place, but some items were clearly concessions. Several beaches on Sand Island would be closed to protect monk seal habitat, and a trail system developed to keep intrusion into bird colonies at a minimum. Eastern Island would be visited only through guided field trips.

Sportfishing would be permitted outside the atoll on a catch-and-release basis, with one fish per person allowed to be brought back for consumption on the island. And the service had agreed to allow some water activities off certain beaches. The number of overnight visitors would be capped at one hundred, but the agreement left open the possibility of large groups of day visitors from cruise ships.

"Ken McDermond really fought hard," Ken Niethammer said, "pushing the basic contract. Problem is the contract is only a memorandum of understanding. It draws a line in the sand, but it turns out to be a dotted one. The people at the bottom, like us, are being overruled by the people at the top."

He sat up and looked directly at me for the first time. "It's hard to decide where to draw the line," he said, softly. "For example, Phoenix wants to take fish to sell in the restaurant. If we exempt them from the 'no commercial fishing' rule, are we still a refuge?" He sighed and rubbed his eyes. "We need some organization with a watchdog interest in what happens out here."

I found that no one at Midway-Phoenix had the job of helping tourists. "They seem to think that just getting folks here and providing rooms and fishing trips is all they need to do," said one of the few navy people at lunch.

Yeoman Dave added, "Fish & Wildlife is going to end up just

being the shadow tenant out here. Phoenix is going to get to do whatever they want. You can't bring tourists out here paying that kind of money and then tell them they can't go anywhere. If they want to walk on the beaches, they'll walk on the beaches. Phoenix is already winning the battles."

Another navy guy said, "They got plans to turn this whole island into a resort eventually, and they'll do it, too."

Yeoman Dave handed me a computer mouse pad with the navy logo and the words CONSERVE ENERGY. "We got a crateload of these sent out by Pearl Harbor," he said. "What a joke. Did you know the reason they keep all the lights and everything blazing around here is you got to run that generator at a certain level? That thing was meant to run a whole town. So for years now they've just kept every light in the place on. And you think Phoenix is going to replace that monster? No way. Suck up that fuel."

Midway's first tourists, a former Pan Am pilot and his wife, were due in the next day. They were in their late seventies. "What if they can't ride bikes?" I asked the person from Phoenix who seemed to be in charge of general logistics. "We'll give them three-wheelers," he said.

"What if they can't ride bikes at all?"

"We have some more golf carts on order."

The retired Pan Am pilot and his wife luckily turned out to be a spry, adventurous pair. They had raised five kids and sailed a boat around the Pacific. The pilot had flown everything from the early clipper ships to 747s. He thought he remembered having been a copilot on a clipper flight that stopped at Midway. That would have been in the late 1930s, when Pan Am had put up a prefabricated hotel building, exactly identical to ones at Guam and Wake, to house guests traveling on the "flying boats." "I remember lunch at a hotel and a lot of sand," said the former pilot. "But now I'm wondering if it could have been Wake instead of Midway."

The first thing my guests did was turn in their three-wheelers for regular bikes. "We may be old, but we're not doddering," the pilot remarked.

I took them out to Frigate Point to scout for monk seals. There were three on the beach, a rare occurrence. The seals slumbered soundly. The pilot and his wife were clearly bored. "Seals are a real problem on the West Coast," the wife said.

The first tourist from Japan, in all likelihood the first Japanese person to visit Midway since World War II, arrived on the next flight, a middle-aged man named Mr. Yoshitani. I asked him if his interest in Midway had to do with the war. He shook his head. "I like to do island hopping," he said. "I read in the paper you can go to Midway. I want to be one of the first to come here. I like Yap the best. Do you know Yap? The women do not wear shirts on top. I was very surprised. Midway is very peaceful. If I knew that, I would bring my wife."

Two veterans arrived. One, Harry Stuart, had recently been released from the hospital after surgery for pancreatic cancer. "He's not in great shape," said his grandson, who had come with him, "but he really wanted to come out here." Stuart had been stationed on Sand Island during the Battle of Midway, working in the administration building, upstairs from what was now the Fish & Wildlife office. The building had taken some bullets from a Japanese Zero, Stuart remembered. "By all rights we shouldn't have won that battle," he said, "We all should have been dead men."

The other, Father Jack, was a retired navy man who had become a priest. He was stationed at Eastern after the Battle of Midway. "It was all bare," he said. "Nothing but blinding white sand."

Winds were kicking up water in the lagoon, and only after a day of threatening to swim to it could the two veterans persuade the Phoenix harbormaster to let a boat go over to Eastern Island. On Eastern, Harry Stuart stood for a long while looking at the memorial. Jack wanted to walk to the end of the runway to see if he could find his old gun station. "Nothing looks the same," he said. "All these plants and birds. None of that was here." I took photographs: Harry at the memorial and Jack standing on a grassy hummock ("This could have been it!" Jack had said). In the photos they both have the same puzzled look.

The NMFS marine mammal biologists were urging Fish & Wildlife to close more of Midway's beaches to allow the seals more pupping areas, and to restrict water activities within a five-hundred-foot buffer zone around both islands. Phoenix was already chafing under refuge restrictions. They wanted to open beaches and add activities such as kayaking and wind surfing. They had mentioned feeding sharks from cages. They wanted to allow, as the navy did, harvesting of lobsters—an important food item for monk seals—for local consumption.

Someone had passed on a letter written from one of the sportfishing captains to Phoenix owner and CEO Mark Thompson: "The seal population is happily on the increase and seems completely at ease with people they see (except those engaged in molesting them in the name of science—like Fish & Wildlife)." And some Phoenix personnel had taken to calling the Fish & Wildlife staff and the NMFS people "seal huggers."

A couple of members of the NMFS monk seal recovery task force had flown in to iron things out with Phoenix. They offered to do an evening "educational presentation on monk seals."

Nearly all of Midway's 150-strong human population showed

up at the old theater to listen to them, filling the dusty green plush seats. The walls were decorated with scenes (PT-109; building the runway at Midway) painted by the Seabee construction crew that had built the sheet piling and filled in the island's east end to extend the runway after the war, as Midway was transformed to a submarine base and then to a spy station. Fish & Wildlife folk filled the first row; the Phoenix staff sat in middle seats directly under the ship's anchor that ornamented the ceiling. "Anybody remember to loosen the bolts on that anchor?" I heard someone in the first row mutter.

A senior biologist from the NMFS Honolulu office stood on the stage next to a screen and explained the status of the seal population: "Rising at Laysan and Lisianski. Rising at Kure since the coast guard left. Falling at French Frigate Shoals for reasons we still don't understand. Stable, we hope, at Midway."

He went on to discuss a new study using the Critter Cam, a small video camera that can be attached to an animal's back. Someone dimmed the lights, and a blurry blue appeared on the screen, with a dark, moving object. Once the camera snapped into focus, we were looking at the shoulders and the back of a seal's head. "He's swimming toward the bottom," the biologist said as the animal humped through the water, shoulders swaying like a linebacker. Sand with patches of coral came into view. The seal nosed around the coral, overturning small pieces. A small shark appeared in the frame, then veered out of view. Then the seal had a dark, writhing mass in its mouth. The light increased as the seal swam toward the surface, going white as it broke into air. The camera adjusted to the bright light, and tentacles whipped across the lens as the seal shook the octopus like a dog.

This amazing *cinema verité* didn't have the desired effect of sensitizing the Phoenix phalanx to the monk seals' plight. The head of the snorkeling and diving concession said, "We walk right past these seals and they don't seem bothered at all." The head of sportfishing asked, "Sticking those camera things on their backs—if you really want to talk about harassing seals, isn't that harassment?"

Mike Gautreaux, the Midway-Phoenix manager, voiced Phoenix's main complaint: "If you restrict too many activities, and close off areas, there's no way we can keep tourists happy and keep good morale among the workers." But this time there was also a note of threat: "If Midway-Phoenix can't make a go out here, then what happens? This place will revert to a sandspit, and you biologists will be living out here in tents."

After the evening program I talked to the NMFS biologist. He looked discouraged. "It's really hard to get the message across about how dire the situation is with these seals," he said. "Midway is important in terms of having one more good egg in our basket if we can build up the population here."

"But what about the seals that were introduced years ago?" I asked. "If you don't know why they died, why expect these seals would be okay?"

"We still don't know, but there could have been several reasons they couldn't make a healthy transition to Midway. We collected them from French Frigate Shoals, and they were already underweight. And also we built their pen on the side near the active sewage outfall . . ."

"Isn't Midway-Phoenix going to be required to put in a new sewage system?"

"Yeah, well, we hope so."

Seven months later, in April 1997, I returned as a journalist to cover the official ceremony transferring jurisdiction over Midway Atoll from the navy to the Department of the Interior. We flew into Midway just after dusk, the lagoon still gleaming with a blue effulgence in the dim light. The headlights of the van that transported us to the barracks illuminated a dark lawn shimmering with dancing albatrosses.

Ceremony day dawned bright and windy. A dais with a podium was set up at the edge of the air terminal parking lot, faced by an assortment of seats. A front row made up of the island's entire collection of office chairs held people in somber suits and the glittering white dress uniforms of navy officers—and one dark-haired man in a black motorcycle jacket. Behind them, on folding metal chairs, sat a row of khaki-clad Fish & Wildlife officials and a few navy yeomen. On benches in the back perched the Thais, Sri Lankans, and Filipinos who kept the place running, and a few members of the cleanup crew. The Sri Lankans were dressed carefully in cricket whites, as though they still adhered to some colonial dress code.

The most numerous clan of Midway's native constituency were spread out as far as the eye could see in the fields behind the dais, lending a certain surrealism to the human drama and its props. Laysan albatrosses clustered so thickly that they blended into solid masses in the far fields like drifts of snow, tending downy chicks the size of bowling pins. They were a visible reminder that sixty years of military history at Midway had played itself out in the midst of one of the world's largest seabird colonies.

The regional officials of Fish & Wildlife, who should have been celebrating the end of an uneasy alliance with the navy that had allowed them only a marginal presence on the atoll for the last decade, were showing not much more enthusiasm than pallbearers at a funeral. Their ascendancy to full custodians of Midway had come at no small price.

Assistant Secretary of the Interior Bonnie Cohen spoke first. She noted that Fish & Wildlife's cooperation with the navy at Midway had begun with "efforts to resolve the hazards of bird/plane collisions." Now the service would continue its conservation work at Midway in a "working relationship with Midway-Phoenix Corporation." Her department, she said, welcomed "a new era of partnerships."

Secretary of the Navy John Dalton's speech was a reminder that it was human history that mattered at Midway. In the Second World War, he claimed, "Midway set the stage for America's victory in the Pacific," and its importance didn't end there: "This part of the world is truly important to our national security. It is clear the Pacific Rim will drive our strategy into the twenty-first century."

"That's a reminder that they can take Midway back if they need it," whispered Nanette, seated on my right.

Then Robert Shallenberger, former DC chief of the division of refuges and now the Midway refuge manager, presented an environmental award conjured up hastily in the weeks before the ceremony to Phoenix Air owner Mark Thompson, the man in the black jacket.

Shallenberger was prepared to face the irony in giving the award to a man whose first act as corporate partner with the US Fish & Wildlife Service was to build a fancy restaurant overlooking the atoll's best beach and bring in a French chef to service what he obviously thought would be corporate jets bearing sportfishing CEOs. Shallenberger had cut his teeth as a field biologist in the Northwestern Islands and learned the harsh realities of federal conservation funding in the service's DC office. He knew well how vulnerable these islands were and how hard it was going to be to get adequate funds to protect them. Handing out an ecological award to a company with no experience in environmental work, with possibly no interest in conservation, was all in a day's work to a man who had managed refuge lands in the midst of oilfields and hazardous waste dumps. His bottom line: "Is it better to have a refuge in an area that is used for mining—or, say, like this one, has five miles of sewage lines—or have no refuge at all?"

Adding Midway to the nation's cash-strapped refuge system meant little in terms of direct support to tackle the myriad problems left behind after over one hundred years of human use and abuse. The National Parks system, with its clear mandate to consider public recreational needs before those of wildlife, was in a somewhat better position, bolstered by its myriad partnerships with private industry. But to maintain land purely for the sake of wildlife had never been a strong goal in the United States.

It was hard enough to monitor one of the remotest places on earth on a shoestring, and even harder to make the public care about a region they had little likelihood of ever visiting. Midway, Shallenberger thought, could help change all that. Midway didn't offer the near-pristine landscape of some of the other islands. Its only high-profile endemic species was the Hawaiian monk seal, and now, after sixty years of military activity, that population was nearly extinct. But the island had buildings, a harbor, and, most important, an airport. Midway could provide a window onto the whole set of places in this island-and-reef wilderness, and maybe support for conservation would follow. It might just be worth it to team up with a company whose work seemed just one step above foreign legionnaire. So the thinking went.

The speeches proceeded against the background clamor of the bird colony and the distant drone of the FIVE system extractor, still struggling to steam-siphon petroleum sludge from Midway's groundwater. Proffering to the Assistant Secretary of the Interior a large wooden "key" to Midway, painted to resemble an albatross, the Secretary of the Navy said, "This is a great day as we gather together to trade guns for gooneys."

Behind him an albatross raised its head in a mating-dance call that sounded like a Bronx cheer.

After the ceremony I asked the Secretary of the Navy: "Certain environmental problems remain at Midway. Where does the navy draw the line as far as its obligation to restore lands it uses to pre-occupation condition?"

His assistant ran interference: "The Department of the Interior," he said, "should be able to handle any remaining problems."

Added the secretary, "These birds look to me like they're doing pretty well." The assistant hustled him away.

I came across Mark Thompson later at the newly opened beach bar, miffed because Fish & Wildlife was orchestrating all the activities for the federal bigwigs. "I'd like to take these people around, show them this place through my eyes. I'd show them what a great small town it is—it's like Middle America in the fifties."

The day had turned warm, but Thompson was still wearing his flight jacket, along with black pants and aviator sunglasses. His environmental award plaque was already affixed to the wall behind him. He lit a cigarette. "I didn't smoke until I got into this project. We're losing $250,000 a month."

"So what made you want to do this?" I asked. "I don't imagine you did it for the birds."

"When I first got into this," Thompson said, "I knew nothing about birds except that they fly. I thought Fish & Wildlife meant the state Fish & Game people. I knew this island, though. I've been flying out here on a regular basis for fifteen or so years. In those days it was usually some form of contract work involving Pacific Basin countries. I got into this when I saw the government was just going to walk away from this place, maybe shut it down. I wanted the airstrip. That's still where I think the money is. The world is going to twin-engine planes, and the law says you have to declare an alternate airport in case of emergency. If they declare Midway, they pay each time."

Were his interests compatible with those of the Fish & Wildlife Service? I asked.

"Left to their own devices they would have obliterated this island," Thompson said. "Did you know they were planning to cut down all the trees because they're not 'native'? [The service was in fact removing all the ironwoods from Eastern Island and doing some FAA-required removal on Sand Island near the airport runways.] What's native about this place?—half of it is reclaimed island."

The year before, Fish & Wildlife had faced a serious threat to the refuge system in the form of a bill passed by the US House of Representatives called, ironically, the National Wildlife Improvement Act. This proposed legislation sought to redefine the basic purpose of wildlife refuges, giving human activities such as recreation, hunting, and fishing the same importance as protection of wildlife. Though the bill was defeated in the Senate, the Clinton administration's response was an executive order mandating that all refuges evaluate current use to determine which are compatible with refuge purposes, and at the same time find ways to generate revenue for the system through cooperative agreements with the private sector. This was the context in which Shallenberger would be operating.

"There is indeed a lot of flexibility in our agreement with Midway-Phoenix," Shallenberger told me after the ceremony. "We wanted it that way. As long as our mandate is clear—that conservation is our mission, we can deal with issues as they come up. My one concern is the lack of adequate funding for this refuge—that it might lead to pressure to do things that are inappropriate . . . to allow activities just to improve economics."

I spent a long evening reading the latest (1995) version of the cleanup plan. Signed by both navy and EPA representatives, it claimed the plan would provide "safe, effective, timely and cost-efficient environmental restoration" to Midway. The next morning I stopped by the Fish & Wildlife office and asked Jon how the cleanup was going.

"We cleaned up all the PCB-contaminated soil. And also the soil with DDT," he said. The contaminated soil was mixed with concrete and water, rolled flat into slabs, and placed in "an isolated cell" in the new landfill, he explained.

According to the latest cleanup plan, some of the PCB-contaminated soil samples contained "moderate levels of Aroclor 1254." This product, manufactured by Monsanto, was heavily laced with some of the more deadly PCBs. Such PCBs were, the document pointed out, "likely to persist in the environment for several centuries."

"At the old landfill," Jon went on, "we did a lot of sampling. We used a standard way to investigate a landfill that doesn't have records of what was dumped there: you dig trenches with a backhoe, down several feet, and you look at what's in there." Although nothing "alarming" was found in the landfill, significant concentrations of PCBs were found in marine sediment adjacent to the landfill. Debris, including electrical components, was removed from the area. The navy, Jon said, would resample sediment in that area for the next couple of years. "The old landfill's now covered with a couple of feet of sand," Jon added. "We'll plant native vegetation. It could become an important habitat area."

A less optimistic picture of the cleanup came from one of the engineers for OHM, who was getting ready to leave Midway at the time. "We pumped out eighty thousand gallons of fuel," he said. "We can't get the heaviest stuff out. We tried pumping hot air into the injection wells to loosen the hydrocarbons. It didn't work. But they'll just sit there until they deteriorate in fifty to a hundred years. We did get 90 percent of the fuel plumes. In some places the stuff was six feet deep." He seemed reluctant to talk about this work. But surely an engineer would know that atolls are not solid, inert structures, like concrete. Like the coral from which they are made, they are a porous bridge between solid and fluid. What still contaminated that groundwater would someday be loosed upon the world.

The day before leaving the atoll I took a "farewell to Midway past" walk. It was a day of small squalls sweeping in from the ocean, low fleets of cloud reflecting the blue water as they moved over the lagoon. I walked out past the wood frame of the new restaurant building. Tropicbirds in their breeding plumage were staking nesting territory under the naupaka, flying courtship loops in the air, quarreling on the ground at the edges of bushes, their feathers flushed with a lovely rose tint that seemed the visible sum of their sexual heat.

Among the ironwoods, albatross chicks sat on their nests,

bottom-heavy with squid au jus. The down around their bills and eyes was thinning out to show adult white feathers sprouting underneath. With many of the buildings torn down, the albatross colonies would have room to expand, and the number of burrowing birds, mainly the night-flying Bonin petrels, would be likely to soar now that rats no longer preyed on their eggs. (This would present a new set of problems to the human population, though, as burrows would appear everywhere and tourists cycling at night with their headlamps on risked collision with disoriented birds.)

The new landfill in the middle of the island had grown into a huge hill marked by lines of bird tracks. At the asbestos dump near the end of the old runway the warning signs had been taken down, since the asbestos had been moved to a new area near the harbor and reburied. Native plants grown in Fish & Wildlife's new nursery had been planted out over the area inside protective cages of orange netting. Several black-footed albatrosses were dancing the fandango among the cages, with great spread-wing bows and sky-pointing shrieks.

At HazMat, everything was gone—the weapons bays, the weapons assembly building, even the huge concrete revetment— nothing left but a flat expanse of sand. Sand had been covering secrets on islands like these for a long time. What would find its way to the surface?

I thought about the barrels buried under the sand at Laysan, only discovered when the rust had eaten them and toxic materials started leaching to the surface and someone started noticing all the dead insects and crabs. Knowing where such poisons are is important, but another question kept coming to mind: what was the navy doing out here when those barrels were buried in the first place? Would enough small pieces of the puzzle ever be recovered that we could appreciate the full legacy of the Cold War among the remote islands of the Pacific Ocean? Not long after I stood on that patch of bare white sand, contemplating the vanished weapons assembly complex, a Freedom of Information Act request from an investigative journalist (writing for the *Bulletin of Atomic Scientists*, November 1999) would net an important previously classified Pentagon document describing the deployment of the US nuclear arsenal between 1945 and 1977. Since Guam has always been important to the strategic air command, the news that that US territory hosted twenty types of nuclear weapons at the time wasn't surprising. Nearly as many had been stored on Oʻahu. Midway was on the list, too, with one type, listed as a nuclear "depth bomb" (most likely an air- or ship-fired antisubmarine torpedo), deployed to the atoll in 1961 and "withdrawn" in 1967.

That evening, my last, I sat out among the Laysan albatrosses nesting in front of Bravo barracks. The birds were settling in for the night, though a few were still taking off and landing. I watched one come in for a landing, maneuvering through buildings and trees and electric wires. A chick near me had the hiccups, its parents gazing on with a look of mild concern. One bird approached and stood in front of me as I lay propped on my elbows, gazing steadily in my face for a moment. The rest ignored me, as though I were a shadow.

Along the beach road the streetlights illuminated two huge satellite dishes, and on two sides the barracks windows cast blank squares of light. Only among the dense trees surrounding the old cable buildings did the night seep in unimpeded. Without this feathered crowd out here on the mown lawn, this place would have the unutterable loneliness of all places where humans settle for reasons other than making a home.

FOURTEEN

Disposable Islands

I had a chance on that October 1996 trip to do something I had wanted to do for a long time: visit that outer ring of emergent reef that magically made the whole burgeoning life of Midway atoll possible. Jon, Nanette, and I motored in a Boston Whaler to the northern end of the lagoon, passing through the deep blue water of the channel dredged for ships—marked by an orange buoy where brown boobies perched, looking, with their heavy-beaked profiles, like mini-pterodactyls—across shallows and coral banks. Miles behind us, Sand and Eastern Islands floated like green lily pads on the bright water.

We anchored and slipped into the water over a type of coralline algae I had never seen before—a delicate blue filigree. Two giant ulua, each the size of a bulldog and as heavily jowled, fell in with us as we swam to the emergent reef that encircles the atoll. I hoisted myself up on the reef wall, which was brown, weathered smooth, and about the width of a levee road. From this perch I could see that the atoll extends outward in a coral shoal a few hundred yards beyond the reef, breaking the force of the huge ocean combers and then dropping off abruptly, the water almost

In 1965 two holes were drilled at Midway Atoll, one reaching volcanic rock at 180 meters and the other at 420 meters. The drill dug down through layers of fossil land shells and sediment that attested to a once-verdant high island. In the lower part of the deeper hole were discovered fossils of tiny one-celled sea animals called foraminifers, believed extinct since early in the Miocene, some 25 million years ago, evidence that marshes had turned to salt swamp as the sea began to invade the drowning island.

Darwin's hypothesis—that "tiny architects" in the form of living coral could have built structures on such an ancient and colossal scale—still presents a challenge to human powers of comprehension. Standing on that reef in 1996, I tried to reconcile Darwin's sense of wonder with the recent news: in the South Pacific the French had exploded their sixth nuclear bomb and announced that they would end their tests. The detonation, in a deep-drilled shaft beneath the lagoon, was not at Moruroa but at nearby Fangataufa Atoll because, according to some, earlier underground tests had created fissures on the coral walls of Moruroa, causing radioactive particles, including plutonium, to leak into the sea.

To the continental mind the ocean is a great wet desert, and its small islands are random outcrops insignificant in themselves, though sometimes of great strategic use. In 1996 the French were still viewing the Pacific Ocean as early Western explorers did: a huge blank spot on the map, an enormous nothingness.

Darwin's legacy had been a view of island worlds as rich microcosms of life, but his vision held little sway in a land-centric culture. The testing of America's most dangerous weapons has happened in the dry desert—the Mojave, the Great Salt Lake Desert—and in the "wet desert" of the Pacific Ocean, and on its islands. US military policy throughout the Pacific had long been shaped by an ethos of islands as throwaway places. Hawai'i residents didn't have to search the farthest-flung islands in the Pacific to encounter that legacy of damage: we occasionally read news about our neighbor Johnston Atoll; we viewed the bombed-out landscape of Kaho'olawe from the shores of Maui.

The extent of environmental abuse I encountered at French Frigate Shoals and at Midway had shocked me, but since first reading in the files at Tern Island about bioweapon field tests in the Pacific conducted during the 1960s, I had been more concerned about the kind of damage that is deeper but less evident. As I had initially discovered reading through the small library at Tern Island, the Bible of every field scientist who works in the Northwestern Islands is the series of *Atoll Research Bulletins* that the Smithsonian Institution put out in the early 1970s. The bulletins made available the huge amount of scientific information collected between 1963 and 1969 in one of the world's largest field studies, the Pacific Ocean Biological Survey Program (POBSP). The Smithsonian-led survey encompassed nearly 4 million square miles of central Pacific Ocean and widely scattered, mostly uninhabited islands and atolls, including the Line and Phoenix Islands near the equator, Johnston Atoll, and the Northwestern Hawaiian Islands. The US military had funded this extraordinary survey. And what they most wanted to know about was the migratory patterns of birds.

The Biological Survey was directed by Phillip Humphrey, curator of birds at the Smithsonian. In October 2000 I tracked down a phone number and called Humphrey, who was then in his eighties and director emeritus of the Kansas Museum of Natural History. He told me that in the summer of 1962 military officials from all four branches—army, navy, air force, and marines—came to the Smithsonian to ask for advice in finding

a research institute that could do "an ecological study of the
central Pacific." Initially the military wanted the study restricted
to an area near Johnston Atoll, but Humphrey said that he told
them, "If we're going to do it, we'll do it my way," and insisted on
a study of the ecology of a much broader area. The army agreed,
offering ships, support personnel, and money, a total of nearly $3
million (a large sum in those days) by the time the study came
to an abrupt halt.

Later that year I asked Robert Pyle, a respected ornithologist
who joined the project as field director in 1966, about the scope
of the Smithsonian project. "We did a lot of open ocean work,"
he said. "The project banded nearly 2 million birds. The army
wanted mainly to know about the dispersal of birds . . . and
which birds nested on what islands."

Pyle made cruises to the Phoenix Islands and Johnston Atoll,
to Kure and to Midway. Midway, he recalls, was packed at the
time with a few thousand military personnel and their families.
He remembers banding birds on all the islands and collecting
birds, killed with shotguns, from huge grids of open ocean.

"Didn't you speculate about what the military wanted this
information for?" I asked Pyle.

"We didn't ask. If the military said, 'We want you to go there,'
we went. Sure, we speculated, but it would just be speculation,
and I'm not gonna talk about it."

It wasn't a secret where the information the scientists gathered was going, or where the blood samples and shipments of
live birds were carried off to. In the first few years, the project
was administered, on the military side, from the army's biological warfare research center at Fort Detrick. The base, located
near the quiet town of Frederick, Maryland, employed over three
thousand military and civilians at that time. It did research on

and development of chemical and biological agents, the latter including bubonic plague, pneumatic plague, anthrax, yellow fever, encephalitis, Q fever, and tularemia.

Deliveries of ticks, blood samples, and live birds were also made to the Deseret Test Center in Utah. This center, off-limits to the public, was located southwest of Salt Lake City in a huge region of desert controlled by the army and air force. It was adjacent to the Dugway Proving Grounds, where, starting in the 1950s, open-air tests of live biological weapon agents were conducted. Several of these disease agents, including tularemia, Q fever, and Venezuelan equine encephalitis (VEE), could potentially be carried long distances, if the host animal was a migrating bird.

What has come to light since is that the military was interested in doing—and did indeed do at Johnston Atoll and other sites—large-scale field tests of biological weapons. The military could not safely test these infectious diseases even within the vast range of their testing grounds in the Utah desert. So they turned to the largest "wet desert" on the planet—the central Pacific Ocean. The fact that migrating birds lived there, crowded onto its tiny island arks or traveling through to elsewhere, presented merely a strategic problem.

Or so the military claimed, when the story of Smithsonian involvement in a biological warfare project broke in the press in 1969. But the military already had ample knowledge, it appears, that wildlife, particularly birds that migrate long distances, could spread some of the diseases they were testing. One of the diseases that may have been tested, VEE, is a close cousin of West Nile virus, similarly transmitted from animal hosts to humans by mosquitoes. (Equines are very susceptible to the disease, and it is often fatal; in humans it produces incapacitating flulike symptoms and sometimes death via secondary infections, such as pneumonia.)

In light of more recent speculations about the origins of the West Nile virus that appeared in New York in 1999, which included the possibility it had been purposely introduced, the question raised in 1969 by a few members of the scientific community may have been dismissed too readily: was the military actually testing birds as hosts and delivery systems for biological agents?

For all sixteen species of seabird that return to nest and breed on Midway's three tiny islands, and for its migrant shore-birds—turnstones, sandpipers, tattlers, plovers, bristle-thighed curlews—the atoll is the hub of a vast wheel, the dry epicenter of a watery universe. So it was too for Johnston Atoll before its military occupation: great colonies of seabirds used to return to nest there. But even during the period in the 1960s when John-ston served as a base for testing nuclear weapons, some seabirds still returned each year to cling tenaciously to the patches of land left undisturbed or to adapt, like the tropicbird, to nesting under the few hedges and exotic shrubs. Migratory shorebirds still flew in to winter there, from their own nesting grounds as far away as the Pribilof Islands in the Bering Sea. Like all the isolated islands and atolls in the Central Pacific, Johnston was knit, by birds, into a vast ecosystem.

Yet in 1964, bioweapons testing with live agents began over open waters off Johnston Atoll, and it continued in 1968 at Eniwetok Atoll in the South Pacific. Although many of the documents describing these tests were reputedly destroyed when President Richard Nixon shut down the offensive biological weapons pro-gram in 1970 (while leaving intact the defensive research pro-gram), a few remaining documents became declassified in the early 1990s. They sketch a harrowing picture of what may have been the world's largest bioweapons field tests.

According to the documents, the tests were to determine whether biowarfare agents could be delivered successfully over a large area by being sprayed from low-flying jets. Among the candidate agents were VEE, Q fever, and tularemia, all three diseases transmissible from animals to humans via tick and mosquito bites. Q fever and tularemia are bacterial diseases that in humans can be severe and sometimes fatal. Animals can be reservoir hosts for these diseases without showing symptoms. What makes them attractive candidates for biowarfare is that all three infectious agents can be disseminated in the air and remain "hot" for some time.

In the largest of the tests at Johnston Atoll the navy anchored barges in a line at intervals of several miles. A jet flew low over the barges, each of which contained caged rhesus monkeys, and released a "weaponized powder." According to Ed Regis, author of *The Biology of Doom*, "The plane sprayed a thirty-two-mile-long line of agent that traveled for more than sixty miles downwind before it lost its infectiousness." Half the monkeys died from the exposure.

Inevitably, seabirds would have been exposed through these tests, and it is likely that some migratory birds were exposed as well. The Smithsonian scientists who provided the military with live bird specimens, ticks, and blood samples during the years of biowarfare testing at Johnston Atoll and at Eniwetok were monitoring the possible spread of disease. But were they also, even if unwittingly, helping the military experiment with animals and insects as delivery systems for biological weapons?

In 1969, the plug was abruptly pulled on the Smithsonian project, shortly after NBC newsman Tom Pettit did a *First Tuesday* segment on chemical and biological warfare (CBW) in the

United States and claimed to have learned from a member of the Senate committee investigating Defense Department activities that "there has even been an ultrasecret test project in the Pacific Ocean, conducted under a cover of a bird-banding study." Phillip Humphrey remembers that after Pettit's program aired, "all hell broke loose" inside and outside the Smithsonian. "People were parading outside with placards with my name on them," Humphrey said. "It was traumatic." The Smithsonian scrambled to protect its good name: Humphrey was removed as director and the program shut down, except for the completion of final reports.

In an article published in *Science* seventeen days after the *First Tuesday* program and clearly intended to vindicate the Smithsonian, Humphrey stated that he learned "fairly early" in the survey "why the military is interested [in the Smithsonian project] in a general sense." He was "sure," he said, that the army wanted to test biological weapons in the Pacific and was looking at the findings of the survey to be certain that any potential test site was safe. At that time Humphrey argued that the Smithsonian study was in fact essential to pointing out the risks of testing live biological agents over open ocean. When I talked to him in October 2000, he still avowed that the army wanted information about the movements of birds.

"They wanted to know the potential danger of these diseases spreading," he told me. "We showed them that there were birds that migrated through the putative test area to the high Arctic. Ruddy turnstones, for example, move between islands in the Bering Sea and the Hawaiian chain. The more we learned, the less feasible this kind of testing became."

It was clear, Humphrey added, that the military planned to go ahead with tests "with or without the necessary science being done." What Humphrey and other Smithsonian officials have never admitted knowing is that shortly after the Smithsonian project got under way, the tests had already begun. So essentially the Smithsonian was tracking effects: that is, the possible spread of disease.

Smithsonian scientists made their first visits to islands of the central Pacific, including Johnston Atoll, in June 1963. The information they gathered would have shown that these islands and the open ocean surrounding them were home to seabirds and migrating landbirds that could potentially carry disease thousands of miles. What the Fort Detrick and Deseret Test Center scientists learned we may never know. A Freedom of Information Act search turned up only two reports about what is almost certainly research linked to the Smithsonian project. Both reports examine the susceptibility of central Pacific seabird species to diseases the military tested. In June 2001 I obtained one report, "Susceptibility of Sooty Terns to Venezuelan Equine Encephalitis Virus," published by Fort Detrick scientists in 1963. (My requests for the second article, "The Susceptibility of Birds to Tularemia: The Wedge-tailed Shearwater and the Black-footed Albatross," published by Dugway Proving Grounds in 1964, were ignored.)

Sooty terns nest on islands throughout the central Pacific and feed over a huge reach of the central and northern ocean. That the study on sooty terns was published in October 1963 suggests that the birds must have been captured on the earliest Smithsonian expeditions, which began with visits to French Frigate Shoals in June, at a time when sooty terns are still to be found in their nesting colonies.

The research at Fort Detrick, reported under a project labeled "BW Agent Process Research," used 257 sooty terns "captured in the wild state." Some of the birds were sprayed with "aerosols of VEE virus." Others were put in cages with VEE-infected mosquitoes of two different species. The report concluded that "sooty terns were found to be highly susceptible to infection with VEE virus by the respiratory route"; in biowarfare terms, this meant that aerosol versions of the virus worked extremely well. The study also confirmed what earlier research had shown: "wild birds could be excellent sources for mosquito infection"— in other words, not just sooty terns but presumably other wild birds could act as host animals for the virus, and mosquitoes that bit them would carry the infection to other animals, including humans.

When a *New York Times* reporter suggested to Humphrey in 1969 that military scientists might be studying birds as "delivery systems" for bioweapons, he called the idea ridiculous. "Birds in a statistical sense may make predictable migrations," he said, "but you don't really know what they are going to do." When I posed the question again in the year 2000, there was a decidedly different tenor to his response: Humphrey was silent for a moment. Then he said, "It was a crazy time, with a lot of crazy ideas. The military was even trying to train bats to use in incendiary warfare."

When *Washington Post* reporter Ted Gup interviewed former Smithsonian officials in 1985, he talked to Sidney Galler, the institution's assistant secretary for science and one of the chief apologists for the Smithsonian back in 1969. Galler revealed that he had worked for the navy from 1948 to 1965, overseeing projects relating to "environmental warfare." "I wasn't interested in the germs," Galler told Gup. "I was interested in the animals and their behavior that could be utilized by an enemy to carry the germs." Some Pacific oceanic birds, he said, "can migrate tremendous distances and reach target areas with about 97 percent accuracy."

In fact, the US military had a long-standing interest in the use of animals as vectors for disease. Spurred by reports of German and Japanese research during World War II, the United States, Canada, and Great Britain began to sponsor research projects on insect vectors in 1942. Japan was experimenting extensively with using fleas and mosquitoes as vectors for disease during the war; after the war it became known that the Japanese had released bubonic plague–infected fleas in Manchuria, initiating outbreaks in which several thousand people died. Camp Detrick (later renamed Fort Detrick) was completed in 1943, and there the United States began to study infectious diseases including tularemia, Q fever, and "neurotropic encephalitis" (probably VEE). But the weakness of the Allies' program was knowledge about how these diseases affected humans—remedied in part, after the war, by the massive amount of information received through the Japanese experiments on prisoners, and directly from Japanese scientists. In 1946, the US military established Unit 406 Medical General Laboratory in Japan. According to historians Stephen Endicott and Edward Hagerman, the body of work at the lab "related to insect and especially mosquito vectors."

Information and personnel moved back and forth between Fort Detrick and Unit 406 in Japan. At Fort Detrick, hundreds of thousands of dollars were spent between 1951 and 1953 on projects with titles like "The Dissemination of BW Agents by Insects" and "On Mosquito Vectors and Encephalomyelitis Viruses as Agents for Biological Warfare." In addition, in 1951 the US Naval Medical Research Unit No. 3 (NAMRU-3) set up

office in Egypt and began a program to study viral and rickett-
sial infections, including West Nile virus. The work organized
by Fort Detrick on insect vectors intensified in the early 1950s
with the initiation of a decade-long series of trials conducted at
various locations, under such fanciful names as Big Itch, Big
Buzz, Drop Kick, Grid Iron, Mayday, and Bellwether. Big Itch,
for example, confirmed that live fleas could be successfully
dropped in "bomblets"; the only hitch, noted in the Dugway
Proving Grounds report, was that somehow fleas managed to
escape from the munitions and "numerous fleas bit the pilot, the
bombardier, and the observer."

At Fort Detrick one of the arthropods studied was the mosquito *Aedes aegypti*, carrier of the yellow fever virus. The study
suggested that since the disease had never occurred in Asia, "the
population of the USSR would be quite susceptible" to it. According to biologist and professor of international security Malcolm
Dando in his book *Biological Warfare in the Twenty-First Century*,
the study concluded that "the difficulties that an enemy would
face in detecting infected mosquitoes and protecting their population would make the *Aedes aegypti*–yellow fever combination
an extremely effective BW agent."

The agent was given a simulated test, titled Mayday, through
the release of uninfected mosquitoes near a residential area in
Savannah, Georgia, in 1956. Within a day many people within
an area of two square miles had been bitten, demonstrating that
mosquitoes could potentially spread disease rapidly to humans.
(Ominously, as Dando notes, "the US Army did not appear to
have considered that the yellow fever virus might have been
transmitted to an animal reservoir population had it been used.")
By 1959, the *Aedes aegypti*–yellow fever mosquito had been classified as a "standard-type biological weapon" and was bred in

large supply at Fort Detrick (along with mosquitoes infected with malaria and dengue; fleas infected with plague; ticks infected with tularemia, relapsing fever, and Colorado fever; and flies infected with cholera, anthrax, and dysentery).

The CIA also appears to have developed an interest in arthropod-borne diseases as covert weapons that could be transported by birds. For example, from 1961—a year before the Smithsonian project began—through 1965 the CIA funded a state university research program for a study titled "The Role of Avian Vectors in the Transmission of Viral Diseases," funded through the CIA's top-secret Project MK-ULTRA. A declassified but heavily redacted CIA document I was able to obtain through FOIA in 2001 describes MK-ULTRA as the umbrella for "research and development of chemical, biological, and radiological materials capable of employment in clandestine operations to control human behavior."

In his 1985 article, Gup reported that the Smithsonian's secretary from 1953 to 1964, Leonard Carmichael, served as director of "the Human Ecology Fund, a . . . conduit for a variety of CIA projects and part of the MKULTRA program." Gup was unable to turn up any proof that the agency and the Smithsonian projects were linked, but the coincidence of dates is suggestive: MK-ULTRA's bird study research continued through the first four years of the Smithsonian project.

All this clandestine activity, even the decision to test bioweapons in select regions of the Pacific, needs to be understood in the context of the times. The United States was deeply concerned in 1959 when Fidel Castro triumphed in the Cuban Revolution and by the subsequent Soviet moves that led to the Cuban Missile Crisis in 1962. By 1962, the year the military approached the Smithsonian Institution about the bird study project, the United

States was also covertly but nonetheless increasingly committed in Vietnam. As Judith Miller, Steven Engelberg, and William Broad documented in *Germs: Biological Weapons and America's Secret War,* use of biological weapons was considered in both Vietnam and Cuba—hence the interest in studying their potential in tropical environments such as the Central Pacific.

In 1972, the United States joined with eight other nations, including the Soviet Union, in ratifying a comprehensive biological and chemical weapons convention. The Soviets, it has come to be known, consistently violated this convention. The United States claims that it has not, although research purportedly for the purpose of developing antidotes to diseases that might be used as bioweapons has continued.

Whether or not bioweapons field tests are a thing only of the past, they may, according to former EPA senior scientist Eileen Choffnes, have left "reservoirs of disease." In a 2001 article for the *Bulletin of Atomic Scientists* titled "Germs on the Loose," Choffnes wrote: "Although the [Cold War biological weapons] programs have ended, the pathogens they released persist in the test sites' animal, bird, reptile and insect populations."

Standing that day in 1996 on the wall of Midway's barrier reef, which cupped like a chalice the atoll's rich life, I looked out on a world that seemed heartbreakingly fragile. Three miles across the lagoon, the islands registered as hardly more substantial than the surrounding reef. One would never imagine that they could support so much life—that congregated on them at that moment were most of the world's North Pacific albatrosses.

It was the decimation of seabird colonies such as these by feather hunters in the early twentieth century that led to the world's first international treaty acknowledging that environmental conservation must transcend national boundaries: the Migratory Bird Treaty Act of 1918, signed by the United States, Great Britain, the Soviet Union, Japan, and Mexico. Migratory birds were, in a sense, our first ambassadors of globalism.

Yet even now, nearly a hundred years later, as it becomes painfully clear that nothing exists apart—as the pesticides and PCBs of Midway begin their long, slow migration to all parts of the earth, as trash dumped in the sea in Southeast Asia accumulates in the belly of a Laysan albatross chick on Midway—we have few international laws that honor the interconnectivity of nature. The military complexes of most countries may be the largest corporate polluters on the planet, but to point the finger primarily at them begs the question: Isn't it the cumulative effect, worldwide, of a thousand forms of industry and carelessness that jeopardize the oceans?

And those birds all come home to roost.

FIFTEEN

Tug of War

By the end of 1997 Midway-Phoenix's new restaurant, The Clipper, was open for business; a young French couple had been brought in to run it. A raised walkway across the sand dunes connected it to a new bar, Captain Brooks' Tavern. The walkway spanned an area where albatrosses ran to get airborne. Its design had not been discussed with Fish & Wildlife, nor had many other things. Nanette had announced that she would be leaving shortly after Fish & Wildlife granted another environmental concession to Midway-Phoenix: "We're trying to restore areas on this island for bird habitat—and in the middle of that we cave in and allow a citrus orchard?" she said. "I can't handle the contradictions of what we're doing out here."

There was some good news. Nanette's native plant nursery produced naupaka, morning glory, and other coastal strand plants to set out in an area that her crew was clearing of *Verbesina* and in all the places where buildings and fuel tanks had stood. The rats were entirely gone from Midway (Fish & Wildlife and the navy had cooperated well on that effort), and the once nearly extinct populations of burrowing birds were now booming. In courting season the Bonin petrels filled the air at night, spooking bicyclists by coming so close they seemed to go right through the spokes. Over on Eastern Island, the ironwood trees were gone, poisoned and chopped down by Fish & Wildlife workers. Of the island's incarnation as World War II military fortress and Cold War spy station, little more than the old antiaircraft gun by the dock and the cracked runway from which Midway's Dauntless bombers took off remained. Nanette would have liked to see the runway broken up and the whole island gradually restored to native habitat, but the historic artifact would probably be left to molder away on its own. Fish & Wildlife was already under fire from a group called the International Midway Memorial Foundation (IMMF) for being more pro-wildlife than pro–military history.

When James D'Angelo, IMMF's founder, ex–air force colonel and World War II history buff, heard that Midway was destined to become a wildlife refuge, he managed to enlist Senator Jesse Helms in an attempt to wrest control of the atoll from Fish & Wildlife and have it designated a National Memorial. A short time before, the service had turned down IMMF's request to install a flagpole (and a flag of IMMF's design) at the Sand Island navy memorial, citing danger to flying birds, and D'Angelo was incensed.

These were the opening volleys in what had become IMMF's Battle of Midway. D'Angelo accused the service of attempting to eradicate "all traces of human habitation on Midway" and claimed the agency had "no sincere interest in keeping Midway Atoll open to the public."

Things were not going well on some other fronts. Reviews of Midway as a tour destination had been mixed. Initially, there was a flurry of ecstatic reports on the fishing and diving there.

Fox Television's *Inside Sportfishing* crew showed up, for example, with Michael Fowlkes raving about "the best inshore fishing you'll ever see in your life" and fishing outside the atoll that was "unreal." "We caught and released over fifty ulua, in the forty- to one-hundred-pound class, the first afternoon we fished," Fowlkes said.

Midway-Phoenix's dream of attracting big spenders who would arrive in private jets and spend their days fishing and their evenings eating and drinking at the French restaurant wasn't panning out, though. The atoll is nearly 8 degrees farther north than Honolulu, and its climate decidedly more temperate and totally maritime. A travel writer for *Forbes* arrived during a rainy spell in May when the fishing boats stayed inside the lagoon, found the spectacle of thousands of soggy albatross chicks depressing, and described the facilities as a "broken-down old military base."

Midway-Phoenix had subcontracted with a nonprofit group called the Oceanic Society to run eco-tours at the atoll. My old cohort from Laysan, Cynthia, was hired as a boat captain and nature-tour leader. She had gotten her divorce, sold her house on Oʻahu, and taken a long trip to Africa with her daughter. Now she was back on one of her beloved Northwestern Islands, this time living communally with the other Oceanic people—a dolphin expert and a seabird biologist—in one of the old navy officers' houses.

But the house was falling down around their ears, and Midway-Phoenix showed little interest in shoring it up. For their part, they had expected Oceanic to sink some money into fixing up headquarters at Midway, but Oceanic was waiting to see whether the tours would really fill up. Oceanic Society led tours all over the world, and the format was pretty much the same: an opportunity for hands-on "research" with a biologist. The society had expected that getting in the water with Midway's resident pod of over two hundred spinner dolphins would be a big draw, but Fish & Wildlife nixed the close encounters as potentially disturbing to the dolphins, who used their time in the lagoon for resting. The service in turn hoped that Oceanic groups would fully embrace activities like weeding out *Verbesina*.

Oceanic tours were pricey, and Midway-Phoenix was imagining they would attract rich retirees who also would flock to the Clipper House for drinks and French cuisine after a hard day out in nature. What they got were dedicated birders and naturalists who would rather walk and bicycle than rent $30-a-day golf carts and preferred to eat three-alarm curry in the mess hall with the local residents.

Other than the wide and beautiful north beach fronting the restaurant, Fish & Wildlife had closed off Midway's beaches to preserve areas where its few monk seals could raise pups undisturbed. A trail system had been created just inland from the shore, with viewing stations where one could scan the coast for seals. Eastern Island, with its beaches finally cleared of debris, was now entirely off-limits except for guided tours led by Fish & Wildlife twice a week, if the weather permitted.

By the time Cynthia arrived, the protection of most beach areas was already beginning to pay off. Eleven seal pups were born at Midway in 1997, and another eleven in 1998. But Cynthia found that on Sand Island, the service didn't have the staff to police the beaches, and when seals hauled out, tourists seemed to forget which beaches were open or closed, and strolled right up to the seals, who fled in panic back into the water. No one was keeping year-round observations on the seals, and it was unclear how many of the pups were surviving. Cynthia started making her own observations early in the morning and near sundown. She made up wooden plaques in the shape of seals, painted them red, and placed them close to where seals snoozed on the beach to warn people they were there and remind them to maintain the required hundred-foot distance. Some Midway-Phoenix personnel began openly calling her an "eco-Nazi."

Any attempt to remain the dispassionate biologist had long gone out the window: Cynthia's sense that her destiny was inextricably linked to monk seals had only increased since Laysan. A surprise encounter at Midway confirmed that sense. Several years earlier, soon after she had started working for NMFS, Cynthia and her coworkers had helped relocate a five-week old newly weaned monk seal from the mouth of the Wailea River on Oʻahu's north shore to Kure Atoll, where it was "enrolled" in Bill Gilmartin's head-start program for monk seal pups. There it joined other young females from French Frigate Shoals and Kure itself.

To protect them from sharks and aggressive adult male seals, "we kept the pups in a large pen that enclosed a shallow reef and a stretch of beach," Cynthia recalled. "We caught live reef fish and lobsters for them. They chased and played with these for the first few weeks, until they got hungry enough to start capturing and eating them." At the end of the summer, Wailea Kai, as Cynthia called the pup, was released at Kure, along with the other pups. At the time many NMFS personnel were critical of Gilmartin's head-start program, doubtful that the fostered pups would make a successful transition to adulthood in the wild. So when Cynthia took binoculars and read the flipper tags of a five-year-old seal snoozing on one of Midway's beaches and discovered it was Wailea Kai, she was thrilled. "We suspected that seals from nearby atolls would migrate to Midway and start making use of the beaches we're now keeping people away from. She didn't produce a pup here, but she may someday—and I'll feel like my life has made some kind of full circle!"

Gilmartin had been advocating a similar head-start program at Midway, and the news about pup seal survival at the atoll seemed to make the issue more critical. In the year 2000 a record fourteen pups were born at Midway, but by 2001 only one had made it through the perilous first year. "They appeared," Gilmartin said, "to be starving."

Low pup survival wasn't a concern just at Midway and Kure. At French Frigate Shoals, the number of pups born in the wake of the departure of the coast guard in 1979 rose rapidly, but then a decade later entered a steep decline. Similarly, the number of seal pups surviving the critical period from weaning to two years of age had risen with exhilarating rapidity to nearly 90 percent after human disturbance was no longer a factor. Then, by 1997, it had plunged to a shocking 8 percent. Sharks took their toll, and the number of seals dying from entanglement in nets and fishing line had increased. But still the extent of the decline was puzzling.

In 1991, NMFS biologists had begun to catalog an unusually high number of juvenile seals that were seriously emaciated. It was possible that some oscillation in ocean temperature, as occasionally occurs, had brought about change in the food available, but it was also possible that seals were competing with fishermen for their food supply. By then Tim Ragen and others had established that lobster was important prey for Hawaiian monk seals, as were reef fish, octopuses, and crabs—the latter three all frequent bycatch in lobster fishing.

It was clear by the late eighties that lobster stocks in waters near French Frigate Shoals were declining precipitously as a result of overfishing, and in 1991 (under pressure from the Marine Mammal Commission) the state lobster fishery was suspended. At the time, little was known about monk seals' diet, and NMFS, pushed by its own subsidiary, the Western Pacific Fisheries Management Council (WESPAC), to reopen the fishery, maintained there was no evidence that lobster were important prey food for the seals.

NMFS reopened the lobster fishery in 1992. Monk seal numbers at the Shoals continued to drop through the 1990s, and lobster stocks continued to decline. In January 2000, several environmental groups sued the Fisheries Service for "failing to properly manage Northwestern Hawaiian Islands lobster and bottom-fish fisheries to avoid harming monk seals." NMFS closed the lobster fishery six months later. It would be more than a decade before the lobster population would show signs of a slow recovery.

Bill Gilmartin, meanwhile, had been closely following the seal census at Laysan. In 1996, the year after we captured and moved the seals from Laysan, no mobbing incidents had been observed on the island, and no seals found with the characteristic injuries. The Laysan seal population had remained stable up to the year 2001, as had the population at Lisianski. Besides Midway, populations at Pearl and Hermes and at Kure had continued to grow slowly. But with the Shoals population little more than half of what it had been in the mid-1980s, the estimated total world population of Hawaiian monk seals still hovered at an only marginally viable thirteen to fourteen hundred seals.

Since retirement Bill had helped found a nonprofit organization called the Hawai'i Wildlife Fund, but he had not lost interest in a head-start program for seals at Midway. He urged NMFS to hire Cynthia as a researcher/observer on the atoll, but the Fisheries Service had not responded. Cynthia was trying to do it all on her own. She gave orientation talks to Midway visitors to teach them protocol toward the wildlife. She attended weekly meetings with Fish & Wildlife and the Midway-Phoenix management. The meetings had started out tense, and they got worse. Rob Shallenberger, with his years of experience in Washington, had acquired some of the skills of a politician. But the position was wearing him down.

The money Midway-Phoenix hoped to make off the airport had so far not materialized, though there was still talk of a "big contract" with Boeing to use Midway as an alternative airport in flights across the Pacific. Midway-Phoenix felt refuge restrictions were holding back the tourism. They had pushed unrelentingly for concessions, and they had won some. Kayaks were allowed, though they had to be launched from swim platforms built to accommodate snorkelers, anchored over patch reef some distance from Midway's beaches.

The limit of one hundred visitors a day was also being reconsidered. One change, a big one, had Cynthia most up in arms: a few cruise ships had been allowed to dock inside the lagoon and send large groups of passengers in to visit Sand Island. "This is an accident waiting to happen," she wrote me. "Surely the ships that lie on the floor of Midway's narrow channel should be a warning that nothing is certain here, especially the weather. Midway would be destroyed if one of these 600-foot-plus vessels went aground."

In June 2000 I returned to Midway to teach a two-week nature writing class for the University of Hawaii–Hilo summer session.

I found that Rob Shallenberger was leaving and his replacement had already arrived.

Midway's next refuge manager seemed like an odd choice, or at least one that seemed to make sense only if Fish & Wildlife had decided that a hard line was the one to take. Ron Anglin was a veteran in refuge management who had worked in Oregon and Nevada, where he had gained a reputation for being able to bring ranchers to the table with wildlife managers. The ranchers had liked his plain speaking, it was said. He was a big man, with a shock of white hair and a ruddy, open face. His attitude reminded me of the gunslinger brought in to clean up Dodge City. "I've dealt with lots of ranchers and cowboys," he told me. "These Midway-Phoenix guys are basically cowboys. They're not going to be getting any concessions out of me."

"The cooperative agreement Fish & Wildlife signed is a strange document," Anglin went on. "There's no teeth in it, and that's a big part of the problem. The service bent over backward in the beginning to accommodate these guys, because they knew they couldn't meet their goals without somebody from the private sector helping run this place. But this kind of cooperative arrangement is like a marriage, and this one's a bad marriage. Midway-Phoenix wanted a gas station out in the middle of the Pacific so they could keep up their military contracts. They never gave a damn about environmental tourism."

Fish & Wildlife had just let go its interpretive ranger, whose main job had been to lead history and nature tours. The money to fund the position was supposed to come from the thirty-dollar refuge fee paid by each visitor, collected by Midway-Phoenix.

"Midway-Phoenix is angry that we are not doing the interpretive tours," said Anglin. "I've told them we'll hire someone as soon as they give us the two hundred thousand dollars they now owe us in refuge fees. There's also a very large fuel bill they need to take care of. If that isn't paid this place is gonna run out of fuel, and there won't be any more deliveries forthcoming from the US government. Midway-Phoenix claims they've sunk $20 million dollars of their own money into this place. But they need to look at what they spent it on. The first million went to building a French restaurant. It would have been much better spent learning how to market tourism to the right people."

Mike Gautreaux was still the Midway-Phoenix manager at the atoll. The year before, at age fifty-six, he had suffered a heart attack, and his family was trying desperately to get him to give up the job, but he had fallen in love with the place. I found him in the former navy commanding officer's suite on the second floor of the hangar. Where the CO's portrait used to hang, behind a huge oak desk, now hung a photograph of Gautreaux as a young marine pilot. He had served for twenty-five years, retiring in 1996, and then got a job with Phoenix Air, flying their Learjets in simulated attacks on navy ships and in practices where they jammed the radar of navy pilots. He had aged considerably since the last time I had seen him, but he still had a boyish, likeable manner.

"Everyone says that Midway-Phoenix folks don't care about the environment," Gautreaux said. "But we're here because we love this place. If we left, in a year the whole island would be taken over by this *Verbesina* weed. So yeah, maybe this was kind of 'field of dreams'—we were naive about what it takes to build up a tourism business; we were slow to get into active marketing and all that. But it's not that we didn't care about the tourism part. It's why we're here.

"Of course if there's a profit to be made here it's going to be the airport. The cooperative agreement acknowledges that we have to make revenue to keep going out here, to keep up our part of keeping the lights on. So all these issues—who pays fuel costs, who pays for interpretive programs, what kinds of activities the tourists get to do—should be up for negotiation."

Fish & Wildlife, however, had just been handed what they had needed all along: a clear mandate in the form of the National Wildlife Refuge System Improvement Act of 1997, which clarified the mission of the refuge system as uncategorically "wildlife first." The act provided new guidelines for assessing what public use programs were appropriate on refuge lands, stating that the primary goal of the refuge system was to preserve and enhance biological integrity and diversity. At Midway, Fish & Wildlife could now put some teeth into their arguments for "appropriate use."

It would be two years before I got back out to Midway again, but I heard snippets of news. In the fall of 2001, Midway-Phoenix lost the $1-million-a-year contract they had made with Boeing to keep the runway open for emergency landings of their 777 jets crossing the Pacific. The island was nearly out of fuel, and Fish & Wildlife was refusing to purchase more until paid back for fuel already purchased. The company began to threaten to pull out, and then, on January 27, 2002, sent the following message to "all the contractors we do business with on Midway":

> The Midway Phoenix Corporation deeply regrets announcing cessation of operations in the Midway Islands. A total lack of flexibility or willingness to cooperate on the part of the Fish & Wildlife Service has resulted in an atmosphere where any expectation of a reasonable financial return is no longer possible.

Cynthia sent me an email a day later:

> The Oceanic Society was about to start the best year we
> have had (despite 9/11) out here with over 200 folks signed
> up. Apparently this didn't impress MPC. Ecotourism never
> seemed to interest them from the beginning; the only aspect
> they enjoyed was the fishing component. This part of the
> USFWS public use program was probably going to be shut
> down this year because of some preliminary findings show-
> ing that their target species the jacks [ulua] were declining
> even though they were operating a "catch and release" pro-
> gram. The decline I believe was due to [the] fact that record
> sized fish were killed in order to weigh them on land and
> claim their official prize.

The failure of tourism at Midway opened the door for some
old battles. In Honolulu, there was talk again of a fisheries station, and one state representative suggested that Midway be used
to house prisoners convicted of drug-related felonies. And there
was one last volley from Midway-Phoenix and their allies.

A series of letters appeared in the *Washington Times*, describing Fish & Wildlife at Midway as "a federal agency running amok"
that had turned what should be a National Monument into "a
defacto private petting zoo for [their] agents." Midway-Phoenix's
statements to the press amplified this theme. A spokesman said
that the service had chopped down many of the ironwood trees
that were crucial for shade and had plans to remove all of them
(this was in fact a suggestion made by Nanette, as part of ridding
the atoll of non-native species, but never seriously considered).

June 4, 2002, would be the sixtieth anniversary of the Battle
of Midway. Midway-Phoenix joined forces with James D'Angelo
of the International Midway Memorial Foundation. Together
they talked Representative John Duncan of Tennessee into intro-

ducing a bill requiring the Secretary of the Interior to name a new federal agency to manage Midway. "Having a wildlife refuge or a national memorial that only bureaucrats can visit does not make a lot of sense," Duncan told the press. "I think the veterans who fought in the Battle of Midway deserve to be better treated."

By June, all the Foreign Nationals had been sent home, the Oceanic Society was gone, Midway-Phoenix had packed up and left, and Fish & Wildlife was down to a skeleton crew. The service had contracted with an engineering firm out of Portland to keep the airfield, the water system, and the electric system running and maintain the few buildings that were not closed up.

For the Battle of Midway celebration on June 4, the navy chartered an Aloha Airlines plane, and I joined other press crew aboard on assignment for the *Christian Science Monitor*. A navy band and honor guard traveled with us. An air force plane flew in an Assistant Secretary of the Interior, a couple of generals, and various Fish & Wildlife officials.

The Midway settlement already had an air of decay. I walked from the airport to "downtown" and noticed *Verbesina* filling in areas that had previously been kept mowed. The albatross chicks were just starting to lose their down and were straying into the roads. I wandered into the bowling alley and looked at the dusty shoes, neatly lined up. The mess hall was closed and locked. The All Hands Club was unlocked, but the liquor was gone.

At the Midway memorial, the monuments were scrubbed to a shine and the grass tightly clipped. "We were up till midnight, mowing," said someone from Fish & Wildlife. There were three veterans of the Battle of Midway, one a striking-looking man of eighty-five, Frank Tompkins, with wraparound dark glasses and a cane. He had manned a machine-gun position "thrown together out of sandbags on Eastern Island during the battle." "Are you glad to be able to be here today?" I asked him. "Hell," he grinned, "At my age I'm just happy to be here, period."

A defensive edge crept into Assistant Secretary of the Interior Craig Manson's voice as he reiterated the department's current position: "There is no *inherent* conflict between conservation goals and public use of refuge lands." The navy fired a twenty-one-gun salute. The albatrosses paid no attention. They had heard it all before.

In the preceding few years, as Fish & Wildlife struggled to maintain a station at Midway, the far end of the archipelago had emerged from obscurity, spurred by one last grand environmental gesture from departing president Bill Clinton that would radically alter what had been mainly a regional struggle over the fate of the Northwestern Islands and reefs. Ironically, a few Hawaiian fishermen provided a spark.

Native Hawaiian Louis "Buzzy" Agard had begun fishing around French Frigate Shoals in 1946 and kept it up for a decade. "I thought I had found the nirvana of the Pacific Ocean," he recalls. "The fish were huge and it seemed like there was an endless supply. It was the way my ancestors must have known it around the Main Islands."

What Agard didn't know, he now admits, is "how fragile that area was." He started flying his own plane in to Tern Island to pick up the fish, flying out as much as 7,500 pounds of fish at a time. But as more and more people started fishing the area, the fish became harder to find. Agard is now one of the directors of a Native Hawaiian/environmentalist alliance working on joint issues of environmental and cultural preservation. He sees a strong link between the two in the Northwestern Islands. "These islands are our ancestors—our *kūpuna*," he said, "the ones who show us the way."

Agard had spent years watching both state and federal agencies allow overfishing. "It's still commercial interests calling the shots," he said in 2002 when I interviewed him. However, there was now growing awareness that the coral reef ecosystems of the world were in danger, from myriad human activities and from climate change. In 1998, El Niño conditions had resulted in the warmest year of the century. Seawater temperatures rose worldwide, and coral reefs exhibited the massive "bleaching" that is indicative of loss of the symbiotic algae that provide nutrients to coral polyps and lend reefs their color. The damage was very high in the world's warmest waters, such as the Indian Ocean, where nearly 60 percent of the reefs were affected, but some bleaching had already occurred even in temperate Hawaiian waters. Such highly visual evidence of the grave danger facing the world's reefs—already weakened by pollution, localized damage from human activities, and the broader consequences of greenhouse gas emissions, such as ocean acidification and sea level rise— was hard to ignore. Coral reefs, one of the world's most diverse ecosystems, were declared the little-explored, species-rich "rain forests of the sea." Seventy percent of the nation's reefs are in the northwestern half of the Hawaiian archipelago, and suddenly the region was put on the national map.

The tug of war over management went national as well. In the year 2000 President Clinton issued an executive order creating the Northwestern Hawaiian Islands Coral Reef Ecosystem Reserve, to be administered by the Department of Commerce, under NOAA, for the "long-term conservation and protection" of the reefs and "related marine resources." But the new order ran full steam into the bureaucratic Sargasso Sea of already-involved federal and state agencies, since it simply mandated that the various interested parties somehow come to a consensus on how to manage what was now the largest protected area in the nation. To accomplish that difficult goal, the order called for setting up a reserve council, with representatives of all interests, including Native Hawaiian, to draw up a "draft operations plan." It called for all of these players to come together to create a National Marine Sanctuary.

Besides the King Solomon division of management between NMFS and Fish & Wildlife, there was the Western Pacific Fisheries Management Council (WESPAC) struggling to keep fisheries open. And the state of Hawai'i was battling to maintain its jurisdiction over waters from shore to three miles seaward around all of the Northwestern Islands except Midway.

The new reserve left state control intact, and WESPAC, the regional fisheries council that operates under a mandate from NOAA, used that door to fight to keep commerce open. But when WESPAC's draft proposing a "fishery management area" was aired at a series of public hearings, they met up with Hawaiians joining with conservationists and doing traditional chants in the aisles, Native Hawaiian fishermen like Buzzy Agard calling for protection of native resources, and a public with growing awareness of what was at stake. Nevertheless, with the various agencies jockeying for power in what Rob Shallenberger characterized as an "egocentric rather than ecocentric" approach to conservation, it was going to be a rocky road sorting out a region that had always been a jurisdictional quagmire.

One immediate benefit of Clinton's order was funding for NOAA to mount the first extensive survey of the region's marine resources. The expedition returned with stunning information. The scientists found massive corals thousands of years old— the marine equivalents of bristlecone pines. They cataloged hundreds of new species of coral, algae, sponges, and inverte- brates. Using divers towed behind boats, and state-of-the-art video equipment laser-linked to record directly onto computer- generated grids, they surveyed transects from Nīhoa up to Kure. Their report began: "The Northwestern Hawaiian Islands . . . support the highest degree of unique reef species (about 25 per- cent) of any large coral reef ecosystem."

Fish of the abundance and size the scientists encountered there have vanished from nearly every other reef in the world. Even the common reef fish—parrotfish, wrasse, goatfish, sur- geonfish, angelfish—were often twice the size of their kind encountered around the Main Islands. Even in the dry statistics of the survey report, the numbers were astounding: a biomass (total weight) of fish three times greater than that found in the Main Islands.

On Northwestern reefs, the divers were surrounded by mas- sive schools of large pelagic jacks and amberjacks, and the occa- sional grouper. Sharks and giant trevally, or ulua, top carnivores seldom encountered anymore around the Main Islands, were everywhere. The ulua, fifty-pound giants, swam up to take nips at the divers' gear. The sharks, fortunately, were less bold, since there were sometimes dozens of them: Galápagos and gray reef sharks and the occasional white-tip or tiger shark.

Up to this point, coral reef research had mostly focused on individual species, often studied in areas already impacted by human activities. These early studies suggested that reef eco- systems followed those seen on land in being structured as a pyramid, with a small number of top predators at the apex, then various "trophic" levels (think position in the food chain) of carnivores feeding on increasingly larger numbers of prey species. This is generally what marine scientists saw around the fished, trafficked, and somewhat polluted Main Hawaiian Islands.

But in Northwestern waters they recorded a whole different kettle. The numbers painted a remarkable picture: "More than 54 percent of the total fish biomass of the Northwestern Hawaiian Islands . . . consisted of apex predators, whereas this trophic level accounted for less than 3 percent of the fish biomass in the Main Hawaiian islands." In other words, while reefs in the Main Islands mainly contain "small-bodied lower level carnivores and herbivores," the largely unfished reefs of the Northwestern Islands are still dominated by the big guys. Later studies, most notably at Palmyra and other Line Islands, would corroborate this new picture of a pristine reef ecosystem as an inverted pyramid, where the slow-reproducing apex predators were maintained in astounding abundance by the sheer productivity of a healthy reef.

But that was later: for a handful of divers at that moment at the beginning of the twenty-first century, off French Frigate Shoals, or Pearl and Hermes Reef, it was like the discovery of a lost world.

It was what they said about sharks that riveted me. I have swum in Hawaiian waters all my life but had never seen a shark before coming to the Northwestern Islands. The clearly intimate knowledge of sharks embedded in Hawaiian tradition had puzzled and fascinated me. If the Northwestern Islands are a near-pristine reef ecosystem, similar to what once existed around the Main Islands, then the earlier Hawaiians knew a sea teeming with sharks. They lived with, made a part of themselves, a marine world of a richness we may never have known existed but for the fact that it still does, in waters surrounding some of the world's remotest islands.

Over the next few years scientific studies would confirm that the archipelago was linked in one vast ecosystem, no longer pristine around the populous islands but very much alive and still remarkably well at the northwestern end. The opportunity to witness part of a shark study as I left Kure Atoll after my volunteer stint in 2005 brought that truth home.

The NOAA ship *Hiʻialakai* picked me up as it completed research tracking the movements of the biggest and most fearsome predator in Hawaiian waters: the tiger shark. As the ship anchored outside the Kure reef, the shark research crew used a large inflatable boat to lay a baited longline in through the natural channel. Hours later, when they picked me up off the island, they checked the line. Well inside the lagoon, they pulled up a twelve-foot tiger shark. It came up tired but still fighting the line, blunt head with gaping mouth a few feet from where I sat in the stern. Though a hull separated me from those rows of teeth, I instinctively clutched my arms to my chest.

With hands in elbow-high leather gloves, one of the researchers leaned far out and grabbed the dorsal fin as the other held the head in close to the boat by the line. A second researcher, Randy Kosaki, a marine biologist who was the NOAA expedition's scientist-in-charge, dropped a loop of rope around the shark's tail, pulling it close to the boat. The shark's fish-white belly turned to the sky, and it went still, in the same rigid response you see in frogs placed on their backs.

A third researcher made a shallow incision in the belly and inserted a tiny transmitter the size of cigarette lighter, then, leaning out over the pontoon side of the inflatable, dexterously sewed up the wound with the aplomb of a dermatologist doing routine skin surgery.

Once these Kure sharks were transmitting, data would soon be complete on a several-year project to track the movements of these top predators. Tiger sharks were considered a near-threatened species around the populous Hawaiian islands; it now appeared that their nomadic ability might be what allowed them to survive in the overfished southern waters.

According to Kosaki, other fish, such as ulua tagged at French Frigate Shoals, had shown up as far south as Hawai'i Island, supporting growing evidence that the Northwestern Islands' waters serve as a crèche for numerous marine species, continuously reseeding the disturbed marine ecosystems around the higher islands.

Here was a stream of life flowing from a world whose existence we had begun to doubt, a gift we didn't know we had—a reminder that even in the Main Islands there was time for restoration.

SIXTEEN

The Last Atoll

September 2005. Cynthia and I were sitting in the middle of Green Island, Kure Atoll. It had been an unusually wet summer, and even in the heat of early September the island lived up to its name. Thick stands of naupaka and tree heliotrope hid the view of Kure's lagoon, the most beautiful in all the Northwestern Islands, but I could see its color reflected in the green-tinted underbellies of low-hanging cumulus clouds. I knew its size from the bone-jarring ride across it in a Zodiac launched from a NOAA research vessel that had dropped me off here six weeks earlier: five miles of shimmering aquamarine water. Green Island curves against the atoll's eastern reef. In satellite photos the reef domes toward the north like the orb of an eye viewed from the side, the convex lens of the island brown-green, the lagoon a luminous vitreous body. Kure, the far end of the Hawaiian chain, seemed like an atoll that had drifted out of time, a last bright eye of tropical ocean not yet dimmed by the chill waters of the north.

Perhaps it was the wonder of having made it there, to the oldest Hawaiian island, the northernmost atoll in the world, ten years after my journeys in this direction began. Or that I was there with my old friend Cynthia, now the manager of a seasonal field camp, and one other volunteer, Katie, and that we three middle-aged women were the entire human population of Kure. Whatever the cause, my nine-week stay on the one-square-kilometer island unfolded with a sense of altered time worthy of a Brothers Grimm fairy tale.

We three humans were the rarest species on the island, and I found myself often painfully aware of the figures we cut in this landscape. Right then Cynthia and I sat on overturned plastic crates, with a square of plywood balanced on another crate between us, in a patch of grass fringed by ironwood trees planted when the island was a coast guard station. Behind us stood the remaining concrete shell of a small building that served us as shelter. The trees were festooned with perching frigatebirds, who drooped among the branches in the warm sun. The clamor and call of seabirds echoed all around us.

The plywood was draped with black cloth, and on it we arranged many small, brightly colored objects. We were both wearing in-camp attire of flip-flops and sarongs. Cynthia's dreadlocks were still long, but her hair had darkened except for its sun-bleached ends. Her deeply tanned skin had weathered in the last four seasons at Kure. Mine was considerably more wrinkled than it was when we were last on an island together, and the hair fringing my forehead had gone entirely gray. We must have looked like a pair of exotic crones reading the future in the pattern spread on the black cloth.

The objects were a few hundred pieces of plastic. In the center of the cloth I arranged the larger pieces: bottle tops, half a plastic clothespin, part of a yellow plastic comb, a turtle, a tiny blue human figure. Cynthia placed in dead center a pink Bic lighter. She tried it a minute before. It still worked.

Many of the pieces were unidentifiable shards. I started to arrange them in diminishing size, fanning outward from the Bic lighter. Last to go down were numerous tiny pellets called nurdles, the basic manufactured plastic grit from which all plastic objects are fashioned.

When we were done the mosaic nearly covered the cloth, spreading out from the center like the wings of a bird. As a design it was quite beautiful. But as a possible augury of the future, it was not a happy one.

We had removed all this plastic a week before from the distended stomach of a dead Laysan albatross. Out of the four-pound bird we took nearly a pound of plastic.

The bird was nearly fledged, with just a few tufts of down still clinging to its neck. It had died on the last day of July, when it was one of maybe twenty fledglings left at Kure. It was unlikely any birds were still being fed by their parents that late in the season, so the chance that these birds would make the transition to living on the wing was slim. This one's development may have been slowed by the bulk of plastic filling its stomach, taking the place of real food and its much-needed liquid content. It was thin and probably dehydrated.

When Cynthia sliced open the bulging, hard mound of stomach, the plastic spilled out like the contents of a piñata. She already had several collections of stomach contents (boluses) taken from albatrosses, soaked and washed free of bile, labeled according to distinctive findings—pink plastic doll bird; blue toothbrush bird—as well as more scientifically, with date and location where they were found. A research foundation in California was interested in distributing them to schools as science projects, to educate about trash in the sea.

A few years before, Cynthia had sailed with the foundation's founder, Charles Moore, on his research vessel, the *Alguita*, into the heart of the central Pacific, a region the size of Texas that oceanographers have dubbed "the garbage patch." The great gyre of North Pacific winds and currents carries trash from all along the Pacific Rim into this calmer center. Moore documented "six pounds of plastic . . . for every pound of naturally occurring zooplankton."

On a night dive off the *Alguita*, Cynthia told me, she encountered multitudes of thumb-sized transparent invertebrates called salps, whose undulating bodies lit up in a dancing shimmer of phosphorescent color.

I looked at Cynthia, thin and sometimes bone-weary, sitting among plastic bags of albatross boluses that still, after long soaking and drying, gave off an acrid odor of bile. Her face lit up, she uncoiled her spine, and brought her arms up in a sinuous wave with the grace of a hula dancer. "They had an unearthly beauty," she said. "I could see straight through them."

She dropped her arms, then added, "And I could see in some of them, suspended in their innards, pieces of ingested plastic."

It had been over a decade since I encountered that first circle of bones and feathers on Tern Island, cupping gently, almost like a feathered nest, its deadly load of plastic. In that time, the amount of plastic trash in the ocean had increased by an estimated tenfold. At Midway, nearly 20 percent of each year's crop of Laysan albatross never make it to fledging, killed off by starvation and dehydration. You would be hard put to find a young albatross with no plastic in its stomach, but biologists were finding that those that didn't survive generally carried a heavy load. Marine debris—plastics, fishing floats and traps, the Medusan tangles of line and net called "ghost nets," which snare seals and turtles and other marine life—were washing up on Northwestern Hawaiian shores at a rate of tens of tons per year.

I had spent many weeks in recent years marooned with biologists, and I continued to be impressed by their sense of purpose in the face of environmental problems massing like an apocalyptic army. I thought of myself as someone whose ecological compass wavered according to the health or sickness of my inner life, while their dedication to the Sisyphean tasks of conservation remained firmly fixed, bolstered by their science training. Now it seemed that they too relied on a few piercing moments, a few indelible images burned into the mind, to drive them forward.

For ten years now I had observed people like Cynthia and Bill Gilmartin—biologists intensely involved in the battle to save an individual species—and wondered what shored them up against a mounting litany of loss. In the case of the monk seal it had been heartbreaking work: small gains, like the growing population at Midway, failing to offset the continuing decline in the overall survival rate of pups. The world population of Hawaiian monk seals was now hovering at about one thousand animals.

Enough funding to support stationing biologists in the field at all the important monk seal rookeries was going to be crucial. Instead, although money was going to research into monk seals' foraging habits, NMFS was cutting back on work in the field. To the biologist who had pioneered the head-start program of fostering seal pups at Kure in 1992 and who thought a renewed head-start program was critical to seal survival, it was the sad tale of the 'alalā, the Hawaiian crow now extinct in the wild, all over again. "By the time we've exhaustively studied the seals," Bill said, "they'll be gone."

Bill still served as an adviser on the Hawaiian Monk Seal Recovery Team, pushing hard for guidelines in handling what seemed to be a growing number of monk seal births around the Main Islands. "Monk seals appear to be recolonizing what must have once been part of their historic range," Bill said. "That presents a unique set of opportunities and problems."

I had read about one of those problems in the news: a seal who had given birth on a beach near one of the resorts had ended up biting a tourist on the butt when he approached its pup in the water. On the Big Island, I had climbed down the steep trail to a tiny, isolated beach near Hilo, where marine biologists and volunteers were keeping a twenty-four-hour watch on a mother and pup. It was a wonder to see the seals there, on the black sand beach along the mouth of a stream that exited a deep, tropical valley, in a landscape I had grown up believing utterly bereft of large native mammals.

But not everyone shared my enthusiasm. It was a small beach, and one of the few on that rocky stretch of coast. The volunteers had strung up a tape barrier in an effort to give the animals enough room, and inevitably ran into confrontations with local beachgoers. I watched an enraged man scream at the volunteers after they asked his young son not to bodyboard in front of the cordoned section of beach. Convincing the humans to make room for the seals was not going to be an easy task. Reestablishing a healthy seal population on the Main Hawaiian Islands would be one more hedge against extinction, but not a solution: wild animals sharing space with humans and the animals that accompany them would always be at risk—if not from disturbance, then from exposure to diseases to which they had no immunity.

Both Bill and Cynthia had been led to the Northwestern Islands through what Cynthia called "a deep involvement with one species," but the focus had shifted for both of them. The private foundation Bill helped set up and now presided over, the Hawaii Wildlife Fund, tackles a wide range of local environmental issues.

On a bad day at Kure, such as the time we spotted a seal pup that had been underweight when weaned and now looked emaciated, Cynthia would say something like, "Bill and I were weaned from our attachment to monk seals by heartbreak. It's too hard to watch a species go extinct, especially when you feel not everything is being done to save it." On good days, like the bright morning after a rare late summer rain greened the seedlings of native grass we planted in an area painstakingly cleared of debris left by the coast guard, Cynthia spoke of a new conviction that "you can't save individual species without first protecting their habitat. Nowhere can you see that truth more clearly than on these small islands." As "manager" of Kure, she had to weigh each act of conservation in light of the full web of atoll life. "It was easier," she said wryly, "when I could wake up just thinking of monk seals."

In the Northwestern Islands, Kure had long been odd man out as the only island under the jurisdiction of the state of Hawai'i. Like most of the other islands, it was placed under navy control during World War II, but President Truman had turned it over to the Hawaiian Territorial government when the war ended, apparently unaware that it was already part of a Federal Bird Refuge. Hawaii's Department of Land and Natural Resources (DLNR) was now nominally in charge but had no money to administer the most northerly land in the archipelago. Other than occasional visits from federal agency biologists to monitor bird and seal populations, the atoll was left alone.

If the place had been pristine, that might have been okay. The atoll was rid of rats, thanks to the DLNR, but human use had left behind introduced weeds, including the rampantly invasive *Verbesina* and a scourge of big-headed ants, a species so ferocious that they attacked skin on the feet of newborn chicks.

Cynthia had talked the state into letting her write a grant proposal for a seasonal "wildlife conservation and restoration" field station at Kure, using solar power and a roof catchment system for water. She would manage the station, providing facilities and support for visiting biologists from spring to fall of the year.

Thus since 2002 she had been working, with very limited resources, toward the conservation of an entire atoll. In addition, Cynthia and other Northwestern Island biologists shared an ambitious vision that was now reaping some rewards.

I had seen fruits of that vision on the boat ride up to Kure. It codified, in a twenty-year plan to restore the ecosystem of Laysan, a new direction in island conservation.

On the way to Kure we had stopped at Laysan to pick up a NMFS crew that had been monitoring seal pupping on the island for the past few months. They were all out on the shore as we pulled up in the Zodiac, with lines of buckets and other gear ready to load. While the Zodiac ferried several loads to our NOAA ship, the *Oscar Sette*, anchored a half-mile offshore, one of the two Fish & Wildlife biologists who would be staying until they were relieved by a winter camp proudly showed me around. It had been a few years since *Cenchrus*—the invasive sandbur that threatened to crowd out native plants—had been totally eradicated. I remembered long hours spent digging out the tough plant with its sticky burrs: it had seemed a hopeless endeavor at the time.

Now areas near our camp where we had dug out *Cenchrus*

clumps were lush with native sedge and morning glory. At the top of the berm sat three small shade houses in which seedlings of endangered native plants, collected with great care from other islands, were growing. Seeds from Nīhoa's stand of endemic loulu palm had already produced a few trees three feet tall to replace its close cousin, the now-extinct Laysan species. To substitute for the extinct Laysan sandalwood, seeds were collected from the last remaining trees of a closely related coastal sandalwood found on O'ahu.

But the showstopper was the Hawaiian caper, *maiapilo* (*Capparis sandwichiana*), the night-blooming plant whose white flowers the naturalist Hugo Schauinsland had praised for their "intoxicating fragrance." The fragrant garden where quick-darting red-feathered honeycreepers (the Laysan *'apapane*) fed, set like a magic raft in a vastly empty northern Pacific, had floated in my mind like a dream of Eden through all the hot and dirty days working on Laysan. Reintroduced, the plant bloomed out of Laysan's sand like an apparition, its pale creamy petals just beginning to curl inward in the morning sun, its delicate fragrance otherworldly among the whiff of guano, the peach-and-earth smell of puncture vine flowers, the sharp, spermatic scent of tree heliotrope.

The Hawaiian caper now blooms under careful nurturance— a far step from its original life among the lush community of plants that once covered the island, its pollen once spread by the *'apapane*. But the new plan to restore Laysan's habitat as closely as possible to its prehuman ecology envisions using pollinating birds and insects to at least partly reconstruct that vanished world.

Sheila Conant, the ornithologist who first fired my imagination with her descriptions of the Northwestern Islands, is one of the authors of this ambitious plan. It reflects the evolution in her thinking (and that of many biologists working with island endangered species) from single species recovery to restoration of entire ecosystems. Indeed, the science of habitat restoration was evolving rapidly among the microcosmic worlds of tiny, uninhabited islands.

On Laysan, there were enough endemic species at risk that it made sense to look at the entire island as an endangered ecosystem. The most obvious threats—rabbits, *Cenchrus* weed—had been removed, and it was now possible to focus on the most tangled knot: how to rid the island of harmful imported insects and rebuild something close to the original interdependent community of insects, plants, and animals.

There were compelling reasons to undertake such an ambitious plan at Laysan. Despite the damage done to the island by introduced alien species, and the tragic loss of species such as the Laysan rail, the island's biota was still relatively intact. And Laysan provided something very rare: a recorded natural history of a nearly pristine island. When Hugo Schauinsland arrived on Laysan in 1896, he found only one non-native plant. Out of the seventy-four insect species he dutifully recorded only four—all beetles—that were not native to the island. No wonder Schauinsland wrote later of a "longing, yearning desire" to be back at Laysan: it was his fortune to see and catalog, only a hundred-some years ago, something very close to the original landscape.

The most dramatic blow to the Laysan ecosystem had been that plague of rabbits introduced to the island shortly after Schauinsland's visit, but the naturalist himself might have been party to the incremental but equally devastating introductions of seeds and insects as stowaways on cargo in an era when today's strict quarantine protocols (everything now brought to Laysan is either frozen or fumigated) were not yet in place. As Conant observes, habitat restoration starts at soil level, with native land snails, arthropods, and mites—and, in Laysan's case, guano—all playing a role. Alien insect species will need to be eradicated, and some native species reintroduced. Successful introductions of a closely related 'apapane, and perhaps even a rail to replace the island's extinct avifauna, will ultimately depend on a restoration of the complex community of plants and insects. But for now the scent of *maiapilo* on the night air of Laysan lends courage to this enormous undertaking.

Cynthia hoped the successes at Laysan would convince the state to get serious about controlling invasive species at Kure. And that would, to some degree, come to pass, but in 2005, when I visited the atoll, the Kure field camp was a shoestring operation. For my last sojourn as a volunteer in the Northwestern Islands, that was just what I wanted. Cynthia kept the three of us busy at our tasks—banding, tagging, counting, weeding, hauling, inventorying nature's store like shopkeepers. But this was a quiet time of year in the cycles of animal life, and there was time to step away from that oxymoronic activity called "wildlife management."

When we did, the atoll asserted itself with a kind of unimpeachable wholeness. I had expected something else in its advanced age, its hovering near the brink of extinction: I had expected diminishment, some barrenness in land and sea, that signaled an approaching end.

Instead, the atoll felt complete in a way that none of the others had. Perhaps it was the round circle of reef entirely visible from the flat concrete roof of the crumbling building that housed our supplies and sheltered us at night. Kure's lagoon nearly vibrated with marine life. On trips to look for entangled marine debris we snorkeled among giant finger corals: stony, slow-growing colonies of organisms that in their collective old age are more venerable than bristlecone pines. Within and along the edges of its jeweled crown of reef, Kure teemed with creatures seldom encountered in the Main Islands: giant groupers, knifejaws, dragonfish, and masked angelfish.

Every time we entered the rich, strange life of the lagoon I thought about my father, who died a few months before I started my voyage to Kure. His life ended at ninety-eight, in the house on the windward coast of O'ahu where I was raised. Perhaps the sound of waves was the last thing he heard, in the pauses between the wheezes of the oxygen machine. He loved the sea, wanting to bathe in it even in his last year, when it took two to support him through the soft sand and the effort left him gasping for breath.

A few hours after they came to take his body away, I sat on the back steps where a gate gave passage out to the beach. Something urged me to open the door to the room where he died. I sensed something—not body, not spirit, but some essence of who he was—pass through that gate, without regret, to enter the water for the last time. When I submerged myself, later that day, the cranial lobes of the coral heads seemed part of him, or he of them.

Now on Kure I pondered what attaches people to place, and how it took more than simply living in a place. The ancient Hawaiians took great pains about where they buried a child's umbilicus, because it cemented an attachment to a particular place. My umbilicus had gone out with the trash from a hospital in Flagstaff, Arizona, which may account for a certain restlessness. But the death of a parent, it seemed, could also bind one to place.

Yet perhaps kinship with the land sprang less from genera-
tional ties and more from an imaginative leap. Certainly that
must have been true for the Hawaiians, whose ancestors had
wandered far in search of new islands. In 2004, the year before
I came to Kure, the famous *Hōkūleʻa*, first replica ever built
of an ancient Hawaiian voyaging canoe, had made its historic
voyage up the archipelago to Kure, the last Hawaiian landfall.
Just inland of the beach on the eastern side of the island, an
arrangement of pieces of coral, capped by offerings of shells, and
a carved stone replica of a traditional adze head commemorate
their visit.

The Polynesians were a venturing culture, spreading across
the Pacific from island to island out of the southeast, undoubtedly
in response to growing populations and shrinking resources—
or maybe sheer adventurousness. At Kure, millennia of island
people pressing west would run out of islands. If ocean voyagers
went on from here, they sailed into an empty expanse, and a
steadily increasing cold.

Reaching the boundaries of their world, the seafaring Polynesians embraced their new home as Hawaiians, and places like
the region called Kaʻū, in the volcano country of the Big Island,
revered historian Mary Pūkuʻi's ancestral home, were the imper-
fect Edens settled by a growing population. Pūkuʻi claimed that
it was the very harshness of the land, its finiteness, that called
forth a fierce allegiance, as expressed in an ancient chant she
often quoted:

> ʻAʻole au I makemake iā Kona,
> ʻO Kaʻū kaʻu
> ʻO ka wai o Kalae e kahe Ana I ka pō a ao
> ʻIke kapa, I ka ʻūpī kekahi wai

I do not care for Kona,
For Ka'ū is mine.
The water from Ka Lae [south end of Ka'ū] is carried all
    night long,
(Wrung) from tapa and from sponges.

The words echo that other proud proclamation: "We are satisfied with the stones, the astonishing food of the land." The people of Ka'ū weathered drought, tsunamis, earthquakes, even volcanic devastation. These people, who had once themselves been foreigners, celebrated in chant and story their attachment to a difficult land.

On the pared-down paradise of Kure I glimpsed something as fundamental as the bones of coral. Despite our romance with the open range, the endless frontier, the inexhaustible paradise, we live with finitude. We move within a sphere of landscape, an imaginary island, a circle of kin. Islanders we are, all of us.

The View from Midway

After completing the shark project at Kure in September 2005, the NOAA ship *Hi'ialakai* stopped at Midway for one day before we sailed for Honolulu. At that time the atoll was still operating with a skeleton crew, while Fish & Wildlife tried to puzzle out how they could put together a visitor plan that would not involve bringing in another corporate partner. The big picture concerning Northwestern Islands and reefs was no less certain, as the push toward establishing a National Marine Sanctuary stalled in a mire of conflicting visions. At Sand Island the settlement looked more derelict than ever, but there was an upside: with the visitor program still shut down, Midway's refuge staff was putting all its energy into restoration. And the atoll had a new and important resident: the Laysan duck.

It had been ten years since I had participated in weekly duck counts on Laysan, watching the one remaining wild population of the Laysan duck forage for brine flies around the island's hypersaline lake. At that time Fish & Wildlife biologists, worried that the ducks were laying all their eggs in that one vulnerable sand-basket, had already begun to consider what other island in the archipelago might provide a second refuge.

The choice of Midway, with its history of environmental damage, surprised me. But because the atoll's airfield makes it more
accessible than other Northwestern Islands, biologists decided to
work with the inherited legacy of introduced problems. Midway
lacks the wetland and hypersaline lake ecosystem of Laysan, so
duck habitat had to be created. A team from both Fish & Wildlife
and the US Geological Survey spent eighteen months testing the
groundwater under several candidate spots for any lingering pollution, then digging shallow seeps, removing non-native plants
around them, and replanting with native bunchgrass.

On my one day in port, resident Fish & Wildlife biologist
John Klavitter took me on a golf-cart tour to the former parade
grounds. When I was last at Midway, five years earlier, the lawn
had already disappeared under an onslaught of alien weeds. Now
native bunchgrass, grown from seed brought in from Laysan,
surrounded a swimming-pool-sized pond of algae-green water.
Under the grass at water's edge huddled three tiny Laysan duck-
lings, keeping out of sight of an avian giant—a Laysan albatross—standing nearby.

John gleefully told me that in spite of some harassment from
Midway's huge population of albatrosses, nineteen of the twenty
adult ducks translocated the year before from Laysan had not only
survived in this and other dug-out ponds, but had produced egg
clutches double the size of those produced on their home island.
Adapting to a Midway diet of various insects after dining mainly
on brine flies at Laysan clearly presented no problems. John was
now preparing for the arrival of thirty-two more ducks from that
island, "hand-picked," he said, "to maximize genetic diversity.
Then we expect ducks will be well established at Midway."

But like most roads to recovery, the ducks' was not smooth.
One day in 2008 John found the bodies of a few dead ducks near

one of the constructed ponds. The next day there were more, and then more. Soon a population that had grown to over 190 birds had been reduced by more than two-thirds. The cause was botulism, a bacteria that is ubiquitous in warm-climate soils and can grow rapidly in stagnant water.

John and his crew then tried various measures to ensure more aeration in the seeps they had created for the ducks, and by the time I flew back to Midway for another visit, in February 2011, the numbers were steadily climbing again.

In the fifteen or so years since the military departed, Midway had emphatically, in the Secretary of the Navy's words, "traded guns for goonies." On Sand Island the power lines and light poles were gone now, and areas cleared of buildings were already heavily colonized by albatross. The total Midway albatross population was nearing 1.5 million, perhaps getting close to carrying capacity. In openings where you could see across the island, the nesting Laysan merged in a shimmering white sea that made me dizzy—even, momentarily, unnerved. The birds were tolerated even in the crumbling dirt roads, where bicycles and golf carts veered around chicks upright in their volcano-shaped nests.

In "downtown" Sand Island, the once-manicured lawns were replanted in native bunchgrass. If funding came through, in another ten years all nonhistoric buildings not in use would be gone, the huge airport hangar replaced by a low-profile visitor's center and BOQ Charlie by appropriately "green" housing. I was perhaps seeing the place for the last time in all its crazy contradictions, with most of its deeply flawed human history still visible. I found myself struck with an odd unease at the prospect of a cleaned-up Midway.

A few visitors were now coming to Midway as part of ecotour

groups vetted under an arduous permitting process. I talked to a man who handled visitor logistics.

He told me that visitors' reactions often followed a predictable trajectory. At first they are stunned, elated, by the density of wildlife, he told me. Then they start to see the place. They see the bolus of plastic cupped within the skeletal remains of an albatross; they see droop-winged albatross chicks crippled by nibbling at flakes of lead paint around derelict buildings. They may be here to capture a perfect photo of an angelic white tern, but they will see it all: the rusting hulks of the bulky-waste landfill; the bird-trapping, crumbling sheet piling; the ghost nets pulled from the reef piled high at the harbor, waiting for a barge to haul them all away.

"Sometimes they weep," he said, "but not just for Midway. If they know anything about Pacific islands, then they know that the damage they see here they could see at a hundred other islands."

"If it were my interpretive call," I said, "I would horrify them more. I would take them on the Toxics Tour, show them what there is left to see and tell them what has been buried. I would show them where the weapons factory stood. In fact, I would have left it standing—it would have made an excellent space for a Museum of Endangered Unsavory Truths."

What does all this mean, on the ground at Midway, as I come to the end of my long journey through this almost—but no longer—forgotten end of the archipelago? I'm no different from all the visitors the logistics man tells me about. "They weep again when they leave," he had reported, "saying this place has moved them to the core." Laysan's profusion of wildlife, the extravagant perfection of Kure's lagoon—these places harbor in my heart:

azure islands, *encantadas*. But Midway, in its damaged beauty, grabs you by the lapels. Midway is a messenger from the world Ocean, an ancient mariner saying, "Learn from the past; look to the future."

It is a crucial time to listen to what Midway tells us about human impact on Pacific islands, for the Northwestern Islands are now making their entrance on the world stage. In the time since I first traveled to French Frigate Shoals to the present visit to Midway in 2011, the region had moved from near-total obscurity to becoming, in 2006, a National Monument, and, four years later, a World Heritage Site.

Recognition as a Marine National Monument was an extraordinary leap and came about in a deliciously ironic way. After the Clinton administration established the Coral Reef Ecosystem Reserve in the year 2000, charging the various state and federal agencies to come up with a management plan that would give both the region's islands and its waters protection as a National Marine Sanctuary, the process became mired in struggles among the stakeholders. Hawai'i governor Linda Lingle removed a major obstacle in 2005 by declaring that the state would grant the same protection for the ring of water around each Northwestern Island that fell within its jurisdiction. (Midway, a federal possession, was the one exception.)

The following year the whole process frogleaped over agency tussles, drafts of environmental plans, and public debates with help from an unexpected quarter. In April 2006 President George W. Bush and his wife, Laura, sat down to dinner with various luminaries, including Jean-Michel Cousteau, to watch a screening of the marine explorer's documentary *Voyage to Kure*. Washington gossip held that Laura was moved by the portrayal of

albatross chicks damaged by plastic ingestion and that Bush saw
the opportunity for an environmental slam-dunk. On June 15 the
White House bestowed National Monument status on 140,000
square miles of Northwestern Islands and waters (an area just
slightly smaller than Montana). Bush used an executive privilege called the Antiquities Act, established in 1906 by Theodore
Roosevelt as a way to quickly provide protection for areas of "historic or scientific interest." There are no set rules for the protections this status provides; in this case Bush decreed that NOAA
would become the lead agency in setting up a marine sanctuary.

Papahānaumokuākea Marine National Monument received
its Hawaiian name a few months later from a group of revered
Hawaiian elders. The name honors the deities of earth and sky
who, according to tradition, are the ancestors of the Hawaiian
archipelago and its people. In the creation chant tracing native
lineage back to these deities, coral polyps are the first life-form
created by the primal union of Papa, earth mother, and Wakea,
sky father. For an island people, all life begins and ends in the sea.

In Judeo-Christian tales of origin, shaped by the bare-bones land
of a great continental desert, the sea is not even a background
murmur. With the views of landlocked cultures still exerting
control over much of Oceania, it is not surprising that we have
been slow to acknowledge that the health of the sea is the true
measure of the health of the planet. Go ask an islander whether
ocean conditions are changing.

Predicted sea level rise in this century could claim anywhere
from 3 percent to 65 percent of terrestrial habitat on the lowest
Northwestern Islands. How does a biologist devoting his life to
restoration projects on a low coral atoll look at the grim possibil-

ity that climate change could undo hard-won gains? "Not happily," John Klavitter admits, as we load gear into a Boston Whaler for a trip over to Eastern Island, to count the ducks and see how the island fared in a bad storm the week before that downed trees and sent waves over one end of the runway on Sand Island, washing out albatross nests along the perimeter.

"At French Frigate Shoals," John says, "we've already seen some erosion, with one tiny island, Whale-Skate, disappearing completely. No one can say absolutely global warming is the cause—these very small islands in a lagoon system are ephemeral. But we can look at the effect and start planning. In that case we lost an important monk seal pupping beach. Those females had to pick less desirable areas. Fewer of their pups survived."

Loss of beach habitat would not heavily impact some species, such as the Laysan duck, but there are secondary effects from sea level rise, such as saltwater beginning to intrude on the groundwater lens that currently feeds the freshwater seeps—the natural ones on Laysan and the hand-dug ones on Midway.

Other effects of global warming—a rise in sea surface temperatures and in ocean acidity—pose serious threats of a different kind. The Northwestern reefs, in their more temperate seas, are less vulnerable to coral bleaching than more southerly reefs, but they are not immune. Ocean acidification could slow down the rate of growth for reefs, essentially moving the Darwin Point southward. The Darwin Point—the latitude at which coral growth can no longer keep pace with rate of subsidence—seems an apt metaphor for an approaching future, with the earth's natural processes overburdened by the accumulated "weight" of the by-products of human industry. If, as various experts warn, we are altering the basic chemistry of oceans, the watery lungs of the planet, then life as we know it may be moving dangerously toward its own Darwin Point.

Eastern was in what one might call an interim disheveled state, made more so by the recent storm. Though the ironwood trees were gone and patches of *Verbesina* had been removed, the weed still covered large areas. The refuge had just received a grant to fund a two-year program to eradicate *Verbesina* on Eastern, but there was never a one-stroke solution in the restoration game. In areas where there had not been a chance to replant with natives thickly enough to keep invasives out, a weed called black mustard was now gaining ground.

"That's the tricky part," said John. "You can't just kill off the weeds you don't want and leave the land bare. We've learned how to clone the native bunchgrass, so we're turning it out and planting it as fast as we can."

On the island we found few of the ducks resident that morning in their custom-made seeps. "After it rains they like to fly over to Sand Island and stand around in the potholes on the roads," John noted, with a hint of chagrin.

"We know that simply building a population of ducks at another low, vulnerable island isn't the end story," said John as we headed down cracked, weed-filled tarmac toward the western end of the island, where John wanted to show me what he called "a small miracle." "Success would be Laysan ducks thriving on the high islands, as they did at one time."

For biologists contemplating a climate-changed future, the tiny, relatively simple ecosystems of Midway and other Northwestern Islands are schools for honing techniques that could someday be used to restore habitat on larger, perhaps even more heavily damaged islands: Kahoʻolawe, for instance.

There was something profoundly satisfying about thinking about Kahoʻolawe, bombed-out waif among the populated
Hawaiian islands, as a duck refuge, from up here in the farthest
reaches of the new National Monument. The movement to stop
the bombing of Kahoʻolawe had pushed the Hawaiian community to find the links between traditional beliefs and conservation. By making central the view of "aloha ʻaina," caring for the
land, as a sacred trust, Hawaiians reestablished their position as
the articulate soul of the land. That Hawaiian spiritual traditions
were the overarching vision in the Monument management plan
felt to me like something new in the conservation world: what
other such plan is infused with a cosmology?

Hawaiian conceptions of a genealogical link between all forms
of life in the archipelago provide a framework for conservation
in the face of a climate-changing future. The indigenous view of
island life as a sea-to-land continuum can move us beyond the
artificial boundaries of set-aside "wilderness" into finding ways
to establish refugia (such as Kahoʻolawe) throughout the chain,
reestablishing the flow of life from one end to the other.

At the western end of Eastern, the dunes that usually build
up on the seaward side of atoll islands had been flattened into
runway, leaving a low expanse, now strewn with storm-washed
debris. Waves had surged more than a hundred feet inland,
washing away chicks and nests, including a short-tailed albatross
chick, the first ever recorded in the Hawaiian archipelago.

Over on Sand Island, John woke the morning after to an
island littered with broken branches and many dead birds. Not
surprisingly, the remote camera set up to keep an eye on the
short-tailed chick was no longer transmitting. It would be days
before John could safely boat over to Eastern to see whether it
had survived the storm.

"My heart sank," John said, "when I made it over to Eastern and saw the devastation. The whole area where the chick had been was washed out, all the albatross nests destroyed, dead chicks everywhere. If any chick could have survived, it would have been that one—it was more than twice the size of the others. But its nest was gone and it wasn't there."

With little hope left, he checked the naupaka bushes a hundred feet inland. There he found the chick, bedraggled but very much alive.

"I didn't want to stress it out any further by picking it up, so I found a flat piece of plastic debris and gave it a sled ride back to its nest site," John said "I fashioned a ring of sand and rubble around it and prayed that its parents would come looking for it soon."

We reached a spot where large decoys painted with the distinctive gold crown and hot-pink beak of the short-tail lay toppled over, one with the head detached from the body. The decoys had done their job, inducing the female who had been showing up at Sand Island to join a male who had chosen this unpromising spot.

There, next to a clump of bunchgrass, sat the chick, covered with dark down and already larger than its adult Laysan neighbors. "If we can get a colony of these birds established here, it hugely increases the chance the species will survive," John commented. "The entire world's population is around twenty-two hundred. Biologists have coaxed a few birds into breeding on a second island in Japan, but most of them are still nesting on the side of an active volcano [on Torishima]."

Two weeks after this visit to Eastern—and a week after I left Midway—an 8.9 earthquake struck the northeastern coast of Japan, triggering a tsunami that surged across the Pacific with the speed of a jetliner. Once again the short-tail chick went on a wild ride. Amid thousands of injured or dead albatrosses he was, once again, a survivor.

On June 11, 2011, the gawky but healthy adolescent left Midway to become a citizen of the North Pacific until, a few years from now, his hormones urge him home.

Acknowledgments

Frankly, I had no idea what I was getting into when I started this project: completing it was only possible with the support of many people. I can't name them all here, but here are a few whose assistance has been invaluable. For help in getting out to the Northwestern Islands I am indebted to Ken McDermond, Ken Niethammer, Barbara Maxfield, Bill Gilmartin, Beth Flint, and the crew members of the NOAA ships *Townsend Cromwell*, *Oscar Sette*, and *Hi'ialakai*. And to Cynthia Vanderlip, who is also an extraordinary mentor in matters biological and a generous friend.

Over the last fifteen years, I've incurred debts of gratitude to a great number of people—more than I can name here. But I would particularly like to acknowledge the generous support of Sheila Conant, Tim Ragen, Crispin Dippel, Kellie Takimoto, George Balasz, Rob Shallenberger, Nanette Seto, John Klavitter, Leona Laniawe, and the warm-hearted service community at Midway, including James Roberson and the members of the Thai house.

Several people have assisted me in reading and commenting on parts or the whole of my manuscript. Special thanks to

Jim Wade, Elizabeth Wales, Elizabeth Grossman, Loralee Mac-Pyke, Sandra Purton, Charlotte Painter, Bill Gilmartin, Cynthia Vanderlip, Rob Shallenberger, and Kapua Kaʻaʻua.

A place to retreat and work uninterrupted can be a godsend for a writer struggling to finish a project. Several special places have given me refuge: Hedgebrook, Ucross Foundation, Island Institute, the Helen Wurlitzer Foundation, and the Virginia Center for Culture and the Arts.

Jonathan Cobb applied his brilliant editing skills to helping me work out various kinks, and copyeditor Christi Stanforth did an excellent fine tuning. The staff of Trinity University Press—Barbara Ras, Sarah Nawrocki, and Tom Payton—have been unfailingly supportive and a pleasure to work with.

My family and friends have listened with astounding patience and good humor to my anecdotes about albatross and the like for the last fifteen years. To all of you, mahalo nui loa me ke aloha.

Notes

6   "poles near thirty feet high": Brigham, "Additional Notes on Hawaiian Featherwork," 14.

30 "ua lawa mākou": www.huapala.org/Kau/Kaulana_Na_Pua .html (accessed January 9, 2012).

54 "Unfortunately I was unable to secure any part of the animal": Henry H. Henshaw, quoted in Dill and Bryan, "Report of an Expedition to Laysan Island," part 1, 8.

55 "The master and several seamen": Shelmidine, "Early History of Midway Islands," 179.

75 "pygmy palms" and "several species of landbirds": Isenbeck, translated by Rothschild and quoted in Ely and Clapp, "The Natural History of Laysan Island," 20.

76 "a kind of palm tree" and "some of the land varieties are small and of beautiful plumage": Brooks, quoted in Ely and Clapp, "The Natural History of Laysan Island," 22.

76 "in the belief that I could throw some light": Wilson, *Aves Hawaiienses*, 2.

78 "I can only compare the sound": Palmer's journal, quoted in Rothschild, *The Avifauna of Laysan and the Neighboring Islands*, part 2, 10.

78 "the egg being large and hard": Palmer's journal, quoted

in Rothschild, *The Avifauna of Laysan and the Neighboring Islands*, part 1, 10.

81 "luxuriantly on the northwest side": Schauinsland, "Three Months on a Coral Island" (1899), quoted in Macintyre, "Laysan Island," 44.

82 "as the many rotten remnants" through "intoxicating": Schauinsland, "Three Months on a Coral Island" (1899), quoted in Macintyre, "Laysan Island," 15–16.

84 "phosphate, guano, and products of whatever nature": Ely and Clapp, "The Natural History of Laysan Island," 39.

84 "Our first impression of Laysan": Dill and Bryan, "Report of an Expedition to Laysan Island," 12.

85 "They swarm over the island by thousands": Dill and Bryan, "Report of an Expedition to Laysan Island," 28.

86 "A few dozen Laysan finches": Wetmore, "Bird Life," 103.

96 "neat little red bird" through "We could not think": Schauinsland, "Three Months on a Coral Island" (1899), quoted in Macintyre, "Laysan Island," 13.

100 "establishing populations": Conant, "Saving Species," 254.

101 "It appears": Conant, "Geographic Variation," 270.

101 "When we translocate a species": Conant, "Saving Species," 256.

102 "failed to consider": Conant, "Saving Species," 255.

106 "At 7 in the morning": Burney, "Log of HMS *Discovery*."

107 "ransacked" the island for "birds, skins, eggs, and feathers": Bishop, *Geographic and Topographical Report upon Nīhoa*, 5.

111 "On Kure Atoll": Hunt, "Rethinking Easter Island's Ecological Catastrophe," 494.

111 "the clearest example": Diamond, *Collapse*, 118.

113 "synergy of impacts": Hunt, "Rethinking Easter Island's Ecological Catastrophe," 485.

184 "Washington had sent word": Fisher, "Populations of Birds on Midway," 105.

199   "an unusual resort": Cushman, "Wildlife Bureau Weighs Ecotourism Policy."

230   "a few remaining documents became declassified": See the
bibliography in Regis, *The Biology of Doom*, for a complete list.

231   "the plane sprayed": Regis, *The Biology of Doom*, 204.

232   "there has even been an ultrasecret test project": Petit, segment on *First Tuesday*, February 5, 1969.

232   "why the military is interested": Boffey, "Biological Warfare,"
742.

234   "Birds in a statistical sense": Gup, "The Smithsonian
Secret," 5.

235   "I wasn't interested" through "reach target areas with about 97
percent accuracy": Gup, "The Smithsonian Secret," 14.

235   "there the United States began to study infectious diseases
including tularemia": Endicott and Hagerman, *The United
States and Biological Warfare*, 31.

235   "At Fort Detrick, hundreds of thousands of dollars were spent
between 1951 and 1953": Endicott and Hagerman, *The United
States and Biological Warfare*, 191.

236   "numerous fleas bit the pilot": Hay, "A Magic Sword or a Big
Itch," 220.

236   "the difficulties that an enemy would face": Dando, *Biological
Warfare in the Twenty-First Century*, 51.

236   "the US Army did not appear to have considered": Dando,
Biological Warfare in the Twenty-First Century, 51.

238   "Although the programs have ended": Choffnes, "Germs on
the Loose," 57.

241   "all traces of human habitation": D'Angelo, personal
communication.

251   "a federal agency running amok": *Washington Times* letter,
March 21, 2002.

251   "a defacto private petting zoo for [their] agents": *Washington
Times* editorial, March 31, 2002.

252   "Having a wildlife refuge": *Washington Times*, May 26, 2002.

254   "the Northwestern Hawaiian Islands": Maragos and Gulko, "Coral Reef Ecosystems," 50.

272   "'A'ole au i makemake ia Konā": Handy and Pūku'i, *The Polynesian Family System in Ka'ū, Hawai'i*, 224.

Selected Bibliography

Abbasi, Zubair. "French Admit Nuclear Tests Cracked Moruroa." *Environmental News Service International Daily Newswire*, May 6, 1999.

Amerson, A. Binion. "The Natural History of French Frigate Shoals." *Smithsonian Atoll Research Bulletin* 150 (1971).

Amerson, A. B., and P. C. Shelton. "The Natural History of Johnston Atoll." *Smithsonian Atoll Research Bulletin* 192 (1976), available at www.sil.si.edu/digitalcollections/atollresearchbulletin/issues/00192x.pdf.

Antonelus, G. A., et al. "Hawaiian Monk Seal Status and Conservation Issues." *Smithsonian Atoll Research Bulletin* 543 (2006): 75–102.

Athens, J. Stephen. "*Rattus exulans* and the Catastrophic Disappearance of Hawai'i's Native Lowland Forest." *Biological Invasions* 11 (2009): 1489–1501.

Auman, Heidi J., et al. "PCBs, DDE, DDT and TCDD-EQ in Two Species of Albatross on Sand Island, Midway Atoll" (1996). Unpublished ms., Michigan State University, East Lansing.

———. "Plastic Ingestion by Laysan Albatross Chicks on Sand Island, Midway Atoll, in 1994 and 1995." In *Albatross Biology and Conservation*, ed. G. Robinson and R. Gales. Chipping Norton, UK: Surrey Beatty and Sons, 1997.

Baker, Jason D., et al. "Potential Effects of Sea Level Rise on the Terrestrial Habitats of Endangered and Endemic Megafauna in the

Northwestern Hawaiian Islands." *Endangered Species Research* 4 (2006): 1–10.

Balasz, George H. "Green Turtle Migrations in the Hawaiian Archipelago." *Biological Conservation* 9 (1976): 125–140.

Baldwin, Paul H. "The Fate of the Laysan Rail." *Audubon* (November 1945): 343–348.

Beckwith, Martha. *Hawaiian Mythology*. Honolulu: University of Hawai'i Press, 1970.

Bishop, Sereno. *Geographic and Topographical Report upon Nīhoa or Bird Island*. Hawaiian Government Survey Pamphlet, 1885, in Pacific Collection, Sinclair Library, Honolulu.

Boffey, Philip M. "Biological Warfare: Is the Smithsonian Really a Cover?" *Science* 163 (September 21, 1969): 791–796.

Brigham, William. "Additional Notes on Hawaiian Featherwork." *Memoirs of the Bishop Museum* 1, no. 1 (1899): 11–24.

Burney, Lt. James. "Log of HMS *Discovery* (15 Feb. 1779–24 Aug. 1779)." Unpublished ms. in Mitchell Library, Sydney, Australia.

Carr, Archie. *The Sea Turtle: So Excellent a Fishe*. Austin: University of Texas Press, 1967.

Choffnes, Eileen. "Germs on the Loose." *Bulletin of the Atomic Scientists* 57 (March 2001): 57–61.

Cleghorn, Paul L. "The Settlement and Abandonment of Two Hawaiian Outposts: Necker and Nīhoa Islands." *Bishop Museum Occasional Papers* 28 (February 1988): 35–49.

Colborn, Theo. *Our Stolen Future*. New York: Dutton, 1996.

Colley, Ben. Untitled, unpublished ms. in Bishop Museum library, Honolulu.

Conant, Sheila. "Geographic Variation in the Laysan Finch." *Evolution Ecology* 2 (1988): 270–282.

———. "Saving Species by Translocation: Are We Tinkering with Evolution?" *Bioscience* 38 (1988): 254–257.

Culliney, John. *Islands in a Far Sea*. San Francisco: Sierra Club Books, 1988.

Cushman, John H. "Wildlife Bureau Weighs Ecotourism Policy." *New York Times*, January 19, 1997.

Dando, Malcolm. *Biological Warfare in the Twenty-First Century*. London: Brasseys, 1994.

Dawson, Theresa. "Dueling Regulations: Council, Sanctuary in Standoff over Control of Leeward Isles." *Environment Hawai'i* 15, no. 6 (December 2004): 1–6.

Diamond, Jared. *Collapse*. New York: Penguin, 2005.

Dill, H. R., and W. A. Bryan. "Report of an Expedition to Laysan Island in 1911." *US Department of Agriculture Biological Survey Bulletin* 42 (1912): 7–30.

Ely, C. A., and R. B. Clapp. "The Natural History of Laysan Island." *Atoll Research Bulletin* 171 (1973): 1–361.

Emory, Kenneth P. *Archaeology of Nīhoa and Necker*. BPMB Bulletin 53. Honolulu: Bishop Museum Press, 1928.

Endicott, Stephen, and Edward Hagerman. *The United States and Biological Warfare: Secrets from the Early Cold War and Korea*. Bloomington: University of Indiana Press, 1998.

Environment Hawai'i. Archive available online at www.environment-hawaii.org. Ongoing, extensive, well-researched coverage of issues relating to the Northwestern Hawaiian Islands.

ERCE. *Final Preliminary Assessment (PA) Naval Air Facility (NAF) Midway Island*. Pearl Harbor: Department of the Navy, Pacific Division, 1991.

Finney, Ben R. *Sailing in the Wake of the Ancestors*. Honolulu: Bishop Museum Press, 2003.

Finney, John W. "Bird Study Held Screen for Army." *New York Times*, February 5, 1969.

Fisher, Harvey I. "Populations of Birds on Midway and the Man-Made Factors Affecting Them." *Pacific Science* 3 (1949): 103–110.

Friedlander, A. M., and E. E. DeMartini. "Contrasts in Density, Size, and Biomass of Reef Fishes between the Northwestern and the Main Hawaiian Islands: The Effects of Fishing Down Apex Predators." *Marine Ecology-Progress Series* 230 (2002): 253–264.

Frierson, Pamela. *The Burning Island*. San Francisco: Sierra Club Books, 1991.

Frierson [Smith], Pamela. "The Ohana: Birth of a Nation or Band-aid Brigade?" *Hawai'i Observer*, May 19, 1977.

————. "Paradise Bombed: The Future of Kaho'olawe." *Hawai'i Observer*, November 10, 1976.

Grigg, R. W. "Darwin Point: A Threshold for Atoll Formation." *Coral Reefs* 1 (1982): 29–34.

————. "Paleoceanography of Coral Reefs in the Hawaiian-Emperor Chain." *Science* 240 (June 24, 1988): 1737–1743.

————. "Paleoceanography of Coral Reefs in the Hawaiian-Emperor Chain—Revisited." *Coral Reefs* 16, suppl. (1997): S33–SA38.

Gup, Ted. "The Smithsonian Secret: Why an Innocent Bird Study Went Straight to Biological Warfare Experts at Fort Detrick." *Washington Post Magazine*, May 12, 1985.

Handy, E. S. Craighill, and Mary Kawena Pūku'i. *The Polynesian Family System in Ka'ū, Hawai'i*. Rutland, VT: Tuttle, 1972.

Harrison, Craig S. *Seabirds of Hawai'i: Natural History and Conservation*. Ithaca, NY: Cornell University Press, 1990.

Harwani, S., et al. "Legacy and Persistent Organic Pollutants in North Pacific Albatross." *Environmental Toxicology and Chemistry* 30 (2011): 2562–2569.

Hay, Alastair. "A Magic Sword or a Big Itch: An Historical Look at the United States Biological Weapons Programme." *Medicine, Conflict and Survival* 15 (1999): 215–234.

Hoogstraal, Harry. "Birds as Tick Hosts and Reservoirs and Disseminators of Tickborne Infectious Agents." US Naval Medical Research Unit (NAMRU) 3, no. 3-TR-62_73 (1972), Department of Navy Bureau of Medicine and Surgery, obtained under the Freedom of Information Act.

Hunt, Terry L. "Rethinking Easter Island's Ecological Catastrophe." *Journal of Archaeological Science* 34 (2007): 485–502.

Hunt, Terry, and C. P. Lipo. "Revisiting Rapa Nui (Easter Island) 'Ecocide.'" *Pacific Science* 63, no. 4 (2009): 601–616.

Kenyon, Karl, and Dale W. Rice. "Life History of the Hawaiian Monk Seal." *Pacific Science* 13, no. 3 (1959): 213–252.

Liittschwager, David, and Susan Middleton. *Archipelago: Portraits of Life in the World's Most Remote Island Sanctuary*. Washington, DC: National Geographic Society, 2005.

Macintyre, Ian G., ed. "Laysan Island and Other Northwestern Hawaiian Islands: Early Science Reports." *Smithsonian Atoll Research Bulletins* 432–434 (1996).

Maclellan, Nic. "Radiation on Johnston Atoll—Cleaning Up the Cold War." *Pacific News Bulletin*, August 2000.

Maragos, J., and D. Gulko, eds. "Coral Reef Ecosystems of the Northwestern Hawaiian Islands: Interim Results Emphasizing the 2000 Surveys." Honolulu: US Fish & Wildlife Service, 2002.

Menard, H. W. *Islands*. New York: Scientific American, 1986.

Miller, Judith, Stephen Engelberg, and William Broad. *Germs: Biological Weapons and America's Secret War*. New York: Simon & Schuster, 2001.

Miller, William S., et al. "Susceptibility of Sooty Terns to Equine Encephalitis." Army Biological Labs, Ft. Detrick, Maryland, October 1963. Unclassified doc. #AD-422353.

Morin, Marie, and S. Conant. *Laysan Island Ecosystem Restoration Plan*. Honolulu: US Fish & Wildlife Service, 1998.

Norris, Robert S., et al. "Where They [nuclear weapons] Were." *Bulletin of Atomic Scientists* 55, no. 6 (November 1999): 26–35.

Ogden Environmental Services. *Base Realignment and Closure* (BRAC) *Cleanup Plan (CLEAN)* February 1995. Pearl Harbor: Naval Facilities Engineering Command.

———. *Cultural Resources Overview Survey*, July 1993.

———. *Final Cleanup Report*, October 1997.

———. *Remedial Investigation Report*, March 1997.

———. *Site Inspection Draft Work Plan*, June 1994.

———. *Supplemental Cultural Resources Overview Survey*, November 1994.

Olson, S. L., and H. F. James. "Fossil Birds from the Hawaiian Islands: Evidence for Wholesale Extinction by Man before Western Contact." *Science* 217 (1982): 633–635.

Pala, Christopher. "Paradise Trashed." *Honolulu Weekly*, November 26, 2008.

Papahānaumokuākea Marine National Monument Management Plan 1998. Available at www.papahanaumokuakea.gov (accessed January 9, 2012).

Papahānaumokākea Marine National Monument Condition Report

2009. Available at http://sanctuaries.noaa.gov/science/condition/pdfs/condition_papa_low.pdf (accessed January 9, 2012).

Petit, Tom. Segment on *First Tuesday*, NBC-TV, February 5, 1969.

Prange, Gordon W. *Miracle at Midway.* New York: McGraw-Hill, 1982.

Ragen, T. J., and D. M. Lavigne. "The Hawaiian Monk Seal: Biology of an Endangered Species." In *Conservation and Management of Marine Mammals*, ed. J. R. Twiss and R. R. Reeves, pp. 224–245. Washington, DC: Smithsonian Institution Press, 1999.

Rauzon, Mark J. *Isles of Refuge: Wildlife and History of the Northwestern Hawaiian Islands.* Honolulu: University of Hawai'i Press, 2001.

Recovery Plan for the Hawaiian Monk Seal. August 2007. Report by National Marine Fisheries Service, Honolulu. Available at www.nmfs.noaa.gov/pr/pdfs/recovery/hawaiianmonkseal.

Regis, Ed. *The Biology of Doom.* New York: Henry Holt and Co., 1999.

Report of Inspection of MKULTRA/TSD, July 26, 1963; MORI DOCID 17748, Memorandum for Director of Central Intelligence, obtained under the Freedom of Information Act.

"Role of Avian Vectors in Transmission of Disease." MKULTRA Subproject #139, October 1961. One-page description obtained under the Freedom of Information Act.

Rose, Roger G., et al. "Hawaiian Standing Kāhili in the Bishop Museum: An Ethnological and Biological Analysis." *Journal of the Polynesian Society* 102, no. 3 (1993): 273–303.

Rothschild, Walter (Lord Rothschild). *The Avifauna of Laysan and the Neighboring Islands.* London: R. H. Porter, 1893–1890. Available from University of Hawai'i at Manoa: www.sil.si.edu/digital collections/nhrarebooks/rothschild (accessed January 9, 2012).

Safina, Carl. *Eye of the Albatross: Visions of Hope and Survival.* New York: Henry Holt and Co., 2002.

Sandin, S. A., J. E. Smith, E. E. DeMartini, E. A. Dinsdale, S. D. Donner, et al. "Baselines and Degradation of Coral Reefs in the Northern Line Islands." *PLoS ONE* 3, no. 2 (2008): e1548. doi:10.1371/journal.pone.0001548.

Shelmidine, Lyle S. "Early History of Midway Islands." *American Neptune* 8 (1948): 179–195.

Steadman, David W. "Extinctions of Polynesian Birds: Reciprocal

Impacts of Birds and People." In *The Growth and Collapse of Pacific Island Societies*, ed. Patrick Kirch, 51–79. Honolulu: University of Hawai'i Press, 2008.

Stewart, C. S. *Journal of a Residence in the Sandwich Islands*. London: Fisher, Son, and Jackson, 1830.

Wagner, W. L., and V. A. Funk, eds. *Hawaiian Biogeography: Evolution on a Hot Spot Archipelago*. Washington, DC: Smithsonian Institution Press, 1995.

Wetmore, Alexander. "Bird Life among Lava Rock and Coral Sand." *National Geographic Magazine* 48 (1925): 77–108.

Wilson, Scott B. *Aves Hawaiienses*. London: R. H. Porter, 1890.

Work, T. H., et al. "The Ecology of West Nile Virus in Egypt." *American Journal of Tropical Medicine* 5 (1956): 579–620.

Index

PAMELA FRIERSON is the author of *The Burning Island: Myth and History in Volcano Country, Hawai'i* and numerous articles and essays about the Pacific world. Raised in Hawai'i, she lived for many years in the American West, where she was a country schoolteacher in Montana, a backwoods homesteader in Idaho, an apple grower near California's Eel River, and one of the founders of the innovative quarterly *Place*. She currently lives on the slopes of Mauna Kea Volcano, growing tropical fruit and working as a writer, photographer, and educator.